RED MAN'S LAND /
WHITE MAN'S LAW

The process of "forest diplomacy," as it is sometimes called, had its own rules which were no less strict than those of European courts and ministries. The blank form here shown was engraved by Henry Dawkins of Philadelphia and New York about the year 1770 for Sir William Johnson, who was Superintendent of Indian Affairs for the Northern Department of North America. Sir William presented these certificates, suitably inscribed, to individual Indian leaders as a public testimonial of "His Majesty's Esteem and Approbation." Unhappily, none of the inscribed copies appears to have survived. The friendship thus solemnized is recalled in the cartouche at the head of the document by two Indian symbols of a treaty accord—the Tree of Peace, and the Chain of Friendship. The white man's principal contribution to the diplomatic process depicted—a peace medal on a chain—is shown being handed to one of the Indians by one of the Europeans.

WILCOMB E. WASHBURN

Red Man's Land /
White Man's Law:

A STUDY OF THE PAST AND PRESENT
STATUS OF THE AMERICAN INDIAN

CHARLES SCRIBNER'S SONS   :   *New York*

TABLE OF CONTENTS

PROLOGUE

The status of the first Americans has long baffled and troubled those Americans who arrived later. The original Americans, once sole occupants of the continent, were reduced during the years following discovery to subordination and dependency.

In this book I hope to describe, in brief compass, the process by which the Indian moved from sovereign to ward to citizen. No attempt will be made to discuss the entire history of Indian-white relations. Rather, I hope to describe and to analyze the steps in the relationship that developed between the first inhabitants of America and the alien political authorities who impinged upon, and sometimes destroyed, their independence. The relationship between white and Indian will be considered primarily in legal terms, though some consideration will be given to non-legal factors.

White assumptions about the status of the Indian do not necessarily derive from the first physical contact with the New World. Rather, they have their origin in classical and Christian assumptions which conditioned the Western European peoples who discovered and conquered the New World. Those concepts provided a guide to Spaniards and to Englishmen alike in their dealings with the American Indian. Part I of this book emphasizes the early Spanish utilization of these concepts. As representatives of the Catholic branch of Christendom, Spain's experiences are pertinent to a consideration of Protestant assumptions about the status of the American Indian in the New World.

The evolution of English colonial, and American post-Revolutionary, attitudes concerning the status of the American Indian are reviewed in Part II. Parts III and IV deal with the contemporary status of the American Indian—in terms of his land and his person—in the light of present-day United States law and policy.

The book seeks to answer the questions: "What is the status of the American Indian in the United States?" and "How did it get that way?" No easy answer can be given, either in terms of present-day law, or of past history, to either question. Thousands of specialized studies of Indian culture and Anglo-American law exist, but none provides a clear-cut answer to the questions. This book seeks to provide the general reader the grounds for forming an intelligent answer to these questions by showing the historical evolution of the assumptions underlying the Indian's present status.

PART *I*

Theoretical

Assumptions

The American Indian was vanquished but is still with us. The now dominant intruders from Europe supplanted him in power but did not destroy him or blend with him. The Indian remains, in body and in spirit, on the land and in the minds of the white man, perhaps not so dominant a figure as D. H. Lawrence suggested in his *Studies in Classic American Literature* (1923), but nevertheless a steady reminder of a relationship that remains a part of the American character.

Though the Indian was supplanted and defeated by the European intruder, it is not solely defeat that created the tradition of Indian subordination and inferiority in American society. That tradition was latent in the civilization of Europe, a heritage of her Christianity and of her classical past.

In the first centuries after the birth of Christ, the Christian message spoke for the weak and oppressed. Its message was one of peace and non-violence. The New Testament message might have been understood and honored by the Indians of the Americas had it been preached as it was on the shores of Galilee. But by the time the American Indian came face to face with the doctrine of Christ it had hardened in a mould of

3

bigotry, intolerance, militancy and greed which made it the mortal enemy of the native American.

The development of a muscular, aggressive, and didactic Christianity has various roots. To a great degree the new look of Christianity reflected the changed status of the sect: from that of persecuted minority to dominant majority. The personal counsels of a humble Christ were reinterpreted—not too successfully—into rules of conduct for proud nation states. War and violence, formerly abhorred, were refurbished and redefined in Christian terms. The theory of just war, which would later underlie the European justification for expansion into America, Africa and Asia, was elaborated. One of the first exponents of the theory, St. Augustine (354–430), asserted that some wars could be considered just, "namely those that avenge wrongs, as when a nation or state has to be punished for refusing to make amends for the wrongs inflicted by its subjects or to restore what it has seized unjustly." "The thing to be considered when any one is coerced," St. Augustine asserted in his Letter (XCIII) to Vincentius (408), "is not the mere fact of the coercion, but the nature of that to which he is coerced, whether it be good or bad. . . ."[1] With the assumption that the Church was in possession of the right, it not only became good to correct evil, but one became guilty, as Ambrose (c. 340–397) put it, who did not prevent an injustice when he had the power to do so. The Christian state, as well as the Christian, was his brother's keeper. Intervention in international affairs was elevated to a moral obligation.[2]

The Crusades to the Holy Land from the eleventh to the thirteenth centuries gave practical application to these theoretical principles of interference in the affairs of others and added to the sorry history of human self-deception, hypocrisy and greed, in the pursuit of the ideal. The Crusades reenforced the self-righteousness of the Christian nations and helped picture the world in terms of the faithful and the infidel and in terms of right and wrong. Not only was intervention justified in terms of Christian theology, but war itself became an act of charity. It is under the very heading of "Charity" that the Spanish theologian of the sixteenth century, Francisco Suarez, treated of war. The evildoer must be chastised, his evil will destroyed, since nothing is more hopeless than the happiness of sinners.[3]

With the discovery of the New World, the theoretical belief, expounded by some Scholastic theorists, and implied by others, that there could be only one Lord of the earth and the Pope was the representative of that power, came to have the potentiality of being realized in fact. Perhaps the Pope could now establish his jurisdiction over the infidels as well as over the faithful, in fact as well as in theory. Columbus, the "Christ Bearer," as his name and his mission implied, seemed to bring closer the day when all the world would be the Lord's. This confident spirit echoes from the famous bull *Inter Caetera* of May 3, 1493, which the Spanish rulers obtained of the Holy Father on Columbus's triumphant return. The Pope noted that "Among other works well pleasing to the Divine Majesty and cherished of our heart, this assuredly ranks highest, that in our times especially the Catholic faith and the Christian religion be exalted and everywhere increased and spread, that the health of souls be cared for and that barbarous nations be overthrown and brought to the faith itself." The Pope's joy was expressed in a practical form by which he did "give, grant, and assign forever to you and your heirs and successors, kings of Castile and Leon, all and singular the aforesaid countries and islands . . . hitherto discovered . . . and to be discovered . . . together with all their dominions, cities, camps, places, and villages, and all rights, jurisdictions, and appurtenances of the same."[4] The Pope expected Spain to convert the Indians, a responsibility which the Spanish interpreted as they saw fit. The Papal gift, and the later Treaty of Tordesillas establishing a Portuguese and Spanish division of the world, avoided the chance of national controversy over the extent of the claims. It did not in itself initiate the discoveries or the conquest. Those enterprises were fully authorized by the heads of state in their policies, charters and agreements with navigators such as Columbus. The papal bulls and international agreements confirmed and solemnized the arrangements that would keep Spaniards and Portuguese in separate spheres of action.

The status of the American Indian was locked into Catholic doctrine and Spanish legalism almost from the moment of discovery. The relationship was not to be merely that of conqueror and conquered. The Indian was condemned by a preexisting theory to a status by which he served as a material resource to be exploited and as a spiritual object to be saved. His dependence was foreordained by his attacker. His status as a member of an independent community or nation could be formally denied even when he was able to maintain that independence against his oppressors.

The most direct and naïve expression of the Europeans' assumption of preexisting status in the New World is contained in the Spanish "Requirement" (*Requerimiento*) which was ordered to be read to the Indians by a notary before hostilities could legally be commenced. The Requirement was

> read to trees and empty huts when no Indians were to be found. Captains muttered its theological phrases into their beards on the edge of sleeping Indian settlements, or even a league away before starting the formal attack, and at times some leather-lunged Spanish notary hurled its sonorous phrases after the Indians as they fled into the mountains. . . . Ship captains would sometimes have the document read from the deck as they approached an island. . . .[5]

The document began with a brief explanation of the Creation and subsequent scattering of peoples.

Of all these nations God our Lord gave charge to one man, called St. Peter, that he should be Lord and Superior of all the men in the world, that all should obey him, and that wherever men should live, and under whatever law, sect, or belief they should be; and he gave him the world for his kingdom and jurisdiction.

And he commanded him to place his seat in Rome, as the spot most fitting to rule the world from; but also he permitted him to have his seat in any other part of the world, and to judge and govern all Christians, Moors, Jews, Gentiles, and all other sects. This man was called Pope, as if to say, Admirable Great Father and Governor of men. . . .

One of these Pontiffs, who succeeded that St. Peter as Lord of the World, in the dignity and seat which I have before mentioned, made donation of these isles and Terra-firma to the aforesaid King and Queen and to their successors, our lords, with all that there are in these territories, as is contained in certain writings which passed upon the subject as aforesaid, which you can see if you wish. . . .

Therefore as best we can, we ask and require you . . . that you acknowledge the Church as the Ruler and Superior of the whole world and the high priest called Pope, and in his name the King and Queen Dona Juana our lords, in his place, as superiors and lords and kings of these islands and this Terra-firma by virtue of the said donation. . . .

If you do so, you will do well. . . .

But if you do not do this, and wickedly and intentionally delay to do so, I certify to you that, with the help of God, we shall forcibly enter into your country and shall make war against you in all ways and manners that we can, and shall subject you to the yoke and obedience of the Church and of their Highnesses; we shall take you and your wives and your children, and shall make slaves of them, and as such shall sell and dispose of them as their Highnesses may command; and we shall take away your goods, and shall do all the harm and damage that we can, as to vassals who do not obey, and refuse to receive their lord, and resist and contradict him; and we protest that the deaths and losses which shall accrue from this are your fault, and not that of their High-nesses, or ours, nor of these cavaliers who come with us. And that we have said this to you and made this Requisition, we request the notary here present to give us his testimony in writing, and we ask the rest who are present that they should be witnesses of this Requisition.[6]

The historian and apostle to the Indians, Bartolomé de las Casas, on reading the *Requerimiento* could not decide whether to laugh or weep. Even the author of the *Requerimiento* had to laugh when told by the historian Oviedo of the difficulty of finding any Indians to whom to read the document on one expedition.[7]

The validity of Spanish actions in the New World was questioned as early as 1511 by Friar Antonio de Montesinos in a fiery sermon in Hispaniola. The King, as a result, called a conference to hear arguments on the question. Two royal preachers, Bernardo de Mesa and the Licentiate Gregorio, advocated some kind of servitude for the Indians' own well being. The resulting Laws of Burgos (1512) effected a com-promise. The Indians were declared to have a right to free-dom and humane treatment, but were to be subject to coercion and were to be kept close to the Spaniards in order to facilitate conversion. The *encomienda* system, by which Indi-ans as well as their lands were placed in the hands of Spanish conquerors, was approved "in view of the Apostolic Grace and Donation and in agreement with divine and human law."[8]

The debate, however, continued. In 1519 Bishop Juan de Quevedo of Tierra Firme (Venezuela) declared to Charles that the Indians were slaves by nature in accordance with Aristotle's dictum that some men are by nature inferior. Las Casas rejected the argument with rage and contempt.[9]

Reports such as that of the Dominican Tomas Ortiz before the Council of the Indies in 1525 provided ammunition for the attractive proposition that the Indians, by virtue of their natural incapacity, had few rights that the Spanish were bound to respect. Ortiz declared that

> On the mainland they eat human flesh. They are more given to sodomy than any other nation. There is no justice among them. They go naked. They have no respect either for love or for virginity. They are stupid and silly. They have no respect for truth, save when it is to their advantage. They are unstable. They have no knowledge of what foresight means. . . . They are incapable of learning. Punishments have no effect upon them. Traitorous, cruel, and vindictive, they never forgive. Most hostile to religion, idle, dishonest, abject, and vile, in their judgments they keep no faith or law. . . . Liars, superstitious, and cowardly as hares. They eat fleas, spiders, and worms raw, whenever they find them. They exercise none of the humane arts or industries. When taught the mysteries of our religion, they say that these things may suit Castilians, but not them, and they do not wish to change their customs. . . . The older they get the worse they become. . . . I may therefore affirm that God has never created a race more full of vice and composed without the least mixture of kindness or culture. . . . We here speak of those whom we know by experience. Especially the father, Pedro de Cordoba, who has sent me these facts in writing. . . . the Indians are more stupid than asses and refuse to improve in anything.[10]

Sweeping condemnations such as that of Ortiz were rejected by Francisco de Vitoria who assumed the *prima* chair of theology at Salamanca University in 1526. In his lectures *On the Indians Lately Discovered,* Vitoria denied that the Indians were of unsound mind.

> This is clear because there is a certain method in their affairs, for they have polities which are orderly arranged and they have definite marriage and magistrates, overlords, laws, and workshops, and a system of exchange, all of which call for the use of reason; they also have a kind of religion. . . . Accordingly I for

the most part attribute their seeming so unintelligent and stupid to a bad and barbarous upbringing, for even among ourselves we find many peasants who differ little from brutes.

Furthermore Vitoria denied the argument taken from Aristotle that the Indians were by nature subject to another's power and incapable of dominion over themselves, "nor does the Philosopher mean that, if any by nature are of weak mind, it is permissible to seize their patrimony and enslave them." Rather Aristotle meant that some, by defect of their nature, need to be governed by others in the manner of children in a state of tutelage while still retaining, however, dominion over their own property. They cannot be classed as slaves, said Vitoria, even though there must be some right to subjugate them if the theory is allowed.[11]

Conversion of the heathen was a frequently acknowledged responsibility, but whether the conversion might be forced or must be voluntary, and under what conditions Spanish temporal authority could be established over the Indians, became the subject of bitter debate.

Pope Clement VI, in his bull *Intra arcana* to Charles V, dated May 8, 1529, asserted that

> We trust that, as long as you are on earth, you will compel and with all zeal cause the barbarian nations to come to the knowledge of God, the maker and founder of all things, not only by edicts and admonitions, but also by force and arms, if needful, in order that their souls may partake of the heavenly kingdom.[12]

Vitoria, on the other hand, rejected the idea of forced conversion. Nor was he willing to justify Spanish hegemony based on the willful refusal of the Indians to accept the Christian faith. Vitoria observed that the Gospel had not been preached to the Indians with sufficient propriety—"nay, on the other hand, I hear of many scandals and cruel crimes and acts of impiety"—but even if it had been properly preached their refusal to believe would have been no cause for making war on them. Quoting the Gospel, St. Thomas, the Council of Toledo, and Pope Gregory, Vitoria insisted that conversion should be voluntary. "It is a sacrilege to approach under the influence of servile fear as far as the mysteries and sacraments of Christ."[13]

But while rejecting the forced conversion of the natives, Vitoria asserted that both the natural law and the law of nations allowed the Spaniards to travel to the Indies and to sojourn there provided they did no harm to the natives. Just as travel and sojourn could not be denied the Spaniards neither could trade. Trade, Vitoria asserted, was justified not only on the basis of the law of nations and the law of nature but also on the basis of divine law.

Should the Indians prevent the Spaniards from enjoying these rights the latter could justly wage war to uphold them if peaceful means proved unsuccessful. Vitoria asserted that the Spanish could build fortresses, seize cities and reduce the Indians to subjection for their own safety if security could not otherwise be had.[14]

Another self-evident proposition to Vitoria was that Christians had a right to preach and to declare the Gospel in barbarian lands. Did not the Lord say "Preach the gospel to every creature"? (Mark 16:15) and St. Paul, that "the word of God is not bound"? (II Timothy 2:9). Moreover, if there was a right to travel and trade among the barbarians there would certainly be a right to teach the truth to those willing to hear it. Were Christians not allowed to preach, Vitoria pointed out, the natives would be beyond the pale of salvation. Furthermore, Christians are "bound" by a duty "to correct and direct them" since "brotherly correction is required by the law of nature, just as brotherly love is."[15]

One would go too far to say with Gilbert Chinard that Vitoria was *"un habile casuiste"* who "took away with his left hand what he seemed to accord so liberally with his right."[16] But it is difficult not to think of Talleyrand's reply to a questioner who asked how one might define the extent of the principle of non-intervention. Talleyrand replied sarcastically that the term "non-intervention" was mysterious and somewhat synonymous with intervention.[17]

Vitoria spoke positively and specifically about conceptions that had never been fully elaborated. His assertion of the rights of nations in an international community in which natural and divine law disallowed the right of isolation can be looked at either as nationalistically oriented or internationally oriented. Some writers, like Scott, have emphasized his importance so far as the independence of states is concerned.[18] Others, like Beaufort, have asserted that Vitoria "is far from admitting the absolute sovereignty of states" and that his "predominant sentiment is that of international solidarity based on right."[19]

What is sure is that Vitoria gave an extended defense of intervention in the international sphere on grounds of Christian charity and on the grounds of objective right, and gave encouragement to the idea of just war under doubtful titles. His substitution of objective violation of right for guilt of the party to be warred against marks, in the eyes of some, a definite break with the earlier Scholastic theory of war. St. Thomas defined just war as that made against a nation which merits it by a fault implying guilt (*culpa*). War thus had a punitive character and was directed against a culpable nation. In Vitoria the enemy need not be morally guilty. Just cause may arise from an objective violation of right by a nation which acts in good faith.[20]

The rational arguments of scholars like Vitoria did not preempt the field. Zealots like the Dominican Bernardino de Minaya, who travelled from Peru to Rome to persuade Pope Paul III to speak out for the suffering Indian, sought practical and immediate solutions to the moral questions raised by the conquest. Minaya had broken with Pizarro when the latter had insisted that he had come to Peru to take the Inca's gold away, not to save the Peruvians.[21] With a letter of introduction from the Empress to the Spanish Ambassador in Rome, Minaya walked to Rome and won the ear of the Pope. The result was the bull *Sublimis Deus,* granted June 9, 1537, by Paul III. The bull declared that

> The enemy of the human race . . . inspired his satellites who, to please him, have not hesitated to publish abroad that the Indians of the West and the South, and other people of whom We have recent knowledge should be treated as dumb brutes created for our service, pretending that they are incapable of receiving the catholic faith.
>
> We, who, though unworthy, exercise on earth the power of our Lord and seek with all our might to bring those sheep of His flock who are outside into the fold committed to our charge, consider, however, that the Indians are truly men and that they are not only capable of understanding the catholic faith, but according to our information, they desire exceedingly to receive it. We define and declare by these letters . . . that, notwithstanding whatever may have been or may be said to the contrary, the said Indians and all other people who may later be discovered by Christians, are by no means to be deprived of their liberty or the possession of their property, even though they be outside the faith of Jesus Christ . . . nor should they be in any way enslaved; should the contrary happen it shall be null and of no effect.[22]

It was a noble try but to little avail. Emperor Charles ordered confiscated and returned to the Council of the Indies all copies of the bull that might have found their way to the New World. At the same time he prevailed upon the Pope, ten days later, to revoke the bull. Minaya, for failing to go through proper channels, was thrown in prison by the general of the Dominican order.[23]

The garish history of Spanish conquest continued to trouble individual Spaniards and in particular Father Las Casas. Las Casas' unmatched fund of knowledge and his unquenchable zeal kept the question of the rights of the Indian before the Spanish Crown. Because of Las Casas' efforts, the King authorized the meeting of a special council of theologians and counselors at Valladolid in 1550–51 to discuss the justness of the wars in the Indies and to

> discuss and determine what form of government and what laws may best ensure the preaching and extension of our Holy Catholic Faith in the New World . . . and to investigate what organization is needed to keep the peoples of the New World in obedience to the Emperor, without damage to his royal conscience, and in conformity with the Bull of Alexander.[24]

Despite the narrow confines of the authorized debate, the clash of fundamental ideas about the justice of the conquest rang forth. Opposing Las Casas as principal antagonist was the humanist scholar Juan Ginés de Sepúlveda. Las Casas's position, which he later expressed in his *Treatise Concerning the Imperial Sovereignty and Universal Pre-eminence which the Kings of Castile and Leon Enjoy over the Indies* (1553), was that the only true title of Spain to the Indies lay in the papal grants but that these constituted a spiritual jurisdiction for the purpose of bringing the Indians to Christ. Force was justified only when the peaceful preaching of the faith was hindered. The Pope had no coercive authority over the Indians and so could not bestow such power on the Spanish. The gospel could be preached, but should be preached peacefully, something the Spaniards had not done. Since they had entered the Indian kingdoms wrongfully, Las Casas believed the King should forcibly evict them and restore the property to its rightful owners.[25] Sepúlveda's position was that "it is right to subjugate by force, if no other way is possible, those who by their natural condition ought to obey others yet refuse to do so."

This natural principle, in Sepúlveda's eyes, was seen in the justness of the rule of a father over his children, a husband over his wife, a master over his servant, a magistrate over the citizens, the king over his subjects, or the rational part of man over his irrational part. As for the Spanish and the Indians:

> Compare then those blessings enjoyed by Spaniards of prudence, genius, magnanimity, temperance, humanity, and religion with those of the little men (*homunculos*) in whom you will scarcely find even vestiges of humanity, who not only possess no science but who also lack letters and preserve no monument of their history except certain vague and obscure reminiscences of some things on certain paintings. Neither do they have written laws, but barbaric institutions and customs.[26]

Sepúlveda, who had just completed a translation of Aristotle's *Politics*, cited the authority of the Greek philosopher for the belief that some people are "from the hour of their birth . . . marked out for subjection, others for rule." The Spanish humanist also quoted approvingly Aristotle's comment that "in one point of view, the art of war is a natural art of acquisition, for the art of acquisition includes hunting, an art which we ought to practice against wild beasts, and against men who, though intended by nature to be governed, will not submit; for war of such a kind is naturally just." Sepúlveda saw as proof that the Indians were by nature slaves not only their abominable customs but their supposed dependence on the arbitrary caprice of the ruler for their livelihood. Their lack of individual ownership based on established rights and their apparent voluntary acceptance of this state was, to Sepúlveda, the certain sign of their abased and servile nature. Sepúlveda's thinking was here again influenced by his understanding of Greek precedent, in particular the Greek description of the state of absolute monarchy—the characteristic form of government of the "barbarians"—as a state of slavery.[27]

It may be significant that the extension of this theory into a belief that the barbarians were by nature fitted only for slavery and that it was the privilege or duty of the Greeks to enslave them arose only in the fifth century B.C. following the Greek victory over the Persians. Both before and after this period Greek thought was largely free from the extreme chauvinism represented by this view of cultural differences. Nor did the actual state of Greek slavery approximate the type of dehumanized slavery that developed in the New World.[28] Yet the doctrine that Spain's victims deserved to be enslaved was attractive to those feeling the "rush" of euphoria brought on by easy victories over the "barbarians" of the New World.

It is perhaps not surprising that Las Casas declared that Sepúlveda did not understand Aristotle. The "Protector of the Indians" answered Sepúlveda with a detailed five hundred and fifty page treatise *(Argumentum apologiae)* in which he asserted that the Indians were rational, superior even to the Greeks and Romans in many respects. Asserting that those who were by nature slaves were few in number and almost mistakes of nature, Las Casas pleaded:

> All the peoples of the world are men . . . all have understanding and volition, all have the five exterior senses and four interior senses, and are moved by the objects of these, all take satisfaction in goodness and feel pleasure with happy and delicious things, all regret and abhor evil.[29]

Both Las Casas and Sepúlveda had (and have) their supporters. Sepúlveda was attacked by Melchior Cano who succeeded Vitoria in the chair of theology at Salamanca, and by Antonio Ramirez, Bishop of Segovia.[30] Fernando Vazquez de Menchaca, a scholar at Valladolid, also denounced Aristotle's theory of slavery as an example of how men try to cover their wars with a "cloak of justice" and as an illustration of that "relaxation of the human spirit, which is almost always caused by the influence and work of those who wish to please power-ful and illustrious princes.''[31] Las Casas was attacked on the other hand by contemporary historians like Oviedo who, ac-cording to Las Casas, were ignorant of the fact that the new lands were discovered principally to convert their inhabitants, and who "ignored the dignity of these rational beings.''[32] Sepúlveda has his supporters even today who uphold "his humane and sanely imperialist views.''[33]

Francisco de Toledo, the Viceroy of Peru during the period 1569–1582, was particularly upset by Las Casas' attacks on the justness of Spain's rule and undertook a historical investi-gation to demonstrate the injustice of Inca rule, on the as-sumption that this would justify Spanish rule. Toledo also arranged for the preparation of a "true history" by Pedro Sarmiento de Gamboa, and a treatise entitled *Defense of the Legitimacy of the Rule of the Kings of Spain in the Indies, in Opposition to Friar Bartolomé de Las Casas* (1571). This anonymous treatise stated the proposition that the Indies had been given to Spain as a reward for her eight centuries of warfare against the Moslems, a justification that had actually been hinted at in the bull *Inter caetera* (May 3, 1493) of Alexander VI. But it also based the justness of Spain's rule on the tyranny of the Incas. It was particularly vehement against those who

> . . . under the guise of zeal try to give these Indians titles and things unappropriate for them which do not belong to them and which God did not choose to give them . . . for they are minors who must be governed. . . .[34]

Toledo's formal historical enquiry into the ancient history of the Incas, the *Informaciones*, was even more convincing in justifying Spain's title. This enquiry was based on "Yes" and "No" answers to "loaded" questions asked certain Indians during a two-year period. Toledo happily informed the King that the enquiry showed that "Your Majesty is the legitimate

ruler of this kingdom and the Incas are tyrannical usurpers."
As lawful sovereign the King must exercise jurisdiction over
the Indians, and "given their weak reason and rude understanding, Your Majesty must devise laws for their conservation and require them to obey these ordinances."[35] That the
Incas were not lacking in reason has been asserted by many.[36]
Toledo himself won much of his reputation as a wise lawgiver
by basing many laws and administrative regulations on the
system developed centuries before by the Incas.[37]

The leading theologian in Spain at the end of the century,
Francisco Suarez (1548–1617), dealt with the justice of
Spain's relations with the Indians in his work *On the Three
Theological Virtues: Faith, Hope, and Charity,* published in 1621
after his death but probably based on lectures given at Rome
in 1583–1584. As noted earlier, Suarez dealt with war under
the heading of "Charity." He refused to accept without qualifications the justification of subjecting barbarian nations
simply because they were barbarians. Such practices, Suarez
observed, had been praised in the Romans by St. Augustine
and St. Thomas. Moreover, he questioned Aristotle's dictum
that some people are naturally fit only for slavery. If peoples
were so barbarous as Aristotle said, war might be justified in
defense of humanity. "But, in my opinion, no people so barbarous have yet been found." Indeed, Suarez asserted, "there
are many unbelievers more gifted by nature than are the
faithful, and better adapted to political life." Furthermore, it
was not enough to say that certain men are merely inferior.
They must be more like wild beasts, naked and cannibalistic
and with no government, to be considered subject to control
on the basis of their natural state alone. He pointed out that
Aristotle justified slavery only against men as different from
the rest of mankind as the body is from the soul.[38]

As for the dominion of the Pope, Suarez asserted that all
Biblical interpretations referred to spiritual dominion, not
temporal. How could the Pope have a temporal kingdom

since Christ himself did not assume it or pass it on? Yet Suarez expressed his absolute belief that the Gentiles "are bound to accept the faith and the law of Christ, as He Himself testifies, when He says (Matthew, xxviii, 19–20): 'Going (therefore), teach ye all nations; baptizing them in the name of the Father, and of the Son and of the Holy Ghost. Teaching them to observe all things whatsoever I have commanded you.' "[39]

The Church did not, however, have the right to compel unbelievers to come in. But in order for Christ's prophecy to be fulfilled the Gentiles must hear the Gospel preached. Buttressing his argument by direct quotation from the Bible, Suarez pointed out that the passage "the word of God is not bound" (II Timothy 2:9) implied the right and obligation to preach the word abroad. And Christ's thrice repeated words to Peter to "Feed my sheep" (John 21:15–17) supported this right,

> . . . for the term "Feed" refers not merely to an indefinite sort of power, but to one coupled with jurisdiction, which is exercised, or rather, is begun, by preaching. Therefore, since this power was given to Peter that it might persist in the Church forever, the Church possesses such right and power.[40]

Stemming from this right to preach was the right to protect preachers of the Gospel and to subdue those who by force hindered or did not permit this preaching. Since the Church has been granted the right to preach the Gospel it must have been granted everything morally necessary for the exercise thereof. Otherwise the grant would be inefficacious. Suarez compared the right to protect preachers with the right to protect ambassadors although

> . . . much more has the Church this right with respect to her own ambassadors who are the preachers of the faith, especially since

the Church, as was proved above, has the power, given by Christ, to expand and to occupy the whole world.[41]

Suarez did not mean to assert here that the Church had the right to occupy the whole world in a temporal sense, of course, but only in a spiritual sense.

It is in light of this right to preach the Gospel that Suarez interpreted the bulls of Alexander VI. He asserted that both Vitoria and John Mair (Joannes Major, the Scotch theologian) agreed with him:

> . . . that the Pope can distribute among temporal princes and kings the provinces and realms of the unbelievers; not in order that the former may take possession of these regions according to their own will, for that would be tyranny . . . but in order that they may make provision for the sending of preachers of the Gospel to those infidels, and may protect such preachers by their power, even through declaration of just war, if reason and a rightful cause should require it. For this purpose, then, the Pope may mark off specific boundaries for each prince, which that prince may not later transgress without committing an injustice. This, as we read, was done by Alexander VI in the case of the kings of Portugal and of Castile.[42]

Of the many theologians and scholars who debated the theory of just war in the late sixteenth century, Alberico Gentili (1552–1608) was one of the foremost. An Italian, Gentili spent much of his life in England and published in London in 1588 and 1589 his *De iure belli*. "Religion," Gentili pointed out, "is a matter of the mind and of the will, which is always accompanied by freedom." Gentili denied the right to wage war with religion as the sole motive.

> Religion is a relationship with God. Its laws are divine, that is between God and man; they are not human, namely, between man and man. Therefore a man cannot complain of being wronged because others differ from him in religion.[43]

Though he excluded atheists from this freedom, he denied that any nation existed which was wholly destitute of religion. As to the belief that some men, after the Greek argument, were slaves by nature, Gentili denied the correctness of the view.

> For, on the contrary, we are by nature all akin. . . . Hence there is no natural repugnance between man and man. . . .
> If man's desires are boundless and there is not sufficient glory and power to satisfy them, that is not a law of nature, but a defect. Moreover, that isolation of the Greeks was insolent, was censured by the Greeks themselves, and is not of great antiquity.[44]

The Protestant Gentili was one of the few who did not assert that it was lawful to make war upon the Indians because they refused to hear the preaching of the Gospel. As Gentili reasoned: "Although it is said 'Go, preach the Gospel to every creature,' it does not therefore follow that any creature which refuses to hear must be forced to do so by war and arms. These are foolish arguments." Gentili did accept the right to make war in defense of the right to commerce, a right he felt fundamental to the law of nations. He noted, however, that while the theoretical right to commerce existed, it was obvious that the Spaniards were not aiming at commerce but at dominion.[45]

The rights of Europeans to preach the Gospel or to trade and travel throughout the world have been asserted with varying degrees of emphasis and conviction from the days of the Spanish theologians to the present. Hugo Grotius (1583–1645), the famous Dutch scholar, while agreeing that "Wars are justly waged against those who treat Christians with cruelty for the sake of their religion alone," nevertheless placed greater emphasis upon the rights of commerce and communication based on the law of nature, and the right to intervene on grounds of humanity.[46] While the right to preach the Gospel has gradually disappeared as a practical cause of just war, it maintains itself in theory in Catholic thinking.[47]

The confusion attendant upon Western claims to rights in non-Christian lands was somewhat systematized by the Jesuit Jose de Acosta (c. 1539–1600). In his *Historia Natural y Moral de las Indias* (1590), Acosta denounced the opinion "commonly held of the Indians" that they were mere brutes, without reason. On the contrary, he noted that those who had studied them and their past history most thoroughly "marvelled that they had so much order and reason among them."[48] Acosta, a missionary in Peru, published in 1588 his *De promulgatione evangelii, apud barbaros, sive de procuranda Indorum salute.* This work is notable for its attempt to categorize the barbarians into three classes. The first class were those who are "not far from right reason and the customs of the human race." Peoples in this class have permanent governments, fortified cities, courts, commerce, and above all writing. In this category were the Chinese and Japanese and other peoples of the Orient. Such peoples ought to be converted, without the help of force, in the manner that the apostles formerly used among the Greeks and Romans. The second class were those barbarians ignorant of writing but having magistrates, permanent governments, religious ceremonies, etc. In this category were the Mexicans and the Peruvians. But such people were very far from "right reason" and the "customs of the human race" despite certain great abilities they possessed. Acosta considered it practically impossible to bring these people to the truth unless they were placed under Christian rule. The third class were those savage men of the woods who lived without laws, without kings, without definite magistrates, and without fixed settlements. In this category were the Caribs. It was men like these about whom Aristotle wrote when he said that certain men must be constrained to civility.[49]

While many other justifications for European travel, settlement or conquest in the newly discovered lands were alleged, at the root of all justification lay the assumption that Christians and Christianity had both a moral right and legal authority to overspread the world. Since this assumption was often accompanied by a belief that the Indians' mental capacity, culture, or sins against nature rendered them naturally subject to European control, the possibility of peaceful relations between the two races on the basis of reason and respect was not to be expected. The English in large measure inherited these assumptions of European culture.

PART *II*

Historical

Survey

1   :   FROM DISCOVERY
       TO SETTLEMENT

England, as part of the family of European nations, was not unaware of the Spanish experience in the New World. Although inactive in overseas exploration by comparison with Spain and Portugal in the fifteenth and sixteenth centuries, England sent out periodic voyages—usually at private cost but with royal authorization—to tap some of the wealth to which the Iberians had fallen heir. These voyages, like Columbus's, sought to reach the rich Orient. The voyages of John and Sebastian Cabot for England in the late fifteenth and early sixteenth centuries, were frustrated—not rewarded—by the discovery of the North American continent. The aim was to sail to Japan and China, and the exploration of the North American coastline was to find the route through the land that blocked the way. The search for a Northwest or Northeast Passage to the Orient continued not only throughout the sixteenth century but into the seventeenth. Always frustrated in its major purpose, it produced several by-products, such as trade with the Kingdom of Muscovy, and the search for mineral wealth in the Arctic by Martin Frobisher in the 1570's.

The record of English achievement in the exploration of

the North American coastline, which recent scholarship has enlarged to include probable pre-Columbian voyages to the fishing areas off Newfoundland, involved increasing contact with the native inhabitants. Frobisher brought back Eskimos from his Arctic voyages whose portraits were the first sketches by English artists of the inhabitants of North America.

More important than direct experience with the inhabitants of the New World, however, was the record of experience which was laboriously brought together by Richard Hakluyt, a scholarly English clergyman, who consciously set out to spur England on to emulate the achievements of the Iberian nations. Hakluyt's method was to collect the accounts of voyages undertaken by the Catholic powers and to supplement them with those of obscure English mariners. The accounts of the former could often be obtained for the price of the books, in Italian, Spanish or Portuguese, in which they were written and published, and the skill to translate them for an English audience. But the cost in labor to search out the English documents and the time and effort to put all the voyages in printed form caused Hakluyt to exclaim: "what restlesse nights, what painefull dayes, what heat, what cold I have indured; how many long & chargeable journeys I have traveiled; how many famous libraries I have searched into; what varietie of ancient and moderne writers I have perused; what a number of old records, patents, privileges, letters, &c. I have redeemed from obscuritie and perishing."[1] Hakluyt, nevertheless, did not begrudge the effort since it accomplished its purpose: to pull Englishmen away from their smoky hearths and out on the great oceans in search of new lands and wealth.

The Indians functioned in most of the accounts of voyages merely as the objects of European desires: whether for labor, for portable wealth, or for land. While Hakluyt fulminated against the crimes of the Spaniards against the New World inhabitants, and while he often suggested the possibility of an alliance between the English and the oppressed Indians of the Spanish areas against their oppressors, neither Hakluyt nor other Englishmen interested in overseas exploits were concerned primarily with the rights of the Indian. The natives were part of the new landscape. Depending upon their power and their relationship to other Europeans, they might be alternatively allies to be cultivated, opponents to be crushed, or inhabitants whose land would be shared by the English. The principal conclusion to be drawn from English thinking of the sixteenth century is that the English refused to be excluded from the new lands. The principal agents of that exclusion were thought to be other European powers, not the Indians. The English would accept no restrictions on their access to the undiscovered lands by other Europeans, and discounted or ignored any restrictions on the part of the native inhabitants.

When the Spanish ambassador in London complained of Drake's piratical voyage around the world in 1577–80, he was told that "the queen does not acknowledge that her subjects and those of other nations may be excluded from the Indies on the claim that these have been donated to the King of Spain by the Pope, whose authority to invest the Spanish king with the New World as with a fief she does not recognise." The Spaniards, in Elizabeth's view, had "no claim to property there except that they have established a few settlements and named rivers and capes. . . . Prescription without possession is not valid."[1a]

The English sovereigns, following European custom, issued grants and charters to their subjects which assumed an ultimate jurisdiction over the lands discovered. Essentially such charters were claims against rival European powers in competition for land in America. English grants extended from sea to sea, though no one knew what territory or what peoples were involved. When specific, the grants prohibited settlements in territory already occupied by other Christian powers. Vis-à-vis the Indians, the grants can be termed "speculative." The letters patent of Henry VII to John Cabot and his sons authorized him to discover "whatsoever isles, countreys, regions or provinces of the heathen and infidels . . . which before this time have bene unknownen to all Christians," and the right to "subdue, occupy and possesse all such townes, cities, castles and isles of them found, which they *can* subdue, occupy and possesse. . . ."[2] When Elizabeth I granted Raleigh liberty to "discover, search, find out, and view such remote, heathen and barbarous lands, countries and territories, not actually possessed of any Christian Prince, nor inhabited by Christian People," and the right to "have, holde, occupie, and enjoy" the same, she similarly assumed that Raleigh would conquer the territories; if he failed, the grant would be of no force. The English sovereigns lost little in authorizing individual entrepreneurs and adventures like Raleigh to undertake expeditions at their own expense. Such an enterprise, whether successful or unsuccessful, would be at the expense of the explorer—and the Indians. If successful, the Crown would gain a new territory and new wealth. If unsuccessful, the explorer would lose his investment and sometimes his life. It was a case of "Heads I win; tails you lose," and the sovereigns played the game with consummate skill.

Most English arguments for title also made use of the Cabots' "discovery" in the Newfoundland area in 1497–98 to strengthen England's right to North America. This was the country's only argument of great priority, for she had slumbered during the hundred years following the Cabot voyages. As in the case of the king's charter, it is doubtful that the argument was accorded much weight even by the English themselves, except as a formal answer to the claims of prior discovery by other nations. Many Oriental regions, unknown in the same sense that many American regions were unknown in the period following Columbus' initial discovery, were "discovered" by Europeans in like fashion but rarely claimed as a result.

"Although many have stated that at the time of the European explorations of the fifteenth through seventeenth centuries discovery was a sufficient basis for a claim to sovereignty," writes William W. Bishop, "it is not clear whether the term 'discovery' meant more than the mere finding of the lands previously unknown to European civilization."[3] Three distinguished students of the question have also concluded that "throughout this lengthy period, no state appeared to regard mere discovery, in the sense of 'physical' discovery or simple 'visual apprehension,' as being in any way sufficient *per se* to establish a right of sovereignty over, or a valid title to, *terra nullius*. Furthermore, mere disembarkation upon any portion of such regions—or even extended penetration and exploration therein—was not regarded as sufficient itself to establish such a right or title."[4] The absurdity of gaining possession of a continent by sailing along its coast line was so obvious that some writers facetiously suggested that Europe would have to be conceded to any Indian prince who happened to send a ship to "discover" it.[5] By itself the assertion had little more effect in restraining other countries from colonizing North America than had the Pope's bulls, which, as Sir Walter Raleigh pointed out, could not gore so well as they could bellow.[6]

It was natural, therefore, to reinforce citations of early discoveries with accounts of actual occupation of the land. Here again the question arose as to how much of the continent passed into the possession of those occupying a portion of it. Did a settlement on the tip of Cape Cod or the Florida peninsula give title to the entire North American continent?

The monarchs were most liberal. Since it cost them nothing to give all, they gave all, with grants usually extending to the South Sea. But with several kings making grants in North

America, international conflicts were inevitable. Final settlement depended on the course of events and the power of the
claimants. "Why shall they," asked the French, "being at 36
or 37 [degrees], advance to 45, rather than we being, as they
admit, at 46, descend as far as 37? What right have they more
than we? This is our answer to the English."[7] An early eigh-
teenth-century English chronicler, on the other hand, expressed the English view of the extent of French sovereignty
in America (which covered vast expanses on French maps) by
asking: "Where then shall we find the Countries of *New-France*
and *Louisiana,* unless it be within the reach of the great Guns
of their Forts on the Rivers of *St. Lawrence* and *Mississippi*
. . . ?"[8]

Unfortunately, international law was not able to resolve the
dilemma. This inability is not to be wondered at, since international law has no central coercive power to establish its
authority; enforcement must rest on the use of power by the
individual sovereign states. Certain conventions, it is true,
grew up in this period, but they developed principally because
it was more expedient for the individual nations to compromise their exaggerated claims than to fight over them. One of
the conventions which appeared at this time was an agreement not to consider acts of violence occurring beyond the
papal line of demarcation in the Atlantic as breaking the peace
in Europe. Neither Spain nor Portugal was willing at first to
concede rights to others within the monopolies fixed by the
line, but other European powers were unwilling to recognize
that they might be barred. Hence, the area came to be excluded, at first by oral agreement and later by treaty arrange-
ment, from the effect of European peace settlements. The
phenomenon of "no peace beyond the line," as it was known,
was not allowed to break the peace that might exist on the
European side of the line. The special legal and moral character of acts committed in the area thus set aside suggests that
the European monarchs realized that their territorial claims

in the newly discovered areas had little basis in law or morality and could be increased, diminished, or surrendered, as expedient, without seriously threatening the vital interests of the mother country. [9]

The type of special relationship between two European powers beyond the ocean is revealed in frequent episodes throughout the seventeenth and eighteenth centuries. In the mid-eighteenth century, for example, the governors of France's colony in Louisiana and England's colony in South Carolina frequently, in the intervals between the formal wars between their masters, complained about the murders and ill treatment committed against their subjects by the Indian allies of the other, ostensibly at the behest, and sometimes with the alleged assistance, of their European partners. The "intervening variable" of the Indian nations—seemingly independent and dependent at the same time—allowed the elements of conflict between the European powers to be clouded with uncertainty. Responsibility could be pinpointed only with difficulty. In such circumstances, it was easy to apply different standards from those used in the European theater of war.

Today we visualize English invasion of the North American continent as the establishment of a military beachhead. The assumption is general that the Indian was a hostile occupant of the territory which the English proposed to settle. Although this was true as soon as English intentions to conquer as well as to settle became evident, it is not an accurate description of the initial Indian attitude. Nothing is so frequently recorded in the earliest chronicles as the warmth of the reception accorded the first colonists. The Indians believed in hospitality. The extent of their hospitality impressed the English; unfortunately, however, they were not impressed with the virtue of the Indians, but only with the power of their own God, who temporarily imbued the Indians with kindness. We read frequently such statements as "God caused the Indians to help us with fish at very cheap rates. . . ."[10] Perhaps such an attitude was natural to a people whose merit was based on salvation through a vicarious atonement. Since earthly success, as well as heavenly salvation, depended on God's will, not on man's effort, God was to be praised, not his terrestrial agents.

Another basis for English suspicion of Indian motives was the inherent fear of the unknown. Indians were strange creatures to the seventeenth-century Englishman, particularly since the sole basis of previous identification was in terms of heathen or infidel opponents of the True Faith. The Indians were expected to react hostilely. Their overt friendliness was often seen as proof of covert antagonism. Captain Christopher Newport, commanding the *Susan Constant, Godspeed,* and *Discovery,* reported after his trip up the James River in 1607 that the Indians "are naturally given to treachery, howbeit we could not finde it in o'r travell up the river, but rather a most kind and loving people."[11] William Symonds, editor of John Smith's *A Map of Virginia* (1612), expressed, with unconscious irony, the often-repeated complaint that the natives were "so malitious, that they seldome forget an injury. . . ."[12]

Nor was the tendency to see evil motives behind good deeds limited to the early colonists. Later writers have assumed that the Indians were secretly hostile to the colonists even when they granted them the most lavish hospitality or supplied food in their periods of want. Alexander Brown in 1898, for example, convinced himself that the Virginia Indians "were really the enemies of the English from the first. . . ." He explained the assistance given the settlers by the Indians in the fall of 1607 as follows:

All accounts agree that for some reason the Indians did daily relieve them for some weeks with corn and flesh. The supplies brought from England had been nearly exhausted; the colonists

had been too sick to attend to their gardens properly, and this act
of the Indians was regarded as a divine providence at that time.
. . . What was the real motive for the kindly acts of the Indians
may not be certainly known; but it probably boded the little
colony a future harm.[13]

Relations, it is true, did not continue friendly for long; treachery was being plotted behind the outward benignity. But was
it Indian treachery or white treachery?

The record of Indian-white relations from the settlement of
1607 to the great massacre of 1622 is one in which English
policy accepted Indian generosity as a matter of course, but
remained harsh and demanding of the Indians. Those demands were not solely for land but for food. The improvident,
ill-disciplined settlers provided a demonstration of how not to
colonize a new country and were only saved by the harsh
discipline of men like Captain John Smith and Sir Thomas
Dale whose harshness was directed not only at the English but
at the Indians. Since survival, in the face of the incompetence
and malingering shown by the settlers was possible only at the
expense of the Indians, the English commanders felt compelled to extort food if necessary from the increasingly disillu-
sioned natives. The proffered hand of friendship was
constantly rejected. As Powhatan, the great "emperor" of the
confederated tribes in the Virginia tidewater area put it:

> What will it avail you to take that perforce [which] you may
> quietly have with love, or to destroy them that provide you [with]
> food? What can you get by war, when we can hide our provision
> and fly to the woods, whereby you must famish, by wronging us,
> your friends?

To Smith, however, the direct way was best: as he put the
matter to Opechancanough, Powhatan's half-brother: "You

know my want; and I, your plenty: of which, by some means, I must have part."[14]

Given the Indian moral requirement for revenge for injuries committed, it is little wonder that a blow would finally be struck and, in keeping with Indian custom, that it would be concealed and sudden. From the Indian point of view, the grievances were real and demanded vengeance. The peace that Pocahontas' marriage with John Rolfe had helped to cement was swept away by the absence of a continuing commitment on the part of the English to respect the Indians' rights.

The massacre of 1622, from the English point of view, erased all previous accounts and provided the English with the "bloody shirt" needed to justify hostilities against the natives whenever convenient. Up until that time it was necessary to see malice in good will or to cite occasional Indian violence against small groups of settlers. Now the English could point to a full-scale war directed against all the settlements and carried out with terrible effects. Hundreds of English were slaughtered and the colony nearly wiped out. It would have been appropriate, of course, to determine whether the Indians were justified in attacking because of previous injuries and because of the English refusal to respect their unqualified sovereignty in the area. The importance of such considerations was admitted by some,[15] but ignored or denied by most. Edward Waterhouse rejoiced that the massacre had occurred:

Our hands which before were tied with gentlenesse and faire usage, are now set at liberty by the treacherous violance of the Sausages [Savages]. . . . So that we, who hitherto have had possession of no more ground than their waste, and our purchase at a valuable consideration to their owne contentment, gained; may now by right of Warre, and law of Nations, invade the Country, and destroy them who sought to destroy us. . . . Now their cleared

grounds in all their villages (which are situate in the fruitfullest
places of the land) shall be inhabited by us, whereas heretofore
the grubbing of woods was the greatest labour.[16]

The Virginia Company seized on the Massacre to order a
war against the Indians, dispossession of those near the settlements, and, as a gesture of mercy, the enslavement rather
than slaughter of the younger people of both sexes.[17] The
company's instructions were hardly necessary. The governor
and council had already initiated a policy of exterminating the
neighboring Indians. "Wee have anticipated your desire by
settinge uppon the Indyans in all places," they wrote
proudly.[18] To aid in the project the natives were lulled into
a sense of false security by the conclusion of a treaty, and the
council in Virginia even went so far as to boast of this bit of
treachery.[19] On one occasion poison was placed in the wine
offered to the Indians on the conclusion of a peace treaty.[20]
When chided by the company for their "false dealing," the
council in Virginia replied that "wee hold nothinge injuste,
that may tend to theire ruine, (except breach of faith). Strata-
gems were ever allowed against all enemies, but with these
neither fayre Warr nor good quarter is ever to be held, nor
is there any other hope of theire subversione, who ever may
informe you to the Contrairie."[21]

Next to treacherousness, "barbarism" was the most convenient accusation to hurl against the Indian in the seventeenth
century. Yet, as John Daly Burk, the historian of Virginia,
pointed out:

Notwithstanding the general charge of barbarism and treachery
against the Indians of Virginia, and of cruelty and tyranny against
Powhatan, with which the early historians abound, not a single
fact is brought in support of this accusation; and in several instances, with an inconsistency for which it is difficult to account,
the same writers speak with admiration of the exact order, which

prevailed among all the tribes of which this empire was composed; and confess at the same time, that this order and security arose from the inviolable observance of customs, which time has consecrated as law and which were equally binding on the King and the people.[22]

Today the character of the American Indian is generally drawn in a derogatory manner. The views of the first explorers and missionaries, who frequently saw heroic qualities in the Indian and whose reports provided the basis for the earlier literary conception of the "noble savage," have long since been buried in the shifting sands of more recent intellectual movements. None of the studies of "the myth of the noble savage" considers the possibility that the early favorable observers of Indian character might not have been entirely deceived in their analysis. All such studies assume that any degree of nobility was a myth: so far have white arrogance and Indian abasement proceeded.[23]

Another common charge against the Indians, which became the basis of the most popular eighteenth- and nineteenth-century justification for dispossessing them, was that they were wandering hunters with no settled habitations. This mode of securing their livelihood, it was charged, was too wasteful in a world in which other countries faced (or thought they faced) problems of overpopulation.[24] The argument that hunters might justly be forced to alter their economy by a pastoral or agricultural people was voiced by many, humble and great, in the colonies and in England. John Locke was perhaps its most famous exponent, although he did not develop the argument logically or clearly.[25] The argument was later expressed most succinctly by Theodore Roosevelt, who wrote that "the settler and pioneer have at bottom had justice on their side; this great continent could not have been kept as nothing but a game preserve for squalid savages."[26]

Again, was not the European creating the myth he wished

to use? Were the Indians in fact nomadic hunters? It was, of course, possible to find examples of nomadic hunting tribes in North America, and the Indians of the eastern coast, those referred to by the early theorists, depended upon hunting as an important part of their economy and an integral function of their social and religious life. But agriculture was also a conspicuously essential part of Indian subsistence, and we may regard with suspicion much of the literature of justification which overlooks this aspect of native life. The English knew well enough how important was Indian food: the early accounts are filled with references to the "Indian fields" along the rivers of Virginia, and little else but native produce sustained the whites in the early years of settlement. It was the Indians who taught the settlers techniques of agriculture, as the familiar story of Squanto and the Plymouth Colony relates, and the Virginia colonists also were instructed by the Indians on how to plant crops and how to retrieve food from the rivers and bays. The natives were hunters, but they were also, and probably more importantly, agriculturists and fishermen.[27]

The literature of justification similarly tends to overlook the fact that the Indians were, for the most part, town dwellers. The great body of contemporary graphic depictions in French, Spanish, and English sources of the sixteenth and seventeenth centuries shows substantial dwellings, palisaded villages, well-planned streets, garden plots, civic and religious centers. Indeed, throughout most of the seventeenth century in Virginia the only true town dwellers were the Indians; the English lived together compactly only during the fearful early years.

The literature of justification has never come to an easy and final solution. Men have thrashed over the morality of expansion without agreement, and the courts have interpreted the "law" involved without consistency.

Sir Thomas More, in his *Utopia* (1516), was one of the first

Englishmen to express himself on the justice of expansion.
When the Utopians, the inhabitants of More's ideal country,
had fully populated their own cities they sent colonists to
build "a town . . . in the next land, where the inhabitants have
much waste and unoccupied ground." The native inhabitants
are invited to dwell with the Utopians—under Utopian laws,
of course, which are considered by the Utopians to be greatly
superior. If the natives are foolish enough to resist this
benevolence, they are driven off the land; if resistance continues, the Utopians have no choice but to make full-scale war
against them. More's ideal people considered this the most
just cause of war: "when any people holdeth a piece of ground
void and vacant to no good or profitable use: keeping others
from the use and possession of it, which, notwithstanding, by
the law of nature, ought thereof to be nourished and re-
lieved."[28]

Sir Walter Raleigh, a hundred years later, was considerably
less positive than More. A people could deceive itself: for
example, "a number can do a great wrong and call it right,
and not one of that majority blush for it."[29] Raleigh noted
sadly and cynically that wars over land ownership were likely
to be inevitable because the "great charter whereby God be-
stowed the whole earth upon Adam and confirmed it unto the
sons of Noah, being as brief in words, as large in effect, hath
bred much quarrel of interpretation." English occupation of
the Bermudas (first "discovered" by the Spanish) was clearly
a moral action because the land had been uninhabited when
the English landed. But what of inhabited areas? Here Raleigh pondered the question which must continue to be at the
heart of all justifications for expansion in a world in which
every individual human being is regarded as possessing
roughly equivalent rights:

> If the title of occupiers be good in land unpeopled, why should
> it be bad accounted in a country peopled over thinly? Should one

family, or one thousand, hold possession of all the southern undiscovered continent, because they had seated themselves in Nova Guiana, or about the straits of Magellan? Why might not then the like be done in Afric, in Europe, and in Asia? If these were most absurd to imagine, let then any man's wisdom determine, by lessening the territory, and increasing the number of inhabitants, what proportion is requisite to the peopling of a region in such a manner that the land shall neither be too narrow for those whom it feedeth, nor capable of a greater multitude? Until this can be concluded and agreed upon, one main and fundamental cause of the most grievous war that can be imagined is not like to be taken from the earth.[30]

Roger Williams, in the 1630's and 1640's, was one of the few Englishmen who dared to dismiss European claims to American soil as unjustified and illegal if the prior right of the Indian were not recognized. Full title was in the Indian, he asserted, from whom alone a valid title could be derived. The colonists should repent of receiving title by patent from a king who had no right to grant it. Williams, said John Cotton, held it "a National duty to renounce the Patent: which to have done would have subverted the fundamental State and Government of the Country."[31]

Williams, despite his brave stand against the royal patent, was eventually forced to request a charter from the English parliamentary government in order to prevent the Rhode Island colony from being devoured by her neighboring English colonies.[32]

The history of Indian-white relations in the seventeenth century, when English colonists first established a permanent foothold in the New World, illustrates how the speculative legal claims of the European sovereigns could coexist with a practical recognition of Indian hegemony in the New World. The facts of the power relationship in the early seventeenth century resulted in an elaborate diplomatic exchange between the English and the Indians in the New World. No sweeping claims to legal title—such as the Spanish Require-ment—were read to the Indians. Rather, the head of each English settlement—whether it was Plymouth or Jamestown —dealt with the Indians who could affect his purpose in the manner of one independent power dealing with another. Threats, cajolery, bribery, force, persuasion, gifts—in sum, all the tools of international relations—were used to facilitate English purchase of, or occupation of the lands to which they aspired. De facto agreements were reached which—if the speculative legal claims of European sovereigns were mean-ingful—would have been totally unnecessary. The two realms coexisted. As English numbers and power grew the actual equality between the parties began to dissolve. Indeed, the breakdown of Indian negotiating power in Virginia and New England dates from about 1675 when the English began to outnumber the Indians with whom they were in contact. The fact that that year marks the outbreak of two significant Indian wars—King Philip's War in New England and Bacon's Rebel-lion in Virginia—during which the Indian power was demon-strably reduced—is not without significance. With their newly acquired predominance of numbers and weapons, the English could disregard justice and exercise mere force. As the Athenians said to the inhabitants of Melos in the famous Melian dialogue reported by Thucydides: "You know as well as we do that, when these matters are discussed by practical people, the standard of justice depends on the equality of power to compel and that in fact the strong do what they have the power to do and the weak accept what they have to ac-cept."[33]

Though the facts of power in the late seventeenth century provided the opportunity for a more aggressive assertion of white dominance over the red man, the assertion was rational-ized in the legal theory of the period. Indeed, as I have at-tempted to show in my book, *The Governor and the Rebel: A*

History of Bacon's Rebellion in Virginia (Chapel Hill: University
of North Carolina Press, 1957; 2d edition, 1968), the most
fundamental issue of the most significant colonial rebellion in
America's history prior to the American Revolution was over
the status of the Indian. Both principals—the governor and
the rebel—were former law students at the Inns of Court in
London. The Governor—Sir William Berkeley—attempted to
uphold the concept that those Indians living in friendship and
subjection to the English Crown were entitled to the same
protection that any of the King's subjects could expect,
whether against the hostile "foreign" Indians or against the
rash, land-hungry Indian-hating frontiersmen.

The rebel—councillor Nathaniel Bacon—asserted that all
Indians were outside the law and could be dealt with as per-
petual enemies of the Crown, whose prerogatives he attempted first to claim and then to subvert. In the "Manifesto"
of July, 1676, justifying the rebels' taking up arms against
the Indians without authorization from the governor, Bacon
noted that a main article of their guilt in Governor Berkeley's
eyes was the rebels' "open and manifest aversion of all, not
onely the Foreign but the protected and Darling Indians."
The Governor and Council, Bacon complained, had asserted
that the English must defend the Queen of Pamunkey and the
Appomattox Indians with their blood though the rebels
charged them with being "Robbers and Theeves and Invad-
ers of his Majesty's Right and our Interest and Estates." The
Manifesto made clear that its objection to the "neighbor Indians" was not only to their alleged, but never demonstrated,
misdeeds. It was to the very idea that any distinction at all
should be made among Indians. Rather, the rebels believed,
all should be "outlawed" as "wholly unqualifyed for the be-
nefitt and Protection of the law." The rebels cheerfully admitted their "Design not only to ruin and extirpate all Indians in
Generall but all Manner of Trade and Commerce with them.
. . ."34

The rebellion ended with the rebel dead, his forces dispersed, and the Governor triumphant. But the issue of the relationship of white man to Indian was not to be so readily solved. The tension between the point of view represented by each side has continued to our own day.

New England's Indian policy in the seventeenth century, like Virginia's, reveals the theoretical conflicts that have marked the white man's relationship to the red man throughout American history. New England's settlement, begun under a religious impulse, is marked by an extensive literature justifying the morality and legality of the settlement. Although New England had its eccentrics like Roger Williams, who denied the King's title, it was more fully represented by divines like John Cotton and governors like John Winthrop who elaborately defended the colonists' right to settle in New England and who justified the colony's strict policy in dealing with the Indians. In New England, as in the other colonies, a distinction was made between the foreign, or independent, Indians who influenced the colonists without being controlled by them; the plantation, or reservation, Indians, who acknowledged a subjection to the Crown but who were authorized to maintain their own local governments under English supervision; and individual Indians who formed a part —albeit a lowly part—of Puritan society.

The governments of New England, in common with most of the other colonial governments, and with the Federal Government later, developed an Indian policy which restricted private transactions in Indian land, which regularized, licensed and supervised the trade with Indians, and which created reservations for those Indians who wished to continue their tribal existence under English domination. The form in which English control was extended over the towns reserved to the "Praying Indians" of Massachusetts in the colonial period foreshadows the development of the entire Indian-white relationship in the United States. The inhabitants of these Indian villages, authorized by the Massachusetts General Court in 1652, were at first allowed to choose their own magistrates who would hear and determine all minor cases, civil and criminal, arising among themselves. Cases involving capital punishment and other matters beyond the cognizance of the Indian judges were to be heard by the Court of Assistants of the colony.

The integrity and self-government authorized the Indian villages lying within the Massachusetts colony were shattered by King Philip's War in 1675–1676. The "Praying Indians" were unthinkingly and unjustifiably tarred with the brush of the colony's enemy Indians and had to be protected by the colonial authorities from attack at the hands of their white neighbors. Following the war, in 1677, the Praying Indians were grouped into four plantations within which all Indians owing allegiance to the colony (except Indian children and servants living within English communities) were required to reside. The provisions of this act of the General Court were designed to provide security to the English in case of another war. The Superintendent of Indian Affairs for the colony, first appointed in 1656, served as the link with the political authorities in Boston. What home rule was allowed the Indians was restricted by an act of 1694 which provided for commissioners for the inspection and care of the plantation Indians. These commissioners, appointed by the governor, could in turn exercise the power of justice of the peace over the Indians in all matters, civil and criminal. They also acted as guardians of the Indians with responsibility for their welfare. The system of commissioners, or guardians, was continued throughout the eighteenth century.

There is no evidence that any reservation ever sent representatives to the General Court, from which one may conclude, in the words of one authority, that "it is reasonable to assume that the Indian reservations were outside the political divisions of the colony and thus did not attain the status of township, the basic political and territorial unit in colonial Massachusetts." As the eighteenth century progressed, Englishmen who purchased land in the Indian towns appear frequently as residents of such towns. Eventually all the Indian towns lost their identity as reservations, though until late in the nineteenth century, Indian villages continued to exist in Massachusetts. The vagueness and provisional nature of much of the Massachusetts legislation concerning Indian reservations suggest that the authorities did not intend the system to be permanent and that they expected the eventual assimilation of the Indians into white society.[34a]

2 : THE EIGHTEENTH CENTURY

Having established strong and vigorous colonies in the trying years of the seventeenth century, the English extended their power over the Indians as occasion warranted and as the weakness of the Indians permitted. Smaller, dependent tribes were gradually amalgamated or destroyed by the eroding effects of white contact. Disease—of which the frequent smallpox epidemics were the most costly—swept away many of the smaller tribes and decimated many of the larger nations. Yet throughout the eighteenth century and into the period of the American Revolution the Indians in several areas, most notably the Six Nations in the present area of New York State, and the Cherokee, Creek, and Choctaw of the southern interior, maintained a power and an independence which kept the colonies adjacent to them watchful and respectful of their needs and rights.

As long as the French maintained colonies in the great inland region stretching from the mouth of the St. Lawrence River in Canada to the mouth of the Mississippi on the Gulf of Mexico, the still powerful Indian nations of the interior could play off the two European powers against each other. The history of the tortuous diplomacy between the Iroquois

Confederation and their Dutch and English neighbors on the one hand and the French in Canada on the other is matched in the south by the contest between England and France for the loyalty and support of Cherokees, Choctaws, Chickasaws and Creeks. Each side competed with the other in presents and offers of support against the other. In the mid-eighteenth century, the King of England was sending annually to the Governors of South Carolina and Georgia as much as £3,000 worth of presents for the Indians of the Southeast. From the Indian point of view, it is possible to see such presents as "tribute" given by the Europeans to the Indians as "protection money" to insure that the Indians did not exercise their power against the white men. From a European point of view, however, the presents were often thought of as symbolic of the dependence of the Indians upon the Europeans and as a practical method of arming auxiliaries against a common foe. There is an element of truth in both Indian and English points of view. Certainly, the presents of guns, ammunition, clothes, useful articles of iron and items of personal decoration such as paint, silver gorgets, hawks bells and the like, came to be expected and sometimes demanded by the Indians as a right due them in exchange for their neutrality or aid. On the other hand, it is also true that the Europeans obtained good will, loyalty and military service in exchange for what was regarded in Indian cultural terms as the evidence of a true friendship and alliance.

Indian affairs continued to be the most important subject matter in the deliberations of the Governor, Council and Commons House of Assembly in South Carolina throughout the eighteenth century. It was only slightly less so in Virginia, Georgia, Pennsylvania, New York, and in other colonies faced with strong Indian nations blocking the path of their future expansion.

The power and unity of the Indian nations even provided an example to the colonists as they sought to form a common plan of resistance to the exorbitant demands of the mother country. It was the Iroquois confederacy which provided Benjamin Franklin with his insightful observation, when attempting to encourage colonial union in the 1750's, that

> It would be a very strange Thing, if six Nations of ignorant Savages should be capable of forming a Scheme for such a Union, and be able to execute it in such a Manner, as that it has subsisted Ages, and appears indissoluble, and yet that a like Union should be impracticable for ten or a Dozen English Colonies, to whom it is more necessary, and must be more advantageous; and who cannot be supposed to want an equal Understanding of their interests.[35]

The defeat of the French in the Great War for Empire (1756–1763) marked the beginning of the end for the de facto independence of the Indian nations. Yet that result is evident only in hindsight. The defeat of the French was followed by a careful policy of conciliation and restraint on the part of the British government toward the native inhabitants of the interior. There was no assumption that Indian rights in the lands claimed by France had been extinguished. Although Indian rights were less formal and less fundamental in European eyes than European claims, they nevertheless did exist as the subject for purchase, for negotiation, or for retention. The Proclamation of 1763, issued by a watchful English government, established a line running along the crest of the Appalachian Mountains, beyond which white settlement was at least temporarily prohibited. The line was one of a package of measures instituted by the imperial government in London to provide a more carefully coordinated and more tightly administered colonial administration for all of the English colonies in North America. By establishing control over colonial expansion the home government sought to avoid the disastrous wars that were often precipitated by frontiersmen

and colonial governments willing to take their chances con-
testing the rich lands of the trans-Allegheny west with their
native inhabitants. The continuing power and de facto sovereignty of numerous Indian nations before, during and after
the Revolutionary War, demonstrate the validity of the home
government's concern.[36]

When the American Revolution burst on the scene, the
revolutionary government moved quickly to duplicate the imperial organization for the management of Indian affairs.
Commissioners were appointed for the Indians in the North,
the middle colonies and in the south, roughly duplicating the
Superintendents of Indian Affairs whom the Crown had appointed for the Northern and Southern Departments of the
colonies. The colonists were aware that they had more to
suffer from Indian adherence to the King's side than their
opponents since the colonists lived scattered from the sea-
coast inland along the frontiers of the Indian nations. The
initial appeal of the Continental Congress to the Indians was,
therefore, that they remain neutral and abstain from warfare
in support of the King's forces. The revolution, they explained, was a white man's quarrel. It did not concern the
Indians. The colonists did not ask them to fight with them
against their "oppressors," as they described the English government. They merely asked them to stay at home.

The imperial agents, on the other hand, sought to enlist the
Indian nations in behalf of the Crown against the rebels. They
attempted to do this while eluding capture by rebel bands
who sought to seize them. Their role was doubly difficult
because of the opprobrium with which Indian raids on the
frontier were regarded by the colonists who were quick to
attribute such attacks to the instigation of the British agents.
The British agents attempted to avoid the charge that they
were setting uncontrollable savages on defenseless women
and children, yet the assertion could always be made whatever
the truth.

In fact, the colonists had the upper hand. The Crown could do little to protect the Indian allies it hoped to recruit because of their remote positions in the interior of the continent. On the other hand, the patriots, roused by the reports of barbaric attacks on defenseless settlers, sent expedition after expedition into the territory of hostile nations, burning the corn and villages of the Cherokee, for example, until the Indians realized the futility of their loyalty to the Crown's agents.

Some of the Indians did notable service, as, for example, Joseph Brant and his Mohawks who, with a Tory regiment, participated in the raid of November 11, 1778, on the Cherry Valley in central New York. Such raids led to swift and savage retaliation by the colonial forces.

As the war with the King's troops drew to a close in the colonists' favor, the Indians—who had for the most part chosen the "wrong" side during the conflict—became increasingly apprehensive. Their assistance to the Crown and their raids on frontier towns had generated resentment and retaliatory expeditions on the part of the colonists. But they had not been defeated or conquered. Neither the preliminary peace nor the definitive treaty of peace between the United States and Great Britain mentioned the Indians. The British, in concluding the Peace of Paris in 1783 had assured them that they had not "given away" their lands to the Americans which, in Indian eyes, they would have had neither the right nor the power to do. Yet persistent rumors of American claims on the basis of such a concession, and of an American claim to their lands on the presumption of conquest, reached and disturbed them. A separate peace with the Indians was clearly necessary. But who would make it? The individual states? The Congress? All could claim some jurisdiction. All had promised officers and men of the revolutionary forces bonuses of land, land that in most cases had to come from the Indian territories.

Article IX of the Articles of Confederation (proposed in

1777 and ratified in 1781) provided that Congress had "the sole and exclusive right and power of . . . regulating the trade and managing all affairs with the Indians, not members of any of the States, provided that the legislative right of any State, within its own limits be not infringed or violated. . . ."[37] The ambiguity, uncertainty, and weakness of the clause is apparent. Attempts were made to coordinate peacemaking after the Revolution, particularly in Pennsylvania and New York where the important interests of the Six Nations were involved. Pennsylvania, with its long tradition of fair dealing with the Indian, a heritage from William Penn, was more willing to coordinate its efforts with those of the Congress. New York, with the powerful Six Nations sitting athwart its main expansion route west, was less willing to concede a significant role to the Congressional commissions sent out to treat of peace. Both states took steps to purchase lands from the Indians in order to provide for the claims of their veterans and the interests of their present and future citizens. Pennsylvania, in accordance with its "ancient usage", sought to satisfy all possible claimants, even if their claims overlapped. New York was more concerned with establishing precise bounds and acquiring land.[38]

The land fever that followed the Revolution was aptly described by Washington, after a tour of the West in 1784:

> Such is the rage for speculating in, and forestalling of Lands on the No. West side of Ohio, that scarce a valuable spot within any tolerable distance of it, is left without a claimant. Men in these times, talk with as much facility of fifty, a hundred, and even 500,000 Acres as a Gentleman formerly would do of 1000 acres. In defiance of the proclamation of Congress they roam over the Country on the Indian side of the Ohio, mark out Lands, Survey, and even settle them. This gives great discontent to the Indians, and will unless measures are taken in time to prevent it, inevitably produce a war with the western Tribes.[39]

The Continental Congress insisted on keeping Indian affairs as much as possible in its hands and not delegating them to the separate states. On August 7, 1786, an Ordinance for the Regulation of Indian Affairs was enacted by which the sole and exclusive right of Congress under the Articles of Confederation to deal with the Indians was once more reasserted. Nevertheless, despite this and other measures to regulate the delicate and critical relationship with the Indian nations, individual states continued to flout the wishes of Congress and individual citizens continued to infringe on the territories of the Indians. On November 3, 1786, scarce three months after the Ordinance reserving such rights to the Congress, Georgia signed a treaty with a small body of Creeks by which Indians claiming to speak for the Creek Nation gave up all lands in Georgia east of the Oconee River.[40]

In 1787, prior to the writing of the Constitution, the Northwest Ordinance, setting forth the manner under which the unsettled areas to the northwest of the existing colonies should be organized, established the basic policy that, as an ideal, has governed American Indian policy since. The Ordinance states:

> The utmost good faith shall always be observed towards the Indians; their land and property shall never be taken from them without their consent; and in their property, rights, and liberty, they shall never be invaded or disturbed, unless in just and lawful wars authorized by Congress; but laws founded in justice and humanity shall from time to time be made, for preventing wrongs being done to them, and for preserving peace and friendship with them.[41]

The Ordinance, growing out of similar Ordinances of 1784 and 1785, drafted by Thomas Jefferson's committee on land disposal, was, in its 1787 form, largely the work of Rufus King and Nathan Dane.

Yet so ineffective were the pronouncements and mandates of Congress that encroachments on Indian land by unauthorized individuals continued. Henry Knox, secretary of war under the Confederation, reported to Congress in July 1788 that unprovoked acts of aggression against the Cherokee Indians by inhabitants of North Carolina were so outrageous "as to amount to an actual although informal war of the said white inhabitants against the said Cherokees." Knox blamed the aggression on the desire for Cherokee lands, and urged Congress to uphold its reputation and its pledged word, expressed in the Treaty of Hopewell, negotiated in 1785 and 1786, by driving the offending whites off. A proclamation was duly issued and an attempt made by the United States to meet its obligations to the Cherokees.[42]

While the Indians had cause to doubt the sincerity of white professions of concern and respect for their rights, their power enabled them periodically to check the encroachments of the white landhunters who eagerly poured into the fertile regions north of the Ohio following the Revolution. In the military responses that usually followed the resulting conflicts over land, the U.S. Army showed that it was by no means capable of asserting its authority in Indian country. On November 4, 1791, the army of General Arthur St. Clair was badly beaten by a force of Shawnees and other Indians, losing six hundred men in the event. The power of the Indian was still a force to be reckoned with. It was not until General Anthony Wayne humbled the Indians at Fallen Timbers, in Ohio, on August 20, 1794, that the Americans could proceed with security into the lands of Ohio which, as a result of the defeat, were ceded by the Indians in the Treaty of Greenville in the following year.[43]

Despite the confusion surrounding the rights and status of the Indians and the jurisdiction and responsibilities of the separate states and the United States in the period following the Revolution, a basic federal Indian policy did evolve in the period. Two men are largely responsible for the formulation of that policy: Henry Knox and Thomas Jefferson. Knox, appointed Secretary of War in George Washington's first cabinet, came to the post with a background of responsibility for dealing with Indian affairs during the Revolution and under the Articles of Confederation. In his first recommendations to President Washington, Knox stated that

> It would reflect honor on the new Government and be attended with happy effects, were a declarative law to be passed, that the Indian tribes possess the right of the soil of all lands within their limits, respectively, and that they are not to be divested thereof, but in consequence of fair and bona fide purchases, made under the authority, or with the express approbation, of the United States.

The different tribes, Knox averred,

> ought to be considered as foreign nations, not as the subjects of any particular State. Each individual State, indeed, will retain the right of pre-emption of all lands within its limits, which will not be abridged; but the general sovereignty must possess the right of making all treaties, on the execution or violation of which depend peace or war.[44]

Knox's humane Indian policy was reenforced by the support of Secretary of State Thomas Jefferson.

One of Jefferson's most significant contributions to Indian law was his emphasis on the right of pre-emption as a valid right of the European migrants to America. The doctrine had been expressed before, and its actuality had been demonstrated by the history of colonial land acquisitions, but Jefferson gave the doctrine new meaning and new dignity. Standing halfway between the preposterous, or exaggerated European claims to title based on "discovery" or observation of the shore line of a continent, and the indefensible, or rather undefendable, claim to total sovereignty on the part of those (the Indians) who could not maintain it, the doctrine of preemption recognized the legal right of the Indian nations to the lands they possessed and at the same time the legal right of the European intruder in the area to purchase the land, *when the Indian nations wished to sell it,* free from the fear that the land might be sold to a rival European power.

The right of pre-emption—which was a governmental and not an individual right—thus provided a legal position more respectful of European logic than the right of discovery and more considerate of the Indian interest than the right of conquest and occupation.

Jefferson clearly expressed his view of the theory in 1792 in response to the query of the British minister. The American right in the Indian soil, he asserted, was

> A right of preemption of their lands; that is to say, the sole and exclusive right of purchasing from them whenever they should be willing to sell. . . . We consider it as established by the usage of different nations into a kind of *Jus gentium* for America, that a white nation settling down and declaring that such and such are their limits, makes an invasion of those limits by any other white nation an act of war, but gives no right of soil against the native possessors.

In 1793, Jefferson reiterated his views in response to queries posed by President Washington to his cabinet:

> I considered our right of pre-emption of the Indian lands [he wrote] not as amounting to any dominion, or jurisdiction, or paramountship whatever, but merely in the nature of a remainder after the extinguishment of a present right, which gave us no present right whatever, but of preventing other nations from taking possession, and so defeating our expectancy; that the Indians had the full, undivided and independent sovereignty as long as they choose to keep it, and that this might be forever.[45]

Jefferson's view was supported by Knox, who pointed out that the Indians possessed the natural rights of man, and could not be divested of their lands legitimately, except in a just war or by appropriate legal means. To the opinion that the Indians had lost their rights by supporting the British in the Revolution, Knox pointed out that Congress in 1788 and 1789 had waived the right of conquest and had conceded the right of the Indians to the lands they possessed.[46]

While Jefferson, Knox and Washington formulated ideal rules for the extinction of Indian title, the more realistic tradition is represented by the comment of Sir William Johnson, the King's superintendent of Indian affairs for the northern colonies, who, in 1765, when asked his views on the dispute between the Wappinger Indians and the heirs of Adolph Philipse over a vast tract of land east of the Hudson River, replied:

> I have laid it down as an invariable rule, from which I never did, nor ever shall deviate, that wherever a Title is set up by any Tribe of Indians of little consequence or importance to his Majestys interest, & who may be considered as long domesticated, that such Claim unless apparently clear, had better remain unsupported than that Several old Titles of his Majestys Subjects should thereby become disturbed: —and on the contrary, Wherever I found a Just complaint made by a People either by themselves or Connections capable of resenting & who I knew would resent a neglect, I Judged it my Duty to support the same, altho it should disturb the property of any Man whatsoever.[46a]

The treaty system, which governed American Indian relations until 1871, explicitly recognizes the fact that the United States government formerly acknowledged the independent and national character of the Indian peoples with whom she dealt. Those treaties were the subject of formal diplomatic negotiations, however much—particularly in later years—the growing power of the United States and the diminishing power of the Indians created the distortions of fair dealing that the Indian Claims Commission is only now correcting. That the solemn treaties of the United States proved ineffective first against the lawless white frontiersmen of the time and later against the forgetful successor governments of the United States is less a commentary on law than it is on honor.

3 : THE NINETEENTH CENTURY

In the early years of the Repub-
lic a prime function of government policy was to regulate
trade between whites and Indians. From the earliest days of
the first explorers until well into the nineteenth century, the
trade in furs played a central role in the relationship between
white and Indian. Throughout the colonial period, various
licensing arrangements sought to regulate the trade, but with
less than outstanding success. Unregulated traders, uncon-
trolled abuses, often sparked Indian resentment and retaliation. Still the trade served a vital function for both peoples:
for the Indian it brought the metal tools and utensils that
provided technological superiority to their possessors (especially if that tool were a musket or rifle) and for the white it
brought the rich furs (of which beaver was the most exotic)
which—in sartorial form—formed the mark of a gentleman in
Europe.

The authority for the relationship between the Indians and
the newly formed United States was established in large measure, be it noted, by the "commerce clause" of the Constitution which provided that the Congress should have the power
"to regulate Commerce with foreign Nations, and among the

several States, and with the Indian Tribes." In keeping with this authority, Congress adopted licensing systems reminiscent of similar restraints imposed by most of the colonial governments. The intercourse act of July 22, 1790, required anyone wishing to trade with the Indians to obtain a license —good for two years—from a properly authorized official, upon posting of a bond of $1,000. The license could be withdrawn if the regulations governing the trade were violated. Persons found trading in the Indian country without such a license were subject to loss of goods and fines. It was not always possible to enforce such laws, however.

Other "intercourse acts" subsequently attempted to regulate the relationship between white and Indian. Enforcement came to depend upon personnel within the War Department appointed to deal with the Indians. These persons received the general designation of "Indian department" even though they constituted only an informal rather than a fixed organization of men and duties.

On April 21, 1806, the office of superintendent of Indian trade was established within the War Department to supervise and run the factory trading system which was established and carried on under government auspices until its demise in 1822. The factory system put the purchase, transfer and sale of Indian goods in the hands of government agents. It was a noble experiement which was abandoned under pressure of independent fur trading interests such as the American Fur Company and their champions in Congress in 1822.[47]

Thomas Jefferson has been accused by some of cynical disregard of Indian interests during his two terms as President (1801–1809) because of his belief that the solution to the Indian problem was their removal west away from the aggressive expansion of their white neighbors in the East. Any president—even Jefferson—must often act *not* as his personal inclinations might suggest, but as necessities of state seem to dictate. But in the early days of the Republic a benevolent friend of the Indian—and Jefferson can in many ways be called such—might indeed believe, both as an intellectual and as a politician, that removal was the most effective and honest solution to the pressures being put upon the tribesmen. This attitude would be conditioned by the assumption that settlement of the western areas by white men would not be soon or significant. The vastness of the continent was only too well known by the man who sent Lewis and Clark to explore it. A more important consideration was the sorrowful knowledge that the federal government could not really protect the Indians against either individuals or states. The nature of English common law, and the limited powers of the central government, both conspired to make guarantees to Indians difficult to carry out.

President Jefferson, the "Great Father," in one of his talks to his "Red Children", in the persons of a delegation of Delawares, Mohicans, and Muncies, had urged them to give up the pursuit of the deer and buffalo and to cultivate and enclose the land. "When once you have property, you will want laws and magistrates to protect your property and persons. . . . You will find that our laws are good for this purpose . . . you will unite yourselves with us . . . form one people with us, and we shall all be Americans. . . ."[48]

In the period following Jefferson's administration, the hope was to be frustrated. The land which the Indians occupied was a prize too great for the United States to acknowledge their rights in, by a tenure as secure as Jefferson envisaged or as a white man expected for himself. "Indian use" and "Indian title" were severely limited forms of possession to those whites whose commitment to Indian-white unity was not so great as Jefferson's. While the obligation of the Indian nations to alienate their land only to the United States continued to be asserted, the right of the Indian to full enjoyment of his land, let alone to legal title to it, was gradually diminished. Attorney General William Wirt, noted as a friend of the Indian in the period of the Cherokee cases in the 1830's, expressed the opinion on March 26, 1819, that the Indians could not even "alienate the natural productions of the soil, the timber growing on it." "I incline to the opinion that the use of the Lands permitted to the Indians is to be considered as personal to themselves as intended for their subsistence and looking to their personal occupation of it, and although they have the right to cultivate and sell the crops which are the production of their own labours, they have no more right to sell the standing timber . . . than they have to sell the soil itself."[49]

In a series of treaties in the early nineteenth century, the U.S. agreed to boundaries of Indian lands and (as in the case of the Choctaw Treaty of Doak's Stand, signed October 18, 1820), promised that those boundaries "shall remain without alteration until the period at which said nation shall become so civilized and enlightened as to be made citizens of the United States, and Congress shall lay off a limited parcel of land for the benefit of each family or individual in the nation." Such treaties did not recognize any immediate right to private property or even such a right at any specific time in the future. Such treaties were routinely approved by the Senate and by the Executive.[50]

In some cases allotments in what is called "fee simple" were made to named individuals as part of such agreements. "Fee simple," which derived from English land law of the late Middle Ages, signified absolute ownership, or the right of the owner to sell the land to anyone, or to allow it to be inherited by his heirs. Such ownership was distinguished from a second type of freehold, the "entail" or "fee tail," in which inheritance and the right of selling were restricted. Allotments in fee simple were normally made to those Indians—sometimes half-breeds—who had adopted the European mode of life. An 1817 treaty with the Cherokee provided, within the reservation set aside, a life estate for every head of a family who wished to become a United States citizen, the tract to descend in fee simple to his heirs, "reserving to the widow her dower." (The dower right, in common law, consisted of a one-third interest, for the life of the widow, in all the land which the husband owned during the marriage. The dower right was modified by statute in many states though alternate provisions were normally provided for the widow). If the allotment was abandoned by its first recipient, however, the land reverted to the United States. In 1819, in a treaty confirming that of 1817, immediate fee simple allotments of 640 acres were made to certain specified capable persons among the Cherokee, and in the Choctaw Treaty of Doak's Stand other allotments in fee simple were made, though presidential consent was necessary for the allottee to sell and convey in fee simple. None of these grants stirred opposition in a Congress. A principal reason was, as Mary E. Young has shown in her study, *Redskins, Ruffleshirts, and Rednecks* (Norman: University of Oklahoma Press, 1961), that such grants were too often simply a form of bribery to win support from influential individuals for the cessions negotiated and to hasten the breakdown of tribal unity. The value of United States citizenship and the protection of American law were not too secure supports for the red man in Georgia in the nineteenth century. Only a handful of the Cherokee and Choctaw received the grants; most of the remainder were eventually forced to remove to the west.[51]

In the case of the northern Indians other methods were sometimes used. In 1817 a treaty with the tribes remaining in Ohio, with the exception of the Miamis, ceded much of the northwestern quarter of the state. In return, the treaty provided annuities and reservations within the ceded territory. The chiefs of the Indian nations were, in effect, made trustees of the reservations, the United States patenting the land in fee simple to the chiefs. The latter could convey shares of the reservation to members of the tribe or their descendants.

These devisees could in turn alienate their possession to any-one provided they had presidential approval for the trans-action.[52]

When President Monroe submitted the treaty, along with other Indian treaties to the Senate, that body treated the Ohio Indians' treaty differently from the other treaties, including the 1817 Cherokee treaty discussed above. The Committee on Public Lands, to which the treaty was referred, objected to it on the grounds that it was "at variance with the general principles" by which Indian affairs were normally handled, which assumed on the part of the Indians an "incapacity to transact their business" and, on the part of the government, "a superintending concern and guardianship over their inter-ests." The committee proposed renegotiation of the treaty to provide for tenure "in like manner as has been practised in other and similar cases." The dilemma was resolved with a timely and generous specie payment to overcome the Indians' objections to the revision of the treaty. As Professor McClug-gage has put it, "The reservation for the Ohio Indians re-mained no more secure than their lands had ever been, which is to say not at all."[53]

When in 1819 a Kickapoo treaty, held at Edwardsville for their lands in Illinois, and providing for a reservation forever for the Kickapoo and their heirs in the Territory of Missouri, was submitted to the Senate, that body, after three months, rejected the proposed tenure under which the Indians were to hold their land. The treaty commissioners persuaded the Kickapoo to agree to an amendment providing that they should hold their new lands "in like manner as the land ceded." Once more the Senate had declined to give the Indi-ans fee simple title in any land.

Jefferson had told the Indians that their hope lay in private property in land. "In this way alone," he had told them, "can you ensure the lands to your descendants through all genera-tions, and that it shall never be sold from under their feet."

The record, of both President and Senate from the turn of the century to the Jackson presidency shows, in the words of Professor McCluggage, "a consistent and clear determination to deny the Indians the security of fee simple title to land."[54]

On March 11, 1824, Secretary of War Calhoun created in the War Department a Bureau of Indian Affairs. The Bureau was established on Calhoun's authority and without special authorization from Congress. Thomas L. McKenney, who was appointed to head the office, preferred to call the bureau the "Indian Office" or, more frequently, the "Office of Indian Affairs." The superintendents of Indian Affairs and the Indian agents were charged with the enforcement of the intercourse acts, but had to rely on local legal officers and courts to bring offenders to justice. The weakness of this system is well known to any student of American history. Apprehending those guilty of crimes against the Indians was second in difficulty only to getting a white judge or white jury to convict a white man of a crime against an Indian. The fruits of permanent bitterness in the Indian mind were left by the inability of the federal government to keep its promises. Though Secretary of War Henry Knox recommended the trial and punishment of offenders against the Indians by military court-martial, the Congress never permitted it, insisting, in all the intercourse acts, that the offenders be turned over to the nearest appropriate civil authorities.

The greatest crisis in the legal relationship between Indian and white arose in reference to the Cherokee cases in the 1830's, about which much has been written. Two strong men were brought face to face by the crisis: President Andrew Jackson and Chief Justice John Marshall. It was the chief justice upon whom was placed the burden of weighing the claims of a vigorous, rising nation against the inherited rights of a faltering race. On his decision hinged the title to the real estate of the nation, the independence of numerous Indian nations, the sanctity of treaty rights, and even the very existence of law and order. Marshall had to consider not only law but conscience and expediency as well. The "natural" rights of the Indians had to be seen in terms of the "speculative" rights of the earlier European monarchs, the "juridical" rights of their successor American states, and the "practical" economic and political demands of the millions who now populated the continent.

Marshall did not hesitate, and his decision has been the basis of all subsequent determinations of Indian right. In the case of *Johnson and Graham's Lessee* v. *McIntosh* in 1823, Marshall declared that the Indians of the United States did not possess an unqualified sovereignty despite the centuries of relations conducted with them in terms of treaties and diplomatic agreements. Their right to "complete sovereignty, as independent nations" was diminished or denied, declared Marshall, by "the original fundamental principle that discovery gave exclusive title to those who made it." "The history of America," the historian-chief justice concluded, "from its discovery to the present day, proves, we think, the universal recognition of these principles." Marshall declared further that the principle of discovery "was a right which all asserted for themselves, and to the assertion of which, by others, all assented." "However extravagant the pretension of converting the discovery of an inhabited country into conquest may appear," wrote Marshall in his decision, "if the principle has been asserted in the first instance, and afterwards sustained; if a country has been acquired and held under it; if the property of the great mass of the community originates in it, it becomes the law of the land and cannot be questioned."[55]

Marshall's decision encouraged the state of Georgia, beginning in 1824, to try to dispossess the Cherokee Indians living within its borders. Hitherto the Cherokee Nation had lived confident in the protection afforded by the many treaties concluded with the English and American governments before and after the Revolution. In all these agreements the Cherokee Nation had been treated as an independent political power possessing proprietary right and political authority in the land it occupied.

The Cherokees had, moreover, in the course of their contact with Europeans, adopted white customs of dress and white modes of cultivation. They had thus, in the words of James Madison, refuted the unfounded claim of the whites that they were nomadic savages, unqualified for formal ownership of land. Yet there was always an answer to Indian claims, and the Cherokees were now opposed on the "strange ground . . . that they had no right to alter their condition and become husbandmen."[56]

In 1828 the Cherokees held a convention to establish a permanent government and write a constitution for their nation. The state, anxious to prevent the creation of further obstacles to Indian removal, replied in 1829 with a series of laws invalidating all statutes and ordinances adopted by the Indians and authorizing the division of their lands. These laws were, of course, in violation of solemn treaties between the United States and the Cherokee Nation. President Jackson, whose frontier upbringing had left him with little sympathy for the Indians, was in complete accord with Georgia. When the Cherokees applied for federal protection against the efforts of Georgia to coerce them in violation of their treaty rights, Jackson replied that "the President of the United States has no power to protect them against the laws of Georgia."[57]

Disappointed by this breach of faith, the Indians initiated legal action before the Supreme Court to prevent Georgia from carrying out its laws in violation of the Cherokee Nation's solemn treaty rights. Two distinguished lawyers agreed to represent the Cherokees: William Wirt, ex-Attorney General of the United States, and John Sergeant, former chief counsel for the Bank of the United States. Before taking the case, Wirt considered the moral and legal issues involved and read extensively on the controversy as it had been argued in Congress. "In making this examination," he said, "I was struck with the manifest determination, both of the President and the States, that the State laws should be extended over . . . [the Cherokees] *at every hazard.* This led me to reflect more seriously on the predicament in which I was about to place myself, and perhaps involve the Supreme Court of the United States."[58]

Chief Justice Marshall, though sympathetic to the plight of the Cherokees, had to consider the incalculable effects a decision in their favor might have on the authority of the Supreme Court: the President's probable refusal to enforce the orders of the court could destroy the authority so painstakingly built up by Marshall.[59] How much effect such considerations had on his decision is uncertain. At any rate, in the action brought by *The Cherokee Nation* v. *The State of Georgia* (1831), Marshall ruled that the Cherokee Nation, though a "State," was not a "foreign State" but a "domestic dependent nation," and that the court had no original jurisdiction of the cause.[60] Justice Smith Thompson dissented "in an opinion of immense power" in which Justice Joseph Story concurred.[61]

The decision on the right of the state of Georgia to impose its authority upon the Cherokees, though not met squarely in this case, was faced in the case of *Samuel A. Worcester* v. *The State of Georgia* (1832). Here Georgia's right to force two missionaries with the Cherokees to obtain a license and take an oath of state allegiance was denied. Marshall, in his decision, held the Georgia statute unconstitutional on the ground that the jurisdiction of the federal government over the Cherokees was exclusive. Georgia, the court ruled, had no power to pass laws affecting the Cherokees or their territory.[62]

Having previously ruled the Cherokees dependent, Marshall now attempted to limit their dependence to the federal government and not to the state of Georgia. But even this ruling was dangerous under the conditions of power which existed. It failed to protect the Indians and it nearly toppled the court's authority. Just what President Jackson's precise feeling in the matter was we do not know; there seems little doubt, however, that he never intended to enforce the decision of the court against an unwilling Georgia. He wanted the Indians removed, by law or without law, in the name of whatever principle might be applied. And they were removed. The court's impotence threw Marshall into a deep gloom. "I yield slowly and reluctantly to the conviction that our constitution cannot last," he wrote to Justice Story on September 22, 1832.[63]

The success of the state of Georgia in defying the federal government encouraged the state of South Carolina, in an Ordinance of Nullification (1832) to declare the tariff act of 1832 "null and void". But on this question Jackson reacted in a different manner. He rebuked South Carolina with the "Force Bill" and thereby bolstered the authority of the central government and the Supreme Court, even causing Georgia to pardon the missionaries upon the withdrawal of their suit. The crisis involving the court and the federal government passed; the only victim was the Cherokee Nation.

On March 3, 1849, the Department of the Interior was created and the Bureau of Indian Affairs transferred from the War Department to the new agency. The assumption underlying the change in status was expressed most effectively by Robert J. Walker, Secretary of the Treasury, in his annual report to Congress on December 9, 1848. Walker noted that the duties performed by the Commissioner of Indian Affairs were bound to increase with the opening up of vast areas of the West and that those duties were more oriented to peaceful pursuits than to warlike ones. More important, however, was the fact that the Indian Commissioner, like the Commissioner of the General Land Office, would be under the supervision of the same Secretary. Because of the close realtionship between Indian treaties, military bounties and land warrants, private land claims, and the public lands, it was logical that there be a coordination of effort in the field. The Indian, thus, by mid-century, was ceasing to be considered a military problem; he now became a potential land resource.[64]

During the Civil War, hostilities with Indians in the West were numerous, and white expansion into Indian lands proceeded apace. With the end of the war, the expansion redoubled in intensity. The overwhelming power the whites could bring to bear on the Indians resulted in demands by frontier editors for their extermination while humanitarians raised an increasingly vocal demand that the Indian be protected from unjustifiable assaults. Secretary of the Interior in 1865 was James Harlan, twice president of Iowa Wesleyan College and an active churchman. The Army, compelled to maintain order on the Plains yet shorthanded because of the exodus from the service following the war, saw merit in supporting a peace commission to make peace with the plains tribes and separate those peaceably inclined from the "hostiles." Congress, as a result of pressure from both the military and humanitarian groups, passed a bill on July 20, 1867, providing for the creation of a commission of military and civilian representatives to make treaties of peace with the plains tribes. General William T. Sherman, commander of the army in the west, and a member of the commission, hoped to concentrate the most powerful Indian nations in restricted areas and to clear Kansas and Nebraska, where population pressures were greatest, of hostile Indians. The commission accepted the necessity of a speedy settlement of the west "by an industrious, thrifty, and enlightened population." The Indians, they believed, should be concentrated, as much as possible, in districts of their own east of the Rocky Mountains. A strong and honest administration of the districts should be set up, agriculture and the mechanic arts introduced, schools established, the English language taught. Annuities of domestic animals, agricultural implements, clothing, and the like, should be granted in the early stages of the enterprise. Missionaries would assist the Indians to adapt to the white man's way of life. The commissioners also recommended thorough reform of the Indian administration, including the creation of a separate Indian Department, and an extension of the commission's powers so that they might continue to meet with those tribes inclined to come within the land reserves that had been selected. Revision of the Indian intercourse laws was also recommended. None of these latter recommendations were put into law, but, by 1873, the shape of American Indian policy following the Civil War had been outlined by the basic conception of creating Indian reserves east of the Rockies, and forcing the Indian nations to reside within their bounds on pain of being declared hostiles and outlaws. Little matter that the Congress failed to make sufficient appropriations to support the Indians in the early years of their new and unaccustomed life and to train them in the new techniques they would have to learn to survive.[65]

The assumption was that the Indians would somehow survive by the hunt, yet game animals were insufficient in the new preserves, and the Indians were frequently forced to return to their former hunting grounds in order to survive. By 1868, the United States was at war with many of the tribes of the Southern Plains. The Peace Commission reconvened in Chicago and on October 9, 1868, adopted a set of resolutions which were sent to the President and the Congress. The Commission recommended that provisions be made for feeding, clothing and protecting all Indians of the plains who currently resided or who would reside in the future on approved reservations. However, the Commission recommended that the government should cease to recognize the tribes as domestic, dependent nations except where already provided for in existing treaties. Otherwise, all Indians should be individually subject to the laws of the United States. The Army should compel the Indians to go to the reservations and the Indian Bureau should be transferred to the War Department. The generals on the commission had succeeded in obtaining a hard line policy.

After Ulysses S. Grant was elected president, and military supervision seemed to be the policy he intended to put into effect, he was approached by a group of Friends, or Quakers, who, in the course of their discussions with Grant early in 1869, were asked to supply the names of candidates for the office of Indian agent. In their response, they requested that an entire superintendency be assigned to the Society, giving it authority to appoint all the employees from the superintendent on down. Agreement was eventually reached on such a scheme, with the Hicksite Friends assuming control of the northern superintendency which included the whole of Nebraska. The Orthodox group was given the central superintendency, including all the Indian tribes in Kansas and the Indian territory with the exception of the Five Civilized Tribes.

The innovations under Grant spilled over into the policy that evolved in the years following. When Congress, on July 15, 1870, prohibited Army officers from holding the post of Indian agent, a practice which Grant, along with his experiments with the Quakers, had followed, the President awarded the agencies to other Christian denominations on terms similar to those made with the Quakers. Grant acted with the support of a civilian Board of Commissioners, of philanthropic background, authorized by Congress in 1869 to be appointed by the President to exercise joint control with the Secretary of the Interior in the disbursement of funds for the support of the reservation Indians.[66]

As the Indian power waned, Congress increasingly took upon itself the power to modify the treaties which it had formerly made. In 1861 a treaty with the Arapahoe and Cheyenne Indians recognized the power of the President, with the assent of Congress, "to modify or change any of the provisions of former treaties . . . to whatever extent he may judge to be necessary and expedient for their best interests."[67] Moreover, Congress frequently ignored or disregarded treaties formerly entered into by enacting laws in conflict with them. Finally, in 1871, the Congress, by a simple "rider" to an appropriations act, abandoned the treaty making system, though upholding the validity of those already made.

The termination of the treaty relationship cleared the way —or seemed to clear the way—for destroying the separate status of the Indian in the United States. No longer able to contest the will of the white man, as expressed through the dictates of the Congress, the Indian waited to see what the new era would bring. He had not long to wait. A massive drive toward "severalty"—the breaking up of tribal lands into individual units for distribution to the members of the tribe— began which culminated in the Dawes Severalty Act of 1887.

The Act had the backing of those who wished the Indian well and of those who wished him ill. About the only group which was not enthusiastic for the bill was the group it was designed to help: the Indians. White reformers, holding persistently to a belief whose falsity rings through the centuries of experience preceding the act, thought that the Indian would (the reformer really meant should) become integrated into white society if he could be taught to value private property and his individual welfare above the interests of his tribe. The white reformer, with a condescension more reprehensible (because based on ignorance) than the greed of the white land grabbers who saw in the severalty legislation a chance to acquire cheaply the surplus land made available by the legislation, took the position that the Indian must be pushed against his will into the white world of competition and individualism. The reformer did not believe that the Indian's values should be respected. The Indian was a child whose perverse will had to be broken until his behavior conformed to that of his loving but stern father.

The catastrophic consequences of the severalty policy are told best in the figures for acreages under tribal control. Of the 138,000,000 acres of tribal land-holdings in 1887, only 48,000,000 remained in 1934.[67a] The 160–acre allotments given heads of families and lesser amounts to other Indians were, more often than not, leased to whites during the period—usually twenty-five years—when the United held title to the land in trust, and afterwards sold for a pittance or lost by default to white neighbors. The surplus land left after the allotments from tribal lands were made went onto the general land market, and were snapped up by land-hungry whites. No longer did many tribal Indians feel pride in the tribal possession of hundreds of square miles of territory which they could use as a member of the tribe. Now they were forced to limit their life and their vision to an incomprehensible individual plot of 160 or so acres in a checkerboard of neighbors, hostile and friendly, rich and poor, white and red.

The blow was less economic than psychological and even spiritual. A way of life had been smashed; a value system destroyed. Indian poverty, ignorance and ill health were the results. The admired order and the sense of community often observed in early Indian communities were replaced by the easily caricatured features of rootless, shiftless, drunken outcasts, so familiar to the reader of early twentieth-century newspapers.

The white world was not immediately prepared to undo its mistake. Although there was quick recognition, by reformers and speculators alike, of the consequences of the Dawes Act upon the Indian land base, a drive began soon after, in the 1890's, to apply the principle of the severalty legislation to the Five Civilized Tribes in Oklahoma, who, with a few other tribes, had been exempted from the original Dawes legislation. By successive acts of Congress, in response to the recommendations of the Commission to the Five Civilized Tribes, first known as the Dawes Commission, the Indians of Oklahoma were stripped of their governmental autonomy and their tribal lands allotted in severalty. The act of June 28, 1898, the Curtis Act, abolished tribal courts and declared Indian law unenforceable in Federal Courts. By the time Oklahoma was admitted to the Union as a state in 1907, the separate character of its famous Indian nations had all but disappeared.

With the damage virtually complete in the areas where severalty was an economic possibility (the Indian inhabitants of the southwestern deserts were fortunately spared the experience by the obvious absurdity of the concept in their lands) white leaders took up the task once again of finding new remedies for the persisting Indian "problem." The commitment to a new approach was foreshadowed in the 1928 report of the Institute for Government Research (the so-called Meriam Survey). That report, by the predecessor to the present-day Brookings Institution, noted how the economic base of traditional Indian culture had been destroyed by the encroaching white civilization. The base could not be restored. Hence the culture could not be restored in its original form.

The report urged that the Indian policy of the United States be designed to fit the Indian to "merge with the social and economic life of the prevailing civilization as developed by the whites or to live in the presence of that civilization at least in accordance with a minimum standard of health and decency." While the report emphasized the desirability of bringing the Indian into a closer working relationship with the white man's civilization, and while rejecting as "impracticable" the "glass case policy" of those who wished to keep the Indian as he always had been, the report also asserted that "He who wants to remain an Indian and live according to his old culture should be aided in doing so." But in any event the government had an obligation to educate the Indian in the most fundamental sense: to teach him how to do things for himself and to see that economic and social conditions supported that process.[68]

The Meriam Survey was the herald of a movement that has continued to our own day which has sought to emphasize education and training as the key to entrance into white society. The assumption that the Indian not only should, but must enter into competition with his white co-sharers of this land has continued. The assumption is held not only by those who uphold white values, but by many who cherish Indian values. Those who uphold the Indian values reason that the prevalent power relationships require that the Indian be able to utilize the white legal, political and economic machinery to maintain his land base and (where it still exists) his tribal identity. Because of the change of policy brought in with the New Deal, the Indian now has a fighting chance to hold onto these two fundamental supports to his Indianness. The New Deal, along with the other sweeping reforms it introduced, called a halt to the policy of breaking up the Indian tribal identity and the tribal ownership of land. The change of policy required a change of heart and a change of attitude on the part of the men controlling Indian affairs. That change was one of the first accomplishments of Franklin Roosevelt, who created an unbeatable and resilient team in Secretary of the Interior Harold Ickes and Commissioner of Indian Affairs John Collier. How difficult it was even for the reforming Roosevelt administration to achieve that change of heart is illustrated in an incident recounted by Secretary Ickes in his *Secret Diary* of the first thousand days of the Roosevelt administration. In the diary, Ickes tells of a crucial meeting in the President's study in the White House which was arranged by the President to bring Ickes and Senator Joe T. Robinson, the Majority Leader of the Senate, together for the purpose of discussing the next Commissioner of Indian Affairs. Robinson had proposed Edgar B. Meritt and had put pressure on Roosevelt to appoint him. Roosevelt asked Ickes to speak to the proposal. Ickes asserted that he had documentary proof tending to show the total disqualification of Meritt for the job. Roosevelt, in his friendliest manner, pointed out to Robinson: "Well, Joe, you see what I am up against. Every highbrow organization in the country is opposed to Meritt, and Secretary Ickes, under whom he would have to work, doesn't want him." Meritt's appointment was blocked and that of John Collier, recommended by Secretary Ickes, was proposed by the President instead.[69]

Ickes' willingness to act decisively in the field of Indian affairs is further revealed in a diary entry for June 8, 1933. In response to a congressional request urging him to prevent the closing of an Indian boarding school, Ickes pointed out to the delegation that:

> we had exploited the Indians from the beginning; that we had taken from them their lands; that we had robbed them right and left; that the diseases they were suffering from were due in a large measure to contacts with the whites and were not unrelated to undernourishment. I said that Congress wouldn't give us money for things needed to be done for the Indians; that Congress had

assisted in despoiling them and that the man who was largely responsible for Indian appropriations in the House of Representatives for many years had gone publicly on record to the effect that eleven cents a day was enough to feed an Indian child. I added that this same man, after he had been defeated for Congress, crowded himself into this Department at a fine big salary, and that it gave me great joy, as one of my first official acts after I came to Washington, to fire him.[70]

With men like Ickes and Collier in control of the executive machinery, and with a frightened nation looking for leadership from an equally dynamic President, it was not long before the Congress reversed its age-old Indian policy and passed the Indian Reorganization Act of 1934, known as the Wheeler-Howard Act, returning to tribal ownership surplus Indian lands previously open to sale, and ending land allotments in severalty. The Act also provided for the acquisition of additional lands by tribes and individuals. In addition it recognized and encouraged tribal organization by authorizing the establishment of tribal governments and the fostering of tribal economic enterprises.

The Indian Reorganization Act extended to the Indian community powers of self-government roughly equivalent to those possessed by incorporated towns in the United States. Prior to the passage of the Act the Indian Service administered the reservations in complete disregard of tribal authority.[71]

Typical of the changes brought about by the Wheeler-Howard Act was the new method of providing credit from federal funds to the Indians. The first general appropriation to supply credit to the Indians had been made in 1911: $30,000 was authorized for the purpose. In succeeding years additional credits were provided. However, under the provisions of this program, government officials purchased the items such as cattle and farm machinery required by the Indians and resold them to the Indians. There was little scope for the Indian to decide on the kinds, types or quality of items he needed. Of over $7,000,000 loaned during the period up to 1937, with minimal participation by the Indian, the government experienced a loss of several million dollars of uncollectable debts.

By contrast, the Indian repayment record made under the Indian Reorganization Act of 1934, which authorized a large pool of credit to be made available to tribal corporations, credit associations, and cooperative groups, has been good and the number of delinquent loans negligible.[72]

The exhilaration of World War II was followed by a return to the depression—economic and psychological—of the past. War no longer provided an outlet for heroism and sacrifice on the battle fronts. War industries closed and the special economic opportunities provided Indians at home dried up. Indians from the war fronts and from the industrial centers returned to the traditional heritage of neglect and poverty on the reservation. Although Indian income during the war year of 1944 was 2½ times that of 1938, one-third of the Indian families resident on the reservations had incomes of less than $500 in 1944 and nearly two-thirds received less than $1,-000.[73] Opportunities open to Indian veterans under the Servicemen's Act of 1944 and subsequent acts gave some the chance to expand their horizons and reorient their lives, but more frequently Indian veterans, like PFC Ira Hayes, USMC, the Pima Indian who helped raise the flag on Iwo Jima, returned temporarily to the reservation and ultimately (as did Hayes) to despair and extinction.

More serious for the Indian was the changed mood of Congress following World War II. Despite the outstanding war record of the American Indian, he had somehow lost some of the sympathy and concern that characterized the pre-war years of white self-doubt, humility and despair. Flushed with victory over alien enemies, flushed with pride in the creation of new instruments of unsurpassed power, flushed with an economic boom which exceeded even the wildest predictions of still-cautious economists, white America sought once more to impose its values on its red brother. The small voice of conscience was drowned out by the stentorian voice of pride.

During the first session of the Eightieth Congress, legislative proposals were introduced to remove restrictions against the alienation of Indian lands, to make these lands subject to taxation, and to throw the allotted Indians upon their own resources regardless of their readiness for such a move. The Bureau of Indian Affairs recognized the power of the Congress to withhold all appropriations from the Indian administration and to remove all trusteeship provisions then in force, should it wish to do so. The Bureau report by Commissioner William A. Brophy, however, noted that in addition to the patent injustice "such precipitate action would inflict on these first Americans, whose property rights do not derive from any benevolence of the United States, it would prove economically disastrous to reduce the resources available to the Indians." Nevertheless, an attempt was made to suggest an equitable basis upon which the government might withdraw its responsibility as trustee. The first factor was the degree of assimilation of a tribe to the surrounding white culture both in terms of Indian acceptance of white habits, and white acceptance of Indians. A second factor was the economic condition of a tribe which might indicate its ability to survive under conditions of federal withdrawal of trusteeship. The third factor was the willingness of the tribe to dispense with the federal relationship, and the fourth, the willingness and ability of the states and communities into which the Indians would be amalgamated to provide public services. Different lists were drawn up by the Bureau of tribes deemed ready for termination and those deemed not ready, or only partially ready.

In keeping with the climate of opinion favoring termination, the Bureau, in 1947, made several moves to minimize its relationship with the Indian tribes. Banking services provided by the Bureau to tribal corporations, credit associations and the like, were reduced, and Indian individuals and corporations were urged to utilize the facilities of local banks.[74]

The movement against tribal authority carried on by the Eightieth Congress had strong roots in the past. Throughout the nineteenth century the U.S. Government sought to "civilize" the Indian by destroying his tribal government and by forcing the individual Indian to take his place as an individual rather than as a collective member of white society. The tribal existence of a number of tribes was dissolved in the nineteenth century: the Choctaws, in 1830; the Kickapoos, in 1862; the Eastern Cherokees, in 1868; and the Winnebagos, who separated from their brothers in Nebraska, in 1875. Despite the dissolution of its ties with the federal government, each is accorded today the rights of an Indian tribe and is so recognized by the United States. As a part of the same movement the Five Civilized Tribes in Oklahoma were by 1906 deprived of their governments, their tribal courts abolished, and their chief executives stripped of their power. They were authorized to continue as tribal entities for the purpose of terminating their tribal affairs.[75]

Suggestive of the enormous pressure to "terminate" the Indian was the fact that 87 bills were introduced in the first session of the Eightieth Congress to require the Secretary of the Interior to issue fee patents, an authority which he already possessed where circumstances warranted, while 46 bills were introduced to direct the Secretary to sell to white men specific pieces of land which had been purchased before the war to build up the Indian land base. Four different so-called "emancipation" bills were also introduced with the purpose of "freeing" the Indian (from his property?) and nine other bills were introduced in the closing hours of the session to force liquidation of tribal property of specific tribes. Little wonder that the Bureau of Indian Affairs wondered how it could meet the needs of Indian veterans returning to reservations which seemed to be on the point of being cannibalized.[76]

Underlying the termination policy of Congress was (and is) an uneasy conscience. The knowledge of the wrongs committed against the Indian has been recognized consciously or subconsciously by even the most hardened patriot. The "spirit of the age" makes dependency, segregation, discrimination and the like somewhat embarrassing to a great nation. The solution? Wipe the slate clean. Abolish the relationship of dependency. The passage of the Indian Claims Act of 1946 (to be discussed in greater detail later) was related to this desire to wipe the slate clean. All the wrongs that weighed on the white conscience, whether or not they could be brought before a court of law, were made justiciable. But the intention of Congress was clearly to unburden itself forever of all the sins of commission and omission committed in the past. After a cut-off date of five years no more past claims could be brought for determination. An Indian Claims Commission would hear and decide on the cases brought, money payments would be made to the later descendants of those whose lands were taken or whose persons were abused, and the book would be closed. The white man could stop thinking about the rights and wrongs of the case. The bill would have been finally rendered and paid. The majority society could get on with the real business of living.

Although culminating in the early Eisenhower period, the termination policy expressed a congressional sentiment spanning both Democratic and Republican administrations of the period. Its spirit, oddly, echoed our foreign policy concern for "liberation" of the "satellites" of Eastern Europe. Both policies expressed high aspirations. Both spoke of "liberation," "freedom," and the like, but the actions that were taken to implement them failed to reach the heights of the rhetoric.

The Hungarian Revolution of 1956 indicated that our commitment to liberation abroad was essentially verbal. We were willing to hope and cheer, but not to act. Similarly, our rhetoric of freedom and liberation for the Indian at home was more a concern for freeing our own conscience and our society of a burden, not so much of meeting the needs and aspirations of the Indians. The Indian was to be "freed" whether he wanted to be or not. The governing interest was that of the white man, not that of the Indian.

The attitude of Congress was expressed with brutal clarity prior to the advent of the Eisenhower administration. House Resolution 698, which passed the House on July 1, 1952, directed the Committee on Interior and Insular Affairs to conduct a detailed investigation of the Bureau of Indian Affairs and particularly how it had performed its function of studying the tribes "to determine their qualifications for management of their own affairs without further supervision of the Federal Government. . . ." The Committee was directed to report to the House the results of its investigations along with recommendations. Among the recommendations specifically called for were (1) a list of those tribes found to be fully qualified to manage their own affairs, (2) legislative proposals designed "to promote the earliest practicable termination of all Federal supervision and control over Indians," (3) a list of those functions of the Bureau of Indian Affairs which could be discontinued or transferred to other federal or state agencies, (4) a list of those states within which further operations of the Bureau of Indian Affairs could be discontinued, and (5) legislative proposals to remove the legal disabilities experienced by Indians under the "guardianship" relationship with the federal government.[77]

The Bureau of Indian Affairs was in little doubt as to what recommendations were expected by the Congress and as to what the consequences would be if they did not produce such recommendations. The Commissioner of Indian Affairs, D. S.

Myer, wrote all bureau officials emphasizing the steps the Bureau was taking to develop "withdrawal concepts and policy." "I think it may be fairly said," the Commissioner pointed out in his memorandum of August 5, 1952, "that current congressional actions with regard to the Bureau of Indian Affairs and Indian appropriations indicate future appropriations will be limited largely to financing items which will facilitate withdrawal." The Commissioner urged all bureau officials to explain to the Indians what was happening, and to try to obtain their agreement on "withdrawal programming" for each tribe. But, he noted, "We must proceed, even though Indian cooperation may be lacking in certain cases."[78]

Here, then, was the usual pattern of Indian policy as exercised throughout American history: a strong expression of interest by the Congress based on a hasty assumption about what was good for the Indian and a more calculating assumption about what was good for the white; the policy phrased in rhetoric evoking images of the Declaration of Independence and the Sermon on the Mount; instructions to the executive to carry out the policy on pain of financial cutbacks or administrative extinction; and an unspoken assumption that the Indians could be cajoled, forced, frightened, or persuaded into recognizing the benevolent intent of the framers.

The twentieth century being somewhat more sophisticated than the nineteenth in such matters, the carrying out of the policy has not been so blatant or so unblushing as have similar policies in the nineteenth and earlier centuries. No "trail of tears," concentration camps, or extermination parties have stained the more recent history of Indian-white relations as they have earlier periods. Moreover, the Indian is finding that he has some sympathetic support for his aspirations and point of view even in the Congress itself. Hence, the cruder aspects of the termination policy have been blunted, and great concern shown for problems it has raised. Timetables have been delayed; court cases have even forced a modification of the congressional purpose. Still, underlying the surface eddies is a great swell of opinion, informed and uninformed, disinterested and self-interested, that seeks to put the Indian on the road to termination, to the extinction of his legal identity as an Indian and to the ultimate (unspoken and unasserted) destruction of his cultural heritage.

The Bureau was given the difficult task of obtaining masses of information from its officers throughout the country, digesting those replies and preparing a report for Congress, all within the space of a few months. A report was duly presented on December 3, 1952, with appropriate regard to the prefigured will of Congress in its recommendations. The report attempted, in a backhanded way, to suggest the importance of studying earlier recommendations, such as the Meriam Report of 1928 and the reports of the Senate Committee on Indian Affairs from 1929 to 1934, but it limited its suggestions to the point that education was the key to Indian assimilation and improvement, and that the Bureau of Indian Affairs had played, and could still play, a role in such a program. The report pointed out that, under the previous recommendations, a number of services formerly provided by the Bureau had been shifted to other agencies, both public and quasipublic, federal and state, and to the Indians themselves. Education and public health, construction of roads, soil conservation, vocational rehabilitation, and other services were among those shifted.

Legislation, the report noted, had also been enacted to transfer responsibility for the maintenance of law and order on certain reservations to state and local authorities. Such legislation was, by 1952, applicable to all Indian reservations in Kansas and New York, the Devils Lake Reservation in North Dakota, the Sac and Fox Reservation in Iowa, and the Agua Caliente Reservation in California.

With the passage of Public Law 280, approved August 15, 1953, Indian lands in California, Minnesota (except the Red

Lake Reservation), Nebraska, Oregon (except the Warm Springs Reservation), and Wisconsin (except the Menominee Reservation) were placed under the criminal and civil jurisdiction of the five states mentioned.[79]

Two weeks prior to the approval of Public Law 280, the Senate passed by voice vote House Concurrent Resolution No. 108 which had previously been adopted by the House of Representatives. This resolution declared it to be the policy of Congress to make the Indians of the United States, as rapidly as possible, "subject to the same laws and entitled to the same privileges and responsibilities as are applicable to other citizens of the United States, to end their status as wards of the United States, and to grant them all of the rights and prerogatives pertaining to American citizenship."

The resolution also declared it to be the sense of Congress, that, "at the earliest possible time" certain named groups of Indians, as well as all of the Indian tribes and individual members thereof located in the states of California, Florida, New York, and Texas, "be freed from Federal supervision and control and from all disabilities and limitations specially applicable to Indians."[80]

Typical of the "Eisenhower way" was the President's willingness to approve Public Law 280, while at the same time criticizing it for failing to provide for consultation with the Indians. Numerous Indian groups had protested that the bill did not provide for Indian consent or consultation. Despite their demands that the President veto the bill, he approved it because, he stated, its basic purpose represented an important step in granting complete political equality to Indians. He urged Congress, however, to enact an amendment requiring consultation with Indian groups and Federal approval before additional states acted to assume jurisdiction under the law.[81]

During the fiscal year 1955, amendments to Public Law 280 were introduced in Congress to require Indian consent before a state could extend its jurisdiction over any Indian reservation. The Bureau of Indian Affairs, however, did not support this proposal, preferring instead an amendment that would require consultation rather than consent. The amendments failed of enactment.[82]

Other organizations friendly to the Indian, while accepting the principle of "ultimate independent management by Indians of their own affairs" cautioned against hasty abandonment of Federal trusteeship. "Termination of Federal supervision in Indian affairs," stated Edward F. Snyder, Legislative Secretary of the Friends Committee on National Legislation, "should follow the attainment by Indians of acceptable health and educational standards and the development of economic resources and experience in business management. It should not be merely an abandonment of protection of Indian property and responsibility for services to Indians."[83]

During hearings before the subcommittee on Indian affairs of the Committee on Interior and Insular Affairs of the U.S. Senate on July 22, 1957, Glenn L. Emmons, Commissioner of the Bureau of Indian Affairs, invoked the conventional assertions of benevolent interest in the welfare of the Indian. "I do not believe there is a man that is more interested in and sympathetic to the Indians in America than I am," declared the commissioner, adding that "I think that the time is overdue in trying to develop the Indian healthwise, educationally, and economically, so that some day he can take over his own affairs." Emmons even invoked the administration of President Jefferson concerning the hope that "some day the Indians should assume their rightful place in our society."

Commissioner Emmons upheld House Concurrent Resolution 108, passed shortly before he took office as Commissioner, as "one of the most constructive acts that the Congress has ever taken relative to the American Indian." The commissioner interpreted the resolution as "a notice to the American Indians that some day the Indian people would reach the age of majority; that some day the time was going to come when they would have to assume their own responsibilities." Emmons likened the Indian situation under the trusteeship of the government to the helplessness of a child under "parental care." His admiration for the Indians hardly knew any bounds. "I say that the Indian people are the finest minority group we have in America," he asserted. "And given an opportunity, they can make their own way."[84]

Senator Richard Neuberger interrupted Commissioner Emmons to point out that the "fire-sale distribution" of the assets of the Klamath tribe, terminated hastily by Congress, had given him pause. "With all due deference to the philosophical principles involved in termination," Neuberger pointed out, "I have had a disdain for termination, because of the specific examples there."

It seems strange that a fundamental declaration such as House Concurrent Resolution 108, which set the policy of termination of federal responsibilities for the Indian, could pass both House and Senate with scarcely a murmur of opposition. In the House it was placed on the unanimous consent calendar. Little discussion took place concerning it, and no one spoke in opposition to it. In the Senate the resolution was endorsed without a word spoken either for or against it. The lack of congressional interest in this declaration, the assumption that it was somehow a "good thing," reflects the fact that the Indian has always been forgotten when he has not been exploited. There was no one to speak for the Indian.[85]

In the hearings that followed the passage of the resolution, no sociologist, anthropologist or other social scientist was heard. The hearings, 1,700 pages of testimony, were designed to carry out the presumed will of Congress, not to determine what was best for the Indian or for the country.

The Bureau of Indian Affairs acted as a compliant accessory of the Congress. It argued for termination even in the case of the Florida Seminoles, two-thirds of whose people were unable to speak English and 80% of whom were illiterate.[86]

The blow-by-blow account of the process by which "termination" was translated from House Concurrent Resolution 108 into law has been told by Gary Orfield, of the University of Chicago, in *A Study of the Termination Policy,* published by the National Congress of American Indians.[86a] Orfield, after a careful study of the legislative history of the resolution and the subsequent enactments, noted the virtual unanimity with which the policy was put into effect. It was a unanimity based on the unconcern and ignorance of the majority of the members of Congress and on the dedicated philosophical conviction of the few members concerned.

The man whose shadow looms over the entire history of termination legislation was Arthur V. Watkins of Utah, chairman of the subcommittee on Indian affairs of the Senate Interior Committee in 1953. Watkins, then sixty-six years old, a devout Mormon and official in the church, a lawyer and a farmer, was to shape all termination legislation not only during his tenure as chairman, but even after he had been replaced as chairman by a Democrat, Senator Murray of Montana, in the Eighty-fifth Congress, organized in 1957 with Democratic majorities. Watkins' view tended to prevail even when they did not coincide with those of E. Y. Berry, a South Dakota Republican, who served as chairman of the House subcommittee on Indian affairs.

Hearings on termination began in 1954, with the consideration of a bill drafted at the request of Senator Watkins to terminate the reservation status of the Indians in Utah. These Indians had not been mentioned in House Concurrent Resolution 108 but Watkins felt that they should serve as an example.

Little time was allowed the Bureau of Indian Affairs to examine the legislation for possible conflict with treaty rights, or for meaningful consultation with the Indians. Tribal meetings, when they were held, were usually presented with a complex piece of legislation previously drafted and asked to signify their approval or disapproval after an explanation had been made. In at least one case, misrepresentation was used by the Bureau to gain Indian assent to a termination bill.[87]

Indian witnesses were often divided, though the great majority were opposed to the legislation. Gradually, however, as it became apparent that Congress, and Senator Watkins in particular, would not rest content with anything less than termination, and as pressures, such as witholding tribal funds, were applied to encourage the Indians, several tribes reluctantly accepted the termination legislation. Questions of tax burdens, adequacy of resources to support local self-government, were hurriedly considered if at all.

Far from realizing or accepting the fact that the reservation system and the trust relationship were part of the treaty agreements made by the federal government in exchange for the land ceded, the peace granted, and the rights conveyed by the proud Indian nations who had contested the way west, Senator Watkins professed to see the Indian as having lost such rights by virtue of his having accepted citizenship and by virtue of his weakened position. Watkins cavalierly dismissed the fact that the termination bills might violate treaty rights. "It is like the treaties with Europe," Watkins remarked when the objection was brought. "They can be renounced at any time." Though he did not believe Indian consent a necessary condition for termination, Watkins constantly talked of "taking off the shackles" and making "free men" of the Indians. Indeed, it was such democratic rhetoric that swayed many liberals in Congress, ignorant of the special relationship the Indian has always had with the federal government. So dominant was Watkins' philosophy of "freeing the Indians" that the termination bills went through Congress with virtually no opposition. On June 17, 1954, two months after the completion of the hearings, the first bill passed Congress, terminating the Menominee tribe of Wisconsin.[88]

The tribe was to be "free" of federal control by December 31, 1958. The act, ostensibly developed by mutual agreement of the Menominees, the Congress, and the Bureau, was called a "monumental step" and a "recognition of the accomplishments of the Menominees in handling their affairs" in the Bureau's annual report.[89]

During the same Congress, legislation was introduced to transfer all the Bureau's health activities to the U.S. Public Health Service. Similar transfer to the Department of Agriculture of all the Bureau's extension work program, such as agricultural assistance and the like, was sought during the same session. Though neither bill was passed during the year, legislation transferring the entire Indian health program to the U.S. Public Health Service was approved on August 5, 1954, by Public Law 568 of the Eighty-third Congress. July 1, 1955, was established as the date of the transfer. Glenn L. Emmons, Commissioner of Indian Affairs, presided over the diminution of his functions. Three thousand six hundred employees and approximately $40,000,000 worth of real property were involved in the shift.[90]

Six "termination" laws were enacted during the 1954 congressional session in compliance with the intent of Congress as expressed in its resolution of 1953. One, covering the Menominee tribe of Wisconsin, became law during the fiscal year 1954. The other five, approved in August 1954, involved the Klamath Indians of Oregon, four Paiute bands of Utah, the Uintah and Ouray Indians of Utah, and the Alabama and Coushatta tribe of Texas. Various time periods, ranging from two to seven years, were allowed for completion of the termination process. In most cases, the legislation required an official tribal roll to be drawn up, to be compiled either by the tribe or by the Bureau of Indian Affairs. The tribal roll was designed to facilitate distribution of the tribal assets upon termination. The termination laws also authorized special education and training programs to fit the Indians for their responsibilities upon termination. One million dollars was provided for the purpose.[91]

Now followed the reckoning. The Menominee tribe, bullied and pushed into termination by a combination of tribal short-sightedness and not-so-subtle congressional pressure, saw that the four-and-a-half years authorized them to get ready for termination were not enough. The tribal leaders next began a series of appeals for an extension of the time by which they would be expected to take over the burdens of local government and the multifarious tax burdens of an economy that was staggering even under federal supervision and support. A series of amendments were authorized during the next few years to extend the time by which the Menominees would be "free." But the delay was won at a high price in tribal funds and congressional irritation. The Department of the Interior supported Senator Watkins and his subcommittee in recommending against extending the deadline in 1955. "The Indians," the Department asserted, "have no vested right to the continuance of the trust relationship."

On the other hand, Senator Murray of Montana, a liberal who succeeded Senator Malone as chairman of the Senate Interior Committee when the Eighty-fifty Congress was organized in 1957, introduced a resolution declaring that "full scale economic development" was the basic objective of Indian policy, and that it should be accomplished without exacting termination of Federal protection of Indian property or any other Indian rights as its price." Senator Murray was supported in his view by Senator Neuberger who pointed to the doleful effects of termination on the Klamath tribe as evidence that the noble philosophical ends of the termination legislation were not realized in practice in the only specific case familiar to him.[92]

Despite the accession of President Kennedy in 1961, the defeat of Senator Watkins, and the death of Senator Neuberger, the Senate subcommittee on Indian affairs continued to reflect Watkins' conservative viewpoint. Senator Church, a young Idaho Democrat, chaired the subcommittee, but, according to Gary Orfield, the real leader was Senator Anderson of New Mexico, chairman of the parent Interior Committee.

Two new conservative members added support to the conservative position: Senators Goldwater of Arizona and Allott of Colorado. Senator Anderson showed increasing irritation as the Menominee stalled for more time. Senator Church also gave the Indians lectures on the virtues of initiative and responsibility. Senator Proxmire, as a witness at one of the hearings for delay, pointed out that the termination procedure "did not stem from the initiative of the people most directly concerned, the Indians," but that "it was thrust on them by Congress, to a significant extent at the instigation of this very subcommittee. . . ." He also noted that "It is apparently believed that no member of the tribe is qualified to hold the top managerial positions in the saw mill which is their chief source of revenue. Yet the same tribe is now scheduled to embark on an adventure in self-financed self-government which would challenge the abilities of almost any group of similar size." It was all in vain. The Menominees, with their rich timber resources, were, in 1961, refused additional time. The Menominees would be free, whether they liked it or not.[93]

The spectacle of the Menominee Indians rent by faction, forced to accept and indeed ask for a fate they did not wish, is a pathetic one indeed. The tribal spirit having been emasculated long since by bureaucratic manipulation, the so-called leaders of the Menominee became more spokesmen for the whites than for their own people. The complicated organization of the tribal government, and the ignorance and unconcern of the majority, provided the trappings of legality and free will to the fateful decline of a once proud people. Outside committees and consultants, supplied by the state of Wisconsin, by the University of Wisconsin, and by the federal government, added to the sea of words in which the tribe sunk from its former status of economic well being and social autonomy. That the loss of both economic and political independence was achieved under the banner of economic and political "liberation" is only one of the many paradoxes of the case. Those who arbitrarily forced the Menominee to abandon the trust relationship which they had been guaranteed in exchange for their land and their acquiescence to the white man's invasion of their country had long since lost their understanding of the meaning of the bargain. Since the record of that time past had been lost, the promises could be forgotten. But one must put the best front on it. To complement the words "emancipation" and "liberation" that provided rhetorical support to the policy, the term "withdrawal," which was used in the earliest discussions of the policy of withdrawing the trust relationship and federal support from the Indians, was replaced by the more neutral word "termination." Termination fitted the image of chains being struck off, rather than the image of a helping hand being removed.

Another paradox of Menominee termination was that the state of Wisconsin was eventually forced to take up many of the trust responsibilities that the federal government relinquished. The Menominee tribe voted to accept a limitation upon its right to sell or mortgage its property and it approved a business plan by which outsiders would manage its property. As Orfield noted: "These were the strange fruits of the termination policy." A policy which had been based on the assumption that the Menominees were as competent as any other citizens to manage their own property was now organized around precisely contrary assumptions. In no other way could termination be supported. The tribal economy could not provide the necessary support for the services needed by a modern community.[94]

In the ten years following the passage of the termination

act, Gary Orfield concluded, none of the major goals of the termination policy were realized. A major goal was to give the Indians full control over their property, both personal and collective. By the time of termination, virtually no trace of this intention to grant economic freedom remained. The Menominees were given more than ample responsibility but they gained no significant new freedoms. The high burden of taxes thrust upon the Indians, the high cost of government services, the low profits of the tribal saw mill, combined to place the Menominees into a worse position than they occupied before termination. The price of "responsibility," Orfield pointed out, may be "bankruptcy."[95]

When the Attorney General of Wisconsin ruled in 1962 that Menominees were subject to state game laws in Menominee County—the new designation of the tribal area—some Indians realized for the first time the extent to which they had sold their birthright.[96] The goal of assimilation, which was so confidently expected with termination, has not been achieved. On the contrary, the small governing elite who represented the tribe at the beginning of the termination question was repudiated by the great mass of the Menominees who have turned more and more to extremist or traditionalist views. A majority of the adult members of the tribe petitioned President Johnson in 1964 to seek the repeal of the termination act. Another goal of termination was the reduction of government expenditures to support necessary services to the Menominees. Far from being achieved, the cost to the federal government has escalated.

In sum, the story of Menominee termination has been the story of a monumental miscalculation. It has been a miscalculation growing out of a mixture of good will, ignorance, and greed in varying proportions. Despite the failure of all the professed goals of termination legislation, the end result may achieve one desired end: the elimination of the Indian problem as an Indian problem. As the land slips from the hands

of the Menominee and the problems of the Menominee become individual problems of poverty, welfare, and disease in
the larger body politic, one may say finally what Orfield has
said perhaps prematurely: "The Menominee tribe is dead, but
for no good reason."[97]

That the termination legislation enacted during the administration of Vice President Nixon will not be repeated
during the administration of President Nixon was suggested
by the position paper on Indian affairs—entitled "A Brighter
Future for the American Indian"—issued by candidate Nixon
on October 9, 1968. In his statement, Mr. Nixon pledged his
administration to the following policies:

1. The special relationship between the Federal Government
and the Indian people and the special responsibilities of the
Federal Government to the Indian people will be acknowledged.
    Termination of tribal recognition will not be a policy objective
and in no case will it be imposed without Indian consent.
    We must recognize that American society can allow many diff-
erent cultures to flourish in harmony and we must provide an
opportunity for those Indians wishing to do so to lead a useful
and prosperous life in an Indian environment.
    2. The right of self-determination of the Indian people will be
respected and their participation in planning their own destiny
will actively be encouraged.
    I will oppose any effort to transfer jurisdiction over Indian
reservations without Indian consent.

Mr. Nixon's campaign promises were followed by a declaration on July 8, 1970, unilaterally renouncing, on the part of
the executive branch, the earlier termination policy, and call-
ing upon Congress, on its part, to repudiate the policy also.
The effect of the presidential declaration remains to be seen.

PART *III*

The Land

1 : BELATED JUSTICE: THE INDIAN CLAIMS COMMISSION

The American legal system, based on English common law precedents and American statute law oriented to white values, has never been able to accommodate within its bounds the different culture and the aberrant status of the American Indian. The goal of justice which such forms sought often resulted in an opposite effect where the Indian was involved. The mechanisms of the white man's law were either incapable of recognizing the cultural and legal separateness of the Indian, or were deliberately designed to destroy that independence.

As World War II drew to a close, attempts were made by the courts to correct the anomalous situation of injustice meted out to an impotent victim through the mechanism of "law." Old wrongs began to be righted. The Court of Claims, in a series of cases, awarded the present members of Indian groups financial satisfaction (no real satisfaction was possible) for wrongs committed a hundred years earlier against their forefathers. In 1944, for example, the California Indians were awarded five million dollars in partial satisfaction of the Senate's failure in 1852 to ratify eighteen treaties made with these tribes. Under the treaties the Indians ceded 75 million acres in return for which they were promised definite reservations of 8½ million acres. They received only 624,000 acres of the poorest land. The award represented the difference between the estimated value of the lands, goods, and services promised them under the treaties and the cost of services since rendered to them by the Federal Government.

In a Court of Claims decision in March, 1945, the Northwestern bands of Shoshone Indians were denied a requested $15,000,000 claim for lands turned over to the United States by the Treaty of Box Elder in 1863. The Supreme Court, in a 5-4 decision, upheld the ruling, supporting the contention that the treaty, which granted rights-of-way across the Shoshone country, did not show intent to recognize Indian title to the territory involved. In the concurring opinion of two of the justices, the inadequacy of judicial decisions in such cases was pointed out and Congress was called upon to provide other remedies. The justices asserted that a moral obligation rested on the whites to do "what in the conditions of this twentieth century is the decent thing to do."[1]

The burden which an Indian claimant formerly labored under in trying to recover for losses against the government is illustrated by the Sioux Pony Claims. Following World War II, reimbursements were made to the descendants of some of the friendly and neutral Indians whose ponies had been taken by soldiers during the Sioux War of 1876. Only three living claimants among those from whom the horses were originally taken could be found in 1946. Payments were made to them. The process of compensation, begun in 1890 with inadequate funds, continued with all deliberate speed. The Bureau of Indian Affairs, in its annual report for 1946, carefully noted that only those Indians who were not hostile then, or their descendants, might receive payments.[2]

As a result of thinking about the legal inequities to which the Indians were still subjected, the Congress passed the Indian Claims Commission Act to hear and determine the many unsettled Indian tribal claims against the United States. The President signed the bill into law on August 13, 1946. The act superseded a law passed in 1863 when various tribes were at war with the United States, which forbade Indians to sue in the Court of Claims. Until the passage of the Indian Claims Commission Act the Indians could bring no claim against the government without a special act of Congress. Numerous grievances arising from treaty violations and the like could not effectively be heard. The discrimination added to the sense of hopelessness and impotence on the part of the Indians.

The significance of the establishment of the Indian Claims Commission derives from the fact that the government recognized claims, and gave jurisdiction to the Commission, in areas not comprehended under existing law or previous practice. The Commission was authorized to hear and determine claims against the United States on behalf of any Indian tribe, band, or other "identifiable group" of American Indians residing within the territorial limits of the United States or Alaska. The claims which it could hear and determine included "(1) claims in law or equity arising under the Constitution, laws, treaties of the United States, and Executive orders of the President; (2) all other claims in law or equity, including those sounding in tort, with respect to which the claimant would have been entitled to sue in a court of the United States if the United States was subject to suit; (3) claims which would result if the treaties, contracts, and agreements between the claimant and the United States were revised on the ground of fraud, duress, unconscionable consideration, mutual or unilateral mistake, whether of law or fact, or any other ground cognizable by a court of equity; (4) claims arising from the taking by the United States, whether as the result of a treaty of cession or otherwise, of lands owned or occupied by the claimant without the payment for such lands of compensation agreed to by the claimant; and (5) claims based upon fair and honorable dealings that are not recognized by any existing rule of law or equity."

No claim accruing after August 13, 1946, was to be considered by the Commission.[3]

The authority to hear and determine claims based upon "fair and honorable dealings" allowed the Commission to consider moral as well as legal claims and numerous judgments have been made under this provision. The sorry record of extortion, deception, and fraud with which the relations of whites and Indians in the United States have been marked, was finally capable of redress in law. While the act has the effect of wiping clean the white conscience about its legal responsibility for past wrongs, it offers cold comfort to those who actually suffered the wrongs. To the descendants of those who suffered it offers financial compensation for lands taken, at rates determined by expert witnesses to be the fair value of the lands at the times they were taken. One wonders whether the belated act of reparation was motivated as much by concern for the victims of white action as by the desire to rub out the memory of that action on the part of those making the reparation. Like other post-World War II policies toward the Indian, the creation of the Indian Claims Commission was also motivated in part by the desire to eliminate the Indian as a separate factor in American society.

The proceedings of the Indian Claims Commission convey the feeling of unconcern and oblivion to which the white man has consigned the Indian. The Commission met, during the 1960s, in a small conference room adjacent to its offices in the new Federal Office Building at Jackson Place which houses similar independent agencies and commissions. The hearing room was low-ceilinged and antiseptic, totally unlike the hearing room of the Court of Claims across Lafayette Park. The commissioners sat on a raised dais, but the atmosphere of dignity and solemnity present in most court rooms was absent. The shift in quarters during July 1970 to a downtown office building has reduced further the dignity of the commission. Lawyers presenting briefs before the commission for the government are often elderly, second-rate members of a little honored branch of the Justice Department. Lawyers for the Indians are often similarly old and uninspired. The commissioners show concern and interest, but are conscious of playing an unimportant and inconspicuous role in public affairs. Their decisions are not printed but reproduced in multilith form. The attempt to distribute justice a hundred years late is difficult to sustain.

In 1965, the Court of Claims ruled in *Seneca Nation of Indians v. U.S.* (173 Ct. Cl. 917) that the Indian Claims Commission Act does not cover pre-1790 claims of Indian tribes based on bad bargains which the tribes may have made with a State in disposing of their lands. The Court of Claims ruled that prior to 1790 the Continental Congress under the Articles of Confederation had not assumed a fiduciary role with respect to Indian lands within state borders.

Late in the administration of President Johnson, on March 19, 1968, a significant change occurred in the Indian Claims Commission: John T. Vance was appointed Chairman of the Commission. After a perceptive study of the workings of the Commission, Vance concluded that its entire history had been misguided. For reasons that are lost in the bureaucratic maze, the Commission organized itself as a court with elaborate legal procedures to hear and determine arguments by lawyers for the Indian groups on the one side and for the Department of Justice, representing the United States, on the other. Nothing in the Act, Vance pointed out, required the establishment of adversary proceedings or of "the same tortured and archaic procedures utilized in settling Indian Claims prior to the enactment of the Indian Claims Commission Act." Indeed, the predecessor bills that eventually resulted in the Indian Claims Commission Act had dropped the word "court" in 1935, the date of the last Indian claims bill introduced with that word in it. The 1946 Act, moreover, provided for an investigation division which, in Vance's interpretation, was to be the agency to gather the information to be presented to the Commission. The Commission was authorized to make its decisions without formal legal proceedings: indeed, the very purpose of the act was to relieve the Indian of the necessity of fighting tiresome battles through the intricate legal apparatus of the white world. In case of disputed decisions, however, appeals were authorized from the Commission's rulings to the Court of Claims.[4]

The Commission, in its early years, not only ignored the express wording of the act creating it, but also the repeated criticisms in Court of Claims rulings that it had failed to exercise its investigation function. Glenn Wilkinson, one of the most knowledgeable lawyers involved in Indian claims matters, in commenting on the amended conclusions of law and final award in the case of the *Pawnee Tribe* v. *U.S.* (1962), which resulted in an award of more than $7,325,000.00, wrote that "If the Court of Claims in this and some of the other early appeals had left the interpretation and determination of the Indian claims to the process of strictly adversary proceedings, it is doubtful whether the Pawnees would have been successful to any extent."[5]

On Vance's accession to the office, an investigation division was finally set up but, because of the personnel freeze in Washington in 1968, the "division" consisted of one man alone. Despite Vance's efforts, the Indian has remained enmeshed in the system. He must have a lawyer to present his case (and yet is often without the wherewithal to obtain one) and he finds an aggressive Lands Division of the Justice Department fighting every case down to the wire, appealing unfavorable decisions, and throwing up questionable defenses against claims. Worse, the intent of Congress that the accumulated claims of the Indians could be resolved in a short space of time by the application of simple justice unburdened by the technicalities of the white man's law has been frustrated. Twelve years after the original termination date of the Commission, Vance pointed out, the adjudication of the claims before the Commission was at best forty per cent complete. Vance's startling conclusion is that "Congress never intended the Indian Claims Commission to operate in the manner that it has for 22 years." The Commission, in sum, "has not accomplished its purpose, but rather has become part of the problem it was created to solve."[6]

The Indian Claims Commission, by an amendment passed in 1967, was scheduled to wind up its activities on April 10, 1972. Commissioner Vance, while remaining on the Commission, was, on July 11, 1969, replaced as chairman by Jerome K. Kuykendall. The commission members—under Kuykendall's leadership—have opposed Vance's ideas and have urged that the commission's life be extended far beyond the deadline. While accepting, without giving credit to Vance, the reforms he introduced to speed up trial procedures, they urged upon Congress the necessity of continuing the court proceedings which the commission mistakenly, in Vance's view, adopted. In a hearing before the Committee on Interior and Insular Affairs of the United States Senate on the status of Indian Claims litigation, on April 10, 1970, the majority of the commission were able to present a persuasive case for continuing their existence. Their argument was predicated largely on the grounds that the Indian must have "his day in court". The power of the phrase is wondrous to behold. There is little or no recognition that the commission was designed to obviate the long, harsh and often incomprehensible journey faced by Indians in the court system. It also ignores the fact that commission rulings are appealable to the Court of Claims and, occasionally, beyond to the Supreme Court. The majority of the commission marshalled support from strategic quarters. Glen Wilkinson, whose comment on the defective character of the adversary process was quoted earlier, attacked the feasibility of building up the investigation division of the Commission. Wilkinson asserted that the purpose of the original bill was to give the Indian his "day in court" and that the commission was designed to be that "court . . . even though it became a commission or agency." A letter was also read into the record from Bruce A. Wilkie, executive director of the National Congress of American Indians, who supported the request for an extension of the life of the commission and upheld the validity of the adversary process in contrast to a system under which he inexplicably and mistakenly assumed that decisions would be made by "government functionaries." Under the barrage of such testimony, the Senators, who have evinced a growing skepticism over the repeated but unfulfilled promises of quick action by the commission in its previous appearances on Capitol Hill, are, nevertheless, liable to take the course of least resistance and extend the life of the commission once more.[7]

2 : ORIGINAL
INDIAN TITLE

It is the prevailing assumption among Americans that the bulk of the land of the United States was simply appropriated from the Indians without benefit of law or compensation. The assumption is persistent, but defective. Thomas Jefferson, in his *Notes on the State of Virginia* (1787), noted

> That the lands of this country were taken from them by conquest, is not so general a truth as is supposed. I find in our historians and records, repeated proofs of purchase, which cover a considerable part of the lower country; and many more would doubtless be found on further search. The upper country we know has been acquired altogether by purchases made in the most unexceptionable form.[8]

The assumption prevalent in Jefferson's time has continued to this day. Felix Cohen, the great authority on Indian law and Associate Solicitor of the Department of the Interior, attributed the belief that America was stolen from the Indians to the desire of Americans to "make our idealism look as hard-boiled as possible."[9] Cohen, in 1947, noted that $800,-

000,000 of Federal funds had to that time been appropriated for the purchase of Indian lands. While the government had not always honored the principle of respect for Indian possessions, it had, Cohen pointed out, honored it to that degree. "To pay $800,000,000 for a principle is not a common occurrence in the world's history," he noted.[10]

Because educated persons as well as ignorant ones have assumed that most of the land of the United States was stolen from the Indians, there has usually been a frightened reaction by responsible officials to any legal decisions that seemed to uphold the right of the Indian to compensation for the taking of what is usually called "original Indian title": that is, land lived upon by the Indians without benefit of any formal recognition of that title by the United States. For example, in the case of *Cramer* v. *United States,* 1923 (261 U.S. 219), the Attorney General of Arizona filed a brief asserting that "Any suggestion by this Court that Indian tribes might have rights in property enforcible in a court of law by the mere fact of occupancy would at least cast a cloud upon the title to the major portion of Arizona."[11]

Despite this warning, the Supreme Court held in *Cramer,* and, in 1941, in *United States as Guardian of the Hualapai Indians* v. *Santa Fe Pacific Railway* (314 U.S. 339), that the Indian right of occupancy, even though not formally recognized, was not terminated by a subsequent statutory grant.[12]

These two cases served notice on purchasers of real property that Indian title could remain as an encumbrance upon grants made in ignorance of, or in defiance of that title. The fundamental constitutional issue of whether the taking by the United States of original unrecognized "Indian title" was compensable, and, if so, whether it was compensable under the strict provisions of the "due process" clause of the Fifth Amendment to the Constitution, was not faced until the case of the *United States* v. *Alcea Band of Tillamooks.* In this case, the Supreme Court, on November 25, 1946, affirmed the judg-

ment of the Court of Claims that the Tillamooks were entitled
to compensation for certain lands which they had been forced
to surrender involuntarily and without compensation. The
Tillamooks, authorized to sue the United States by a special
statute of 1935 for "any and all legal and equitable claims
arising under or growing out of the original Indian title,
claim, or rights in, to, or upon the whole or any part of the
lands and their appurtenances occupied by the Indian tribes
and bands" involved in the legislation, proved their original
Indian title to designated lands and demonstrated an involun-
tary and uncompensated taking of such lands. The government, fighting the case in the Court of Claims and in the
Supreme Court, urged that in the absence of some form of
official "recognition," original Indian title could be appropriated without liability on the part of the sovereign.[13]

The Supreme Court had not previously had an occasion to
pass on the precise issue brought before it in the Tillamook
case. In only one act prior to 1935 had Congress authorized
judicial determination of the right to recover for a taking of
nothing more than original Indian title, and no case under
that act, passed in 1929, reached the Court. Prior to 1929,
adjudications of Indian claims against the United States were
limited, the Court pointed out, "to issues arising out of treaties, statutes, or other events and transactions carefully designated by Congress." The Court, aware of the sensitive nature
of the relationship between Congress and its Indian wards,
always carefully and narrowly interpreted the congressional
acts in deciding the merits of disputes arising under them.
The 1935 act, however, admitted to judicial consideration
what had always been a political question: the manner of
extinguishing Indian title. The sovereign, in effect, had
waived his immunity to prosecution for an arbitrary taking of
lands held by original Indian title.

The Court reviewed the early evidence of treaty-making
and noted "the striking deference paid to Indian claims." "It

was usual policy," it noted, "not to coerce the surrender of lands without consent and without compensation." Although later practice became less responsible, the Court concluded that "Something more than sovereign grace prompted the obvious regard given to original Indian title." The Court rejected government interpretations of certain decisions, which seemed to suggest that an Indian tribe could not recover compensation on the basis of original Indian use and occupancy. It rejected, in addition, the dichotomy between "recognized" and "unrecognized" Indian title which the government sought to establish in order to rule out the Tillamooks' claim. The Court accepted the paramount power of Congress to extinguish the Indian right of occupancy, but pointed out that "The power of Congress over Indian affairs may be of a plenary nature; but it is not absolute." The power implied an obligation.

Three members of the Court dissented in the case and presented an opinion, written by Mr. Justice Reed, pointing out the dangerous implications of the decision, if applied to all Indian tribes having claims against the United States. The dissenters conceded that distinctions had traditionally been made between plenary authority over tribal lands and absolute power, but asserted that they knew of no authority for holding that Indian lands unrecognized by specific actions of Congress were protected by the Fifth Amendment. Whatever the moral justice of the claim, the dissenters concluded that "Never has there been acknowledgment before of a legal or equitable right to compensation that springs from the appropriation by the United States of the Indian title." They therefore concluded that no rights arose from the Tillamooks' original Indian title and no compensation was due.[14]

On the basis of the Supreme Court's decision in the first Tillamook case, the Court of Claims heard evidence on the amount of the recovery and entered a judgment for the value of the lands as of 1855, when the principal taking occurred, plus interest from that date. The value of the land was $3,000,000, and the interest granted by the Court of Claims was $14,000,000. The Supreme Court, which agreed to consider the question presented by the award of interest, ruled, on April 9, 1951, that the granting of interest in such cases was justifiable only when the taking entitled the claimant to just compensation under the Fifth Amendment. Since the jurisdiction act of 1935 authorizing the Tillamooks to sue did not authorize interest, and since none of the opinions in the case expressed the view that recovery was grounded on a taking under the Fifth Amendment, the Court reversed the ruling of the Court of Claims.[15]

The coup-de-grace to claims for compensation under the Fifth Amendment was rendered in the case of the *Tee-Hit-Ton Indians, An Identifiable Group of Alaska Indians* v. *the United States,* decided by the Supreme Court on February 7, 1955. The Tee-Hit-Ton Indians, a small group of Tlingit Indians residing in Alaska, claimed compensation for a taking by the United States of certain timber from lands allegedly belonging to them. They established "original Indian title" or "Indian right of occupancy" to the lands in question. But, because of uncertainty concerning the compensable nature of this right, about which several court decisions disagreed, the Supreme Court agreed to hear the case. In its majority decision, delivered by Mr. Justice Reed, the Court took a hard line, holding that Congress had never granted the Indians of Alaska permanent rights in the lands occupied by them, but, in the legislation dealing with Alaska, had deferred such a determination until a later time. The majority asserted that "No case in this Court has ever held that taking of Indian title or use by Congress required compensation." The Court rejected the precedent of the first Tillamook case, which it pointed out had been modified by the second Tillamook case, and the precedent of another case, *Miller* v. *United States* (159 F. 2d 997), which held that a taking of lands held by original

Indian title was compensable under the Fifth Amendment. That the practical and imagined "threat" of such cases encouraged the court to strike hard at the doctrine is suggested by the footnote in the majority decision which noted the disproportion between the principal and interest granted the Tillamooks by the Court of Claims. The footnote cited the Government's argument that "if aboriginal Indian title was compensable without specific legislation to that effect, there were claims with estimated interest already pending under the Indian jurisdictional act aggregating $9,000,000,000." The Court was at pains to disallow a Fifth Amendment defense to the Indians. "Generous provision has been willingly made to allow tribes to recover for wrongs," the Court noted, but "as a matter of grace, not because of legal liability." In an opinion notable for its pejorative references to "tribal" ownership as opposed to individual ownership, to "savage tribes," "stages of civilization" and to "nomadic" patterns of land use among the Indians, the Court bolstered the "hard line" conclusion that "The line of cases adjudicating Indian rights on American soil leads to the conclusion that Indian occupancy, not specifically recognized as ownership by action authorized by Congress, may be extinguished by the Government without compensation." The majority, however, did not wish to be holding the monkey of responsibility for a harsh policy toward Indian claims. "Our conclusion . . . leaves with Congress, where it belongs, the policy of Indian gratuities for the termination of Indian occupancy of Government-owned land rather than making compensation for its value a rigid constitutional principle."[16]

In a powerful dissent from the majority opinion, Justice Douglas, with whom Chief Justice Warren and Justice Frankfurter concurred, challenged the majority's interpretation of section 8 of the first Organic Act for Alaska (1884), which stated that "the Indians or other persons in said district shall not be disturbed in the possession of any lands actually in their use or occupation or now claimed by them but the terms under which such persons may acquire title to such lands is reserved for future legislation by Congress. . . ." The minority read the passage as recognizing Indian title—not as reserving the question whether they had any rights in the land. The opinion delved into the legislative history of the act and noted that the words "or now claimed by them" were added by an amendment offered by Senator Plumb of Kansas in order to assure that the Indians would have as many rights after the passage of the bill as before. Plumb, during the debate on the bill, had humorously commented that:

> I do not know by what tenure the Indians are there nor what ordinarily characterizes their claim of title, but it will be observed that the language of the proviso I propose to amend puts them into very small quarters. I think about 2 feet by 6 to each Indian would be the proper construction of the language "actually in their use or occupation." Under the general rule of occupation applied to an Indian by a white man, that would be a tolerably limited occupation and might possibly land them in the sea.

The minority opinion concluded that Congress in the 1884 Act recognized the claims of the Indians to their Alaskan lands. Because of the uncertainty and ignorance surrounding the whole question of Alaska at the time, no attempt was made to lay out bounds or specify precise titles. That the Congress did seek to save to the Indians all the rights claimed, reserving to a later period the resolution of conflicting claims and tribal boundaries, seemed clear to the minority. The minority bitterly rejected the assumption of the majority that Congress reserved for some future day the question whether the Indians were to have any rights to the land.[17]

Recent decisions concerning Indian title have reflected a broadened understanding of the different Indian cultural patterns and a heightened awareness of the need to adjudicate Indian claims in terms of equity and morality rather than on the basis of narrow legality. For example, in *U.S.* v. *Seminole Indians of the State of Florida,* 1967 (180 Ct. Cl. 375), the Court noted that although proof of Indian title depends on a showing of actual, exclusive and continuous use and occupancy for a long time by the Indian tribe in question, it is also necessary to consider the nature of the use: whether primarily for agriculture, hunting, or trade, whether utilized seasonally or nomadically, and the like. Actual possession in the strict sense, the Court ruled, is not essential and Indian title may be established through the tribe's intermittent contacts in areas they control.

The Seminole decision was a rebuke to the government which had appealed the prior decision of the Indian Claims Commission on the grounds that it was not supported by the evidence. The peculiar insistence of the Lands Division of the Justice Department in stubbornly fighting and appealing even the weakest case reflects the bureaucratic ethos at its worst. The Lands Division has lost sight of the humane and benevolent purpose of the Indian Claims Commission Act and has acted as though it must fight, obstruct, extend, delay, and frustrate any effort on the Indians' part, or inclination on the government's part, to settle claims with generosity and good will. The attitude derives in part from professional pride, but it also reflects an irritation at the Indian claimants which seems to be a part of the mental equipment of those in government dealing with Indians.

In the Seminole case, the Court of Claims, in an opinion delivered by Judge Linton M. Collins, upheld the Indian Claims Commission in its conclusion that the Seminole Indians justifiably had Indian title to most of Florida. To the government's objection that the Seminoles occupied only a handful of settlements before being joined by 2,500 Creeks (from whom the Seminoles had derived earlier) following

American attacks in the period 1814–1819, the court pointed out that

> Had the Seminoles chosen to live by food-raising alone, we would regard the "village" evidence (stressed by the government) as a persuasive consideration in limiting the Seminoles' "title" to the land falling within the compass of their permanent homesites, *i.e.,* the northern half of the peninsula. . . . But the Seminoles—as was the case with many other Indian groups—survived not simply through farming, but by food-gathering and hunting as well. In other words, Seminole land-use clearly encompassed more than the soil actually "possessed." Therefore, other aspects of the Seminole pattern of life demand consideration.

The Court of Claims noted also that the use and occupancy essential to the recognition of Indian title "does not demand *actual* possession, whereas the key to Indian title lies in evaluating the manner of land-use over a period of time." "Physical control or dominion over the land," the court asserted, "is the dispositive criterion."

The Court of Claims also laid down a liberal rule to determine the cultural identity of the Seminoles. It noted that the remnants of the original inhabitants of the Florida peninsula —some twenty-five groups with an estimated 50,000 population in 1512—were absorbed by the Seminoles who moved into the peninsula in the eighteenth century. "Cultural assimilation," stated the court, "extinguishes the identity, but not the people." "Therefore," the court went on, "whatever land rights were possessed by those absorbed may be recognized as inhering in the culture that emerges." The Seminoles were first clearly denominated as Seminoles in 1765. The fifty years between 1765 and 1823 when the United States negotiated a treaty of cession—the Treaty of Moultrie, September 18, 1823—"would have been sufficient, as a matter of law, to satisfy 'the long time' requirement essential for Indian title.''[18]

In *Confederated Tribes of the Warm Springs Reservation of Oregon v. U.S.,* 1966 (177 Ct. Cl. 184), the Court of Claims also affirmed, as in the Seminole case, that Indian title does not apply only to those areas where the tribe had permanent villages or habitations, but included those areas over which the tribe had control even though used only seasonally or intermittently.

In the same decision the Court of Claims concluded that the period of time during which a tribe must have used and occupied land sufficient to acquire Indian title to the land could not be fixed precisely but must have been long enough to have allowed the Indians to transform the area into domestic territory. Conquest by one Indian tribe of another a few years before the arrival of the whites would not by itself confer aboriginal title to the area on the conquering tribe.[19]

The Tlingit and Haida Indians of Alaska, like the Tillamooks, brought suit against the United States in the Court of Claims, in accordance with the previously cited Act of Congress of 1935 (49 Stat. 388) for the failure or refusal of the United States to compensate the Tlingit and Haida for lands and property rights taken by the United States without the consent of the Indians and for the failure of the United States to protect the interests of the claimant Indians following the purchase of Alaska from Russia in 1867.

The Court of Claims, in 1959, found that the Tlingit and Haida had occupied the lands in question and that the United States had taken the land thus entitling the Indians to compensation under the Act. A separate determination of the amount of the liability was made in a decision by the Court of Claims on January 19, 1968.

The court rejected the government's contention that a "value to the Indians" formula, which would tend to exclude the value of minerals and other resources not used by the Indians prior to the coming of the white man, should be used by the court in awarding damages. It held instead for a "fair market value" of the property which it defined, "in the absence of an actual market," as "the estimated or imputed fair market value based on sufficient evidence which justifies a conclusion as to the fair market value which would be established when an informed seller disposes of his property to an equally informed buyer."

The "fair market value" formula, which derived from earlier decisions, requires that proper consideration be given to the natural resources of the land, including mineral resources, whether or not they were of economic value at the time of cession, or merely of potential value. The court asserted, moreover, that the value of the land was the same, whether it was held by aboriginal title or in fee simple. The value of land held by Indian title, in other words, was not merely "the value of its primitive occupants relying upon it for subsistence."

The Court of Claims rejected the contention of the Indians, however, that the Tlingit-Haida had compensable proprietary exclusive fishing rights, title to which might be established by proof of aboriginal Indian title to adjacent land areas. The court cited a long legal tradition which has held that fish are capable of ownership only by possession and control. An Indian tribe might exclude non-Indians from fishing in navigable waterways within its reservation if the grant of the reservation included, as part of the grant, the right to fish in designated areas free from interference. But outside such areas, "no citizen has any right to the fish nor to exclude any other citizen from an equal opportunity to exercise his right to possession."

The court, therefore, ruled that the Tlingit and Haida possessed no fishery rights based on aboriginal ownership of the land and that no right of recovery was established by the jurisdictional act of Congress under which they sued. In a dissent to the opinion on the fisheries, Judge Nichols noted how strange it seemed that the fishing rights of the Indians were rejected when the Court of Claims itself in its original opinion (147 Ct. Cl. 341, 177 F. Supp. 468) had noted that the most valuable asset lost to the Indians was the fishing rights. Nichols agreed that the supposed value of the fish was not an appropriate valuation technique and that no one can own exclusive fishing rights in navigable water. But just as a person owning a building on Fifth Avenue might claim it was worth more because of its favorable location without asserting any proprietorship in the flow of automobiles and pedestrians past his door, so Judge Nichols argued, could the Indians claim an enhanced value in the land bordering on bays and coves even though they could obtain therewith no ownership in the fish. Nichols concluded: "I hope this decision is not taken as authority that, should an island such as Cuttyhunk, Block Island, or Tangier [Island in Chesapeake Bay] be taken by eminent domain, the court in setting a valuation must utterly ignore the fact that fishing goes on from there."[20]

What of the lands of Indian tribes which formerly existed under the sovereignty of an alien European or European-derived power? This question has arisen in the case of Indian tribes, such as those in the formerly Spanish or Mexican areas, and even in those areas formerly under the sovereignty of an Anglo-Saxon state, such as the Republic of Texas during the years of its existence.

In the *Lipan Apache Tribe, etc., Mescalero Apache Tribe, etc., and the Apache Tribe of the Mescalero Reservation, etc.* v. *the United States,* the Court of Claims, in 1967, reversed the decision of the Indian Claims Commission dismissing the petition of the Indians for failure to state a cause of action under the Act. The Commission had held that the Lipan and Mescalero Apaches, who had been driven from their ancestral lands in Texas in 1858 and 1859 by Texas and United States troops, had no right of occupancy to the lands they had once held because such a right had not been accorded by the Republic of Texas prior to its annexation by the United States in 1845 and therefore did not exist after Texas' admission to the Union. Even if the Indians possessed such rights, the Commission believed, they could not have recovered in their suit against the United States which before and after annexation did not have any proprietary interest in the public lands of Texas.

The Court of Claims, however, in reversing the decision ruled that

> Indian title based on aboriginal possession does not depend upon sovereign recognition or affirmative acceptance for its survival. Once established in fact, it endures until extinguished or abandoned.

The Indian Claims Commission, the Court of Claims ruled, should not have inquired whether the Republic of Texas accorded or granted the Indians any rights, "but whether that sovereign extinguished their pre-existing occupancy rights." The court took notice of the policy of President Lamar, second chief executive of the Republic, and of certain legislation enacted during his tenure of office (December 1838–December 1841) which reflected his policy of expelling or exterminating hostile Indians and resettling friendly Indians on reservations. However, the court ruled that the total picture of Indian-white relations in Texas in the period of the Republic could be interpreted as well to show that the Republic accepted, or acquiesced in, Indian title as the converse.

Moreover, when the new State of Texas, as one of its first legislative acts, on April 29, 1846, declared that it recognized no title at all in Indian tribes within the State of Texas, it was in fact without right or authority. Only the Federal Government could abrogate aboriginal title by unilateral action, declared the court. "It makes no difference that the lands were State-owned," the court went on; "the Federal Government's power stemmed, not from the ownership of public lands in this instance, but more importantly from the general grant of the right to deal with Indians." The Constitution had vested the right and authority to deal with the Indian tribes in the Federal government.

The court, therefore, reversed the Indian Claims Commission and remanded the case to it for further consideration.[21]

The effect of the Court of Claims decision in *Lipan Apache* has affected succeeding rulings of the Indian Claims Commission. In *The Caddo Tribe of Oklahoma, et al,* v. *U.S.,* decided August 30, 1968, the Commission withdrew its order and opinion issued October 27, 1961, which was based on the assumption that the Caddo, as residents of Texas, had no right to any land there that needed to be considered by the United States since the Republic of Texas did not acknowledge Indian title and the United States had never acquired a greater obligation. The Caddo, by a treaty with the United States of July 1, 1835, had voluntarily relinquished possession to all lands east of the Mexican border and promised to remove themselves from U.S. territory. The Caddos left Louisiana and moved into Mexico only a few months before the Battle of San Jacinto made Texas independent. During the years of the Republic, 1836–1845, the Caddos remained in Texas, though their right of occupancy was never recognized by the Texas Congress. When Texas entered the Union, the United States concluded an agreement with State authorities to relocate some of the Indian tribes within Texas' boundaries. The Caddos were persuaded to settle on one such reservation, under the protection and supervision of the national government, in 1854. In the years that followed, white Texans harassed and attacked the Indians, culminating in an attack by

250 white settlers on May 23, 1859, when many of the Caddo men were away from the reservation fighting with United States troops against the Comanches in the north. The local Indian agent decided that the Indians could not be protected unless they removed themselves from Texas, and he organized an emergency march to the Washita River in Oklahoma of 300 Caddo Indians. The Washita River area became a permanent reservation for the Texas Indians.

The Indian Claims Commission, in its 1968 ruling, noted that the Caddos were placed on the Oklahoma reservation "in discharge of an obligation of the United States to them, not as a gratuity." Moreover, when the Caddo, by the Treaty of 1846, placed themselves under the protection of the United States, they did not cede whatever rights to land they may have had. The obligation of the United States to the Indians, furthermore, could not be ignored or repudiated solely because the United States had no public lands in Texas. The Commission, therefore, issued a new Order and revised Findings of Fact. The Caddo were, thus, finally if belatedly rescued from the apparently endless round of misfortune that has befallen them from the time of their first dealings with the United States.[21a]

3 : ALASKAN
INDIAN LANDS

The land problems of the Indians, Eskimos and Aleuts of Alaska remain unsolved to this day. Neither Russia, during its occupation of the periphery of Alaska, nor the United States, during the first hundred years of its possession of this vast land, formally or legally established a system of land tenure to govern the land rights of the natives. "The truth of the matter is," as Secretary of the Interior Stewart Udall put it in 1968, "that the claims of the Alaska natives were almost literally swept under the rug in the past." The Congress and the country at large had never, until that time, addressed themselves to the problem.[22]

The Census of 1970 counted 51,000 Indians, Eskimos and Aleuts out of a total state population of 300,000. Though racially distinct from the Indians to some degree, the Eskimos and Aleuts (numbering 35,000 in all) are considered "Indians" for the purposes of American law. The more numerous Eskimos are concentrated in the western half of Alaska. The Aleuts live along the Alaska Peninsula and the islands of the Aleutian chain. The Athapascan Indians, numbering about 5,000, live along the Yukon River and in the upper Kenai Peninsula around Anchorage. In southeast Alaska, in the narrow strip along the west coast of North America, are the Tlingit (about 8,000), the Haida (1,000), and the Tsimpshians (1,000).

Most of the Indians live in villages and small settlements along streams and ocean inlets, not in reservations. Their tenure has been both insecure and restricted by the absence of a clear-cut determination of their proprietary rights in general and by the stringent rulings by the Department of the Interior concerning native allotments made under the Alaska Native Allotment Act of 1906 (34 Stat. 197). Under the 1906 Act, no more than 160 acres of non-mineral land could be allotted to any native head of family or adult of 21 years of age. Such allotments were to be "in perpetuity, and shall be inalienable and nontaxable until otherwise provided by Congress." A 1956 amendment to the act permitted natives to sell the land allotted to them with the approval of the Secretary of the Interior.

A legal opinion of the Solicitor of the Department of the Interior, June 27, 1956, held that an allotment right of an Alaskan native under the Alaska Allotment Act was limited to a single entry and that the allotment could not embrace a grant of incontiguous tracts of land.[23] By a memo of September 21, 1964, however, Acting Solicitor Weinberg advised the Secretary of the Interior that the Secretary could make an allotment of incontiguous tracts of land, that he could consider native custom and mode of living, and that he could consider customary seasonability of occupancy in determining whether an applicant for an allotment had shown substantial continuous use and occupancy of the land. The 1964 memo represented a change of previous policy regarding allotments, which interpreted standards in terms of white settlement. The 1964 memo denied the intent of Congress to superimpose the requirements of the general homestead laws on the Alaska Allotment Act. It pointed out that incontiguous tracts of land in several different locations, taken as a whole, can compose a single Indian home unit. An Alaskan native home may include a fishing site, a hunting and trapping site, reindeer headquarters and corrals and tracts regularly used for other purposes. The decision, which cited the Report to the Secretary by the Task Force on Alaska prepared in 1962, is typical of the more sophisticated, if grudging, recognition paid by the agencies of government to the cultural uniqueness of Indian communities.

Despite the existence of the allotment privilege, only 100 grants of title under the act were made in the half century between the enactment of the 1906 act and 1962.[24]

By an Act of May 1, 1936 (49 Stat. 1250), the Secretary of the Interior was empowered to designate as an Indian reservation in Alaska any area of land which had been reserved for the use and occupancy of Indians or Eskimos by the Act of May 17, 1884 (23 Stat. 26), described below, though the designation of such a reservation was made conditional upon approval by a majority of the Indian or Eskimo residents of the area affected. Six validly created reservations were established under this law; a number of others were rejected by their native residents. On the whole, both native and non-native Alaskans have been hostile to the idea of reservations. The native antipathy to reservations is based in part on the Alaskan natives' knowledge of the condition of Indian reservations in the original forty-eight states.

The Act of May 17, 1884 (23 Stat. 24), providing a civil government for the Territory of Alaska, declared that the natives "shall not be disturbed in the possession of any lands actually in their use and occupation or now claimed by them, but the terms and conditions under which such persons may acquire title to such lands is reserved for future legislation by Congress." A similar provision is contained in the Act of June 6, 1900 (31 Stat. 321) concerning a civil government for Alaska.

Because of the Federal guarantee that the Indians shall not

be disturbed in their use and occupation of lands, Secretary of the Interior Stewart Udall, during the Johnson administration, refused to allow lands to be patented to the State under the land selection provisions of the Alaska Statehood Act, July 7, 1958 (72 Stat. 339) in the face of the persisting claims of the natives using and occupying such lands. "To allow these lands to pass into other ownership," Secretary Udall asserted, "would pre-empt from Congress the power to exercise its right and obligation to decide this issue, and would deny the Alaska Natives an opportunity to acquire title to lands which in many instances, it is generally admitted, they have openly and continuously used and occupied from a period that antedated the purchase of Alaska by the United States."[25]

Rather, Secretary Udall pointed out that it was incumbent upon Congress to determine the extent to which it wished to recognize or to extinguish aboriginal title in Alaska. "Congress may convert the aboriginal titles into full ownership, or it may extinguish the titles completely, or it may recognize the titles to a limited extent," Udall pointed out.[26]

The Governor of Alaska reacted vigorously to Secretary Udall's ruling, filing a suit on February 10, 1967, requesting a mandatory judgment against the Secretary to force him to issue patents to lands which the State had selected, but which were claimed by certain Indian natives of Alaska. The State contended that the Alaska Statehood Act vested selection rights absolutely in the State regardless of the natives' claims of aboriginal occupancy. The United States District Court for the District of Alaska granted the State's motion for summary judgment. Upon appeal to the Ninth Circuit Court of Appeals, however, the District Court's judgment was reversed. The court ruled that the State's claim could not be exercised until the natives' claim of aboriginal title had been adjudicated.[26a]

While the lawsuit filed by the State of Alaska was pending, the administration of President Johnson set the stage for a quick decision on the matter. In his Message to the Congress on Goals and Programs for the American Indian, March 6, 1968, President Johnson recommended prompt action to give the native peoples of Alaska title to the "lands they occupy and need to sustain their villages," "rights to use additional lands and water for hunting, trapping and fishing to maintain their traditional way of life, if they so choose," and "compensation commensurate with the value of any lands taken from them."[27]

The failure of the Indian Claims Commission and the Court of Claims to move rapidly on Indian claims prompted Secretary of the Interior Udall, in 1968, to propose a solution of the Alaskan Native claims not by reference to judicial decisions but by the direct determination of Congress. The Department's original recommendation and proposed bill of June 1967 provided for a grant of land to the villages and the adjudication of the remaining issues by the Court of Claims. But the prospect of twenty or thirty years of litigation in the Claims Commission or Court of Claims would have condemned an entire generation, and one desperately in need, to uncertainty and continued poverty. Udall proposed, therefore, that the committees of Congress concerned with Interior and Insular affairs "sit as a court and determine these issues."[28] Udall proposed, in other words, that the committees of Congress assume the function that may well have been the function Congress thought the Indian Claims Commission would assume: to hear and determine claims in an informal, liberal and generous manner.

The Alaska bill of the Department of the Interior, submitted in 1968, proposed a land settlement of up to 50,000 acres per village and up to $180 million in cash. The total amount of land going to the natives under such a settlement would be 8 to 10 million, much less than the 40 million acres and $500 million proposed in the bill favored by the Alaska Federation of Natives. Secretary Udall, in explaining how the monetary figure was determined, noted that it was based on a figure of $3,000 per person and that "it was practically picked out of the air" in negotiations with the Bureau of the Budget. The argument made by the Department of the Interior to the Bureau of the Budget was that Congress should be no less liberal with the natives of Alaska than it had been in the instance of the most liberal treatment given any Indian group in the United States. Udall pointed to the settlement with the Seneca Indians on the Kinzua Dam issue which averaged $3,-000 per person. In addition to the monetary settlement, the Department of the Interior's bill called for the continuation of aboriginal uses on other lands for 50 years, and the creation of an economic improvement corporation to be managed by the natives themselves. The 50,000 acres granted each village would be in trust status, but any native group with an acceptable plan would be granted the lands in fee upon application.[29]

The issue, Secretary Udall noted, was no longer whether the natives possessed any rights to be respected. The issue was, rather, "How much land? How much money?"[30] The debate over the question of "How much land?" and "How much money?" raged for three years, with the debate centered within the Interior and Insular Affairs Committees of the United States Senate and House of Representatives. At one end of the spectrum were the natives themselves, who never had been consulted about their fate from the time the United States purchased Alaska from the Russians. Their attempt to retain the largest possible land base—one that would sustain their traditional activities of fishing and hunting, and provide income from mineral leases and future economic utilization of the land by themselves and by others—was opposed at the opposite extreme by the representatives of the mining and other extractive industries, who saw the native possession of large areas of Alaskan land as a hindrance to the commercial exploitation of the state's mineral treasures. As

George Moerlein, Chairman, Land Use Committee, Alaska Miners Association, put it in testimony before the Senate Committee on Interior and Insular Affairs, "It is my firm belief that the Government of the United States is neither legally nor morally obligated to grant any of the claims put forth by the various native groups or by the native land claims task force; . . ." The proposal of the Alaskan native land claims task force to provide native title to 40 million acres— ten per cent of the land area of the state—was denounced by Moerlein as a threat and impediment to the future of Alaska, which he believed was tied to its extractive industries. The high royalties he expected the Indians to charge for mineral and oil leases would discourage exploration and exploitation. Needless to say, Moerlein condemned the "illegal land freeze placed upon Alaska by Mr. Udall" which Moerlein and others saw as slowing down Alaska's advancement. While most of Alaska's commercial boosters at least gave lip service to Indian rights, Moerlein was adamantly committed to the survival of the fittest. The native villages located where they are because of proximity to game and/or fish have, according to Moerlein, no economic justification. "Just as mining towns have been allowed to die when the ore played out, so should most of the native villages." Moerlein's solution to the Indian problem was to take them from their present homes, educate them for "useful, productive work" wherever new industries might develop, dissolve their special status and protection under the Bureau of Indian Affairs, and put them in direct competition with Alaska's non-native citizens.[31]

The denouement came in the summer of 1970 on the floor of the Senate and House of Representatives. The bill reported out of the Interior and Insular Affairs Committee of the Senate was a massive and complex piece of legislation but was in essence a simple compromise package, with land and dollars lumped in easily remembered arbitrary figures. Up to ten million acres of Alaska's 350 million acres were authorized in grants to village corporations, in grants to individuals, and in grants to native corporations. Monetary compensation was raised from figures in previous bills to $1,000,000,000, $500,000,000 of it from the United States Treasury over a twelve-year period, and the other $500,000,000 to be provided by a revenue sharing provision in the mineral leasing of the public lands and lands which would be patented to the State of Alaska under the terms of the Alaska Statehood Act. Once the $500,000,000 figure had been reached, the royalties would cease. In the meantime, however, the money would go into a Native-owned Services and Development Corporation and into a Native-owned Investment Corporation. The Services Corporation would provide professional, technical and financial assistance to individual natives and to village corporations in the selection and management of their land. The Investment Corporation would conduct business for profit activities, returning the profits to the native stockholders.

The bill, designed to make a final settlement of all native land claims based upon aboriginal right, title, use, or occupancy of land in Alaska, including any aboriginal hunting or fishing rights, also requires the Secretary of the Interior to develop a program for ending Bureau of Indian Affairs control over the affairs of the native people of Alaska within five years. The responsibility for the welfare of the Indian people of Alaska would become the State's with the exception of native public health services administered by the United States Public Health Service and certain educational programs.

This "termination" clause was the basis for a sharp fight on the floor of the Senate during the debate on the bill on July 14 and 15, 1970. Senator Fred Harris of Oklahoma, supported by Senator Edward Kennedy of Massachusetts, spoke feelingly of the error of forced termination as it has been applied generally to the Indian of the United States. The two senators supported an amendment proposed by the Alaskan

Federation of Natives to strike the termination clause from the bill. They also sought to raise from two to three the number of native members on the five-man board of the Alaska Native Commission, charged for seven years with preparing a final membership roll of Natives and a roster of Native villages, and with determining questions of land entitlement and boundaries among native claimants. Harris and Kennedy also sought to raise from 10 to 40 million acres the land settlement provisions of the bill. All of these attempts to modify the bill on the floor were unsuccessful. The bill had been carefully prepared with a greater degree of unanimity on the part of the interested parties than is usual in legislative proposals. The floor leadership was skilled. Senator Henry Jackson of Washington, Chairman of the Interior and Insular Affairs Committee, managed the bill with great effectiveness, proposing the only substantial amendment that did carry (47 to 35), which eliminated the possibility of huge windfall profits to those taking out leases on potentially rich oil producing lands. The committee's bill had authorized noncompetitive leasing of lands not known to be oil producing. Jackson's amendment provided for competitive bidding for leases wherever the demand for such leases indicated the possibility of the presence of subsoil wealth. A further factor in the passage of the bill (for which Harris eventually voted "aye" and Kennedy—still desirous of more for the natives—"nay") was the comprehensive knowledge and forensic skill of the junior senator from Alaska, the Democrat, Senator Gravel. With the senior senator, Senator Stevens, a Republican, providing timely support, Gravel was able to spike all appeals from the liberal wing with forceful oratory, apt allusions and a more comprehensive grasp of the Alaskan situation than any other senator.

The Alaskan Native Claims bill passed 76 to 8 and was sent to the House of Representatives. It did not, however, reach the floor of the House during the session. Indeed, some members of the House Interior and Insular Affairs Committee felt that the bill was altogether too generous to the Indians. Although the bill did not become law in 1970, a renewed legislative and executive effort was made in 1971 to achieve a settlement. The possibility that a more generous land settlement, nearer to the natives' desires, might be authorized, seemed possible as the White House lent its support to the native cause. The natives of Alaska, under the proposals being hammered out, may achieve both self-determination *and* termination. It is a solution that could not be achieved, in all probability, in any of the other fifty states. It may occur in Alaska because of the strength, sophistication and unity of the native population, because of the huge "pie" to be divided, and because of the high degree of good will on the part of the whites—both in Alaska and in Washington—concerned. Whether the goal of "maximizing the participation by Natives in decisions affecting their rights and property" can in fact be achieved, as the 1970 bill asserted, "without (1) establishing any permanently racially defined institutions, rights, privileges, or obligations; (2) creating a reservation system or lengthy trusteeship; or (3) ultimately adding to the categories of property or organizations enjoying special tax privileges or to the legislation establishing special relationships between the United States and the State of Alaska," remains to be seen.

4 : THE OKLAHOMA
INDIANS

The Alaskan Indians, Eskimos
and Aleuts were fortunate in being off the beaten path and in
being "discovered" by Europeans and Americans at a relatively late stage in history. Less fortunate were the tribes
whose descendants now inhabit the state of Oklahoma. Some,
most notably the Five Civilized Tribes (the Cherokees, Choctaws, Chickasaws, Creeks and Seminoles) played important
roles in early American history as powerful nations whose
favor was sought by the French, Spanish and English governments. Once American hegemony was established in the
Southeast, and white population began to overwhelm the Indians in their original homes, the situation changed. No attempt will be made to recount the shameful story of how these
proud nations were forced to "remove" to the lands set aside
for them in Oklahoma. Suffice it to say that the Five Civilized
Tribes, and numerous other Indian nations or portions
thereof, including Cheyenne, Arapaho, Apache, Comanche,
Kiowa, Caddo, Delaware, Wichita, Kaw, Otoe, Tonkawa, Pawnee, Peoria, Ponca, Shawnee, Ottawa, Quapaw, Seneca,
Wyandotte, Iowa, Sac and Fox, Kickapoo, Pottawatomi and
others, found themselves, in the course of the nineteenth

century, in an area which the United States, in its early removal treaties, had promised the Indians should "in no future
time, without their consent, be included within the territorial
limits or jurisdiction of any State or Territory."[32]

Most of the tribes removed to the Indian Territory were
well organized when they moved there. They maintained
their own schools, their own legislative assemblies, their own
courts. Administrative rulings and court opinions in the early
years of their residence there consistently upheld the power
of self-government exercised by the Five Civilized Tribes.
The independent position of the Indian nations was, however, gradually eroded. In the Civil War the Five Civilized
Tribes adhered to the Confederacy and, as a result, Congress,
in 1862, authorized the President to abrogate existing treaties. In 1866 new treaties were negotiated with these Indians.[33]

Meanwhile the westward movement of white settlers continued at an increasing pace and the isolation of the Indian
Territory soon became a thing of the past. Because Indian
courts had no jurisdiction over non-Indian settlers, the Indian
Territory became a refuge for outlaws from neighboring
states. By an act of May 2, 1890, a portion of the Indian
Territory was created into the Territory of Oklahoma. In
1893 Congress began to destroy the autonomy of the tribes
by dissolving the tribal governments of the Five Civilized
Tribes and allotting their lands in severalty. New courts were
established by Congress and the enforcement of tribal laws
was gradually forbidden and tribal courts abolished.[34]

The instrument by which the destruction of tribal identity
was accomplished was the Commission to the Five Civilized
Tribes, commonly referred to as the Dawes Commission,
which was established by an Act of March 3, 1893 (27 Stat.
612, 645). After three years of negotiation the Commission
was unable to reach an agreement with the tribes. Therefore
an Act of June 10, 1896 (29 Stat. 312, 339–340) was passed

directing the commission to prepare rolls of tribal members as a preliminary to allotment. It was made clear that the breakup of the tribal governments and the allotment of the land in severalty would proceed, whether the Indians agreed or not. Reluctantly, the tribes began to fall into line. By an Act of June 28, 1898 (30 Stat. 495), known as the Curtis Act, an allotment plan was instituted and Indian law declared unenforceable in Federal courts. The plan was so much in violation of the rights which the Indians had been guaranteed when they were moved to Oklahoma that it was necessary for the government to make further concessions to the Indians before they would proceed with the plan.[35]

The coup de grace was given by the enabling act of June 16, 1906 (34 Stat. 267) which made possible the admission into the Union of both the Indian Territory and Oklahoma Territory as the State of Oklahoma. On November 16, 1907, the two units were admitted to the Union as the State of Oklahoma with the provision that the laws in force in the Territory of Oklahoma at the time of the state's administration should be in force throughout the state. Though the Federal jurisdiction over the Indians and their lands was reserved, the destruction of the tribal governments and the aggressive activities of white Oklahomans resulted in the passage of an act of May 27, 1908, repealing the restrictions on the sale of classes of lands hitherto protected by the Federal Indian relationship, and imposing taxes on such lands.

The hope was to terminate the tribal governments by March 4, 1906, at the latest, but the necessity for additional time to permit the allotment of tribal land caused the Congress to authorize the continuance of the tribal existence and governments until the distribution of the tribal property. To complete the indignities heaped upon the Five Civilized Tribes, an act of April 26, 1906, gave the President of the United States the power to remove the principal chief of the Choctaw, Cherokee, Creek, or Seminole Tribe, or the governor of the Chickasaw Tribe, for failure to perform his duties, and the right to "fill any vacancy arising from removal, disability or death of the incumbent, by appointment of a citizen by blood of the tribe." Other controls over tribal affairs were given to the Secretary of the Interior. A few residual activities of tribal concern—mostly expressed in litigation growing out of the tribes' earlier status—have remained despite the largely successful assault on Indian sovereignty.

The hurried nature of the dissolution of the governments of many once proud nations now resident in Oklahoma has resulted in a complex web of confused judicial and administrative rulings on matters of taxes, allotments, inheritance, restricted tribal funds, leases and membership in the tribes. Despite the nominal recreation of tribal organizations by some tribes under the provision of the Thomas-Rogers Oklahoma Indian Welfare Act, of June 26, 1936 (49 Stat. 1967), Oklahoma's Indians have lost the coherence and strength which once characterized them.[36]

Despite the decline from their earlier lofty position, there have been signs that the Five Civilized Tribes should not yet be counted out. During the period of termination legislation in the Eisenhower administration, an Act of August 25, 1959 (73 Stat. 420) provided for the final termination of the Choctaw Tribe over a six year period. The termination period was, by subsequent legislation, extended to August 25, 1970. Although requested by the tribe at the time, the Indians later claimed that they had been deceived. They thought the bill merely gave them control over tribal assets and the right to appoint the Principal Chief of the Tribe. They were assured by officials of the Bureau of Indian Affairs at the time that they would not be deprived of eligibility for Federal education, health and other services deriving from their status as Indians.

A bill (H.R. 15866), to repeal the act of August 25, 1959, was introduced in the summer of 1970. The plea of the Choctaw—the only one of the Five Civilized Nations for which such a bill was written—to reverse the termination legislation of 1959 was fully supported by Commissioner of Indian Affairs Bruce in testimony before the subcommittee on Indian Affairs of the Committee on Interior and Insular Affairs of the United States Senate on July 14, 1970, as well as by the chiefs of each of the Five Civilized Tribes. What gave special point to the plea was the fact that in May of 1970 the Supreme Court determined that the Cherokee Nation, the Choctaw Nation and the Chickasaw Nation—not the State of Oklahoma—were the owners of the bed of the Arkansas River for the 100 miles from Muskogee, Oklahoma, to Fort Smith, Arkansas. If the Choctaws were deprived of their tribal status and of the trusteeship relationship with the Federal government, they would probably find it impossible to act to take advantage of the ruling (a vast amount of data must be assembled at considerable expense and with considerable technical skill) in the litigation that will be necessary to establish the exact extent of the assets to which they now have title. The Chickasaw Nation, which has lived since 1837 in one of the four districts of the Choctaw Nation, is also involved because the Choctaw Termination Act of 1959, enacted without the concurrence of the Chickasaws, provided for the sale of jointly owned lands without reference to the desires of the Chickasaws.

The move to repeal the Choctaw Termination Act of 1959 was the first demonstration of the Nixon administration's determination to repudiate the termination policy of the 1950s. With the support of Democratic leaders such as Senator Harris of Oklahoma, it may well succeed.[36a]

5 : THE PUEBLO INDIANS
OF NEW MEXICO

Another group of Indians living under a special tradition and with a unique history are the so-called "Pueblos" of New Mexico. The "pueblos," or towns, which the Indians inhabit, mostly in the Rio Grande Valley, have been lived in for a longer period than any other settlements in the United States. When "discovered" by the Spaniards, the Pueblos had their own tightly organized governments, a closely knit community life, and a well organized agricultural system, utilizing irrigation. Though reduced to obedience by the Spaniards, the Pueblos were always able to maintain internal administrative autonomy and to preserve their cultural integrity.

Under Mexican administration the tradition of local autonomy under the central government persisted. Title to Pueblo lands remained in the name of the individual pueblos; no individual Indian held title to such lands. The Pueblo Indians were considered wards of the government though they had the title "citizens." Their land could not be alienated without the authority of the central government.[37]

By the Treaty of Guadalupe Hidalgo, signed February 2, 1848, the residents of the territory ceded by Mexico could elect to retain their Mexican citizenship by making a declaration to that effect. Those failing to make such a declaration "shall be considered to have elected to become citizens of the United States." None of the Pueblo Indians elected to retain Mexican citizenship; hence, although some doubted their status, they became citizens of the United States. For many years after the accession of New Mexico to the United States the Pueblos were not considered Indian tribes within the meaning of existing statutes. When a question concerning their status arose in 1869 as the result of an attempt by the United States to invoke a section of the Indian Intercourse Act of June 30, 1834, making unauthorized settlement of tribal lands a Federal offense, the territorial judge dismissed the suit, pointing out that no person had ever been authorized by Congress as an agent for any of the twenty-one pueblos. Chief Justice Watts of the Supreme Court of New Mexico Territory declared that

> the transfer of eight thousand of the most honest, industrious, and law-abiding citizens of New Mexico to the provisions of a code of laws made for savages, by the simple stroke of the pen of an Indian commissioner, will never be assented to by congress or the judicial tribunals of the country so long as solemn treaties and human laws afford any protection to the liberty and property of the citizens.

The Chief Justice went on to say that

> This court has known the conduct and habits of these Indians for eighteen or twenty years, and we say, without the fear of successful contradiction, that you may pick out one thousand of the best Americans in New Mexico, and one thousand of the best Mexicans in New Mexico, and one thousand of the worst pueblo Indians, and there will be found less, vastly less, murder, robbery, theft, or other crimes among the thousand of the worst pueblo Indians than among the thousand of the best Mexicans or Americans in New Mexico.[38]

The United States did not accept defeat gracefully. Under the Appropriation Act of May 29, 1872, provision was made for an agent for "the Pueblo Agency," thus putting the Pueblos on a par with other Indians. The United States thereupon again attempted to invoke the Intercourse Act of 1834. Again the territorial court denied the applicability of the statute to the Pueblos and in 1876 was upheld by the Supreme Court of the United States, in *United States* v. *Joseph* (94 U.S. 614). In its decision, the Supreme Court pointed out the centuries old history of the Pueblo people.

> The Pueblo Indians, . . . [declared the court] hold their lands by a right superior to that of the United States. Their title dates back to grants made by the government of Spain before the Mexican revolution,—a title which was fully recognized by the Mexican government, and protected by it in the treaty of Guadaloupe Hidalgo, by which this country and the allegiance of its inhabitants were transferred to the United States.[39]

With the admission of New Mexico to statehood in 1910, the administration of the federal affairs of the area was shifted from Santa Fe to Washington, and the Pueblo Indians came more and more to be treated as other tribes were treated. The New Mexico Enabling Act specifically provided that "the terms 'Indian' and 'Indian country' shall include the Pueblo Indians of New Mexico and the lands now owned or occupied by them."

The constitutionality of this extension of Federal control over the Pueblos was in 1913 upheld in *United States* v. *Sandoval* (231 U.S. 28). The Supreme Court, in *Sandoval*, reversed its position in *Joseph* and asserted that the Pueblos were not "beyond the range of Congressional power under the Constitution."[40]

The *Sandoval* decision thoroughly dismayed the Pueblos. In the years that followed attempts were made to facilitate the acquisition of title by white men in the Pueblo lands, as in the bill introduced by Senator Bursum of New Mexico, in the Sixty-seventh Congress, "to quiet title to lands within Pueblo Indian land grants and for other purposes." Despite the support of the Harding administration for the bill, determined opposition organized by the New Mexico Association on Indian Affairs and the General Federation of Women's Clubs helped to defeat the bill. The Bursum bill eventually was replaced by The Pueblo Lands Act of 1924 to settle the status of all lands within the Pueblo area. The act provided that "no sale, grant, lease of any character, or other conveyance of lands, or any title or claim thereto, made by any pueblo as a community, or any Pueblo Indian living in a community of Pueblo Indians, in the State of New Mexico, shall be of any validity in law or in equity unless the same be first approved by the Secretary of the Interior." The constitutionality of the act was upheld in several cases.[41] Thus, while maintaining a corporate identity, the Pueblos have gradually lost some of the powers of sovereignty and control over their lands and destinies that they once had. The application of the Indian Civil Rights Act of 1968 (dealing with the constitutional rights of the Indian) will compress the Pueblo jurisdiction still further. Still, the Pueblo Indians maintain their tight discipline, living compactly and peacefully as they have for centuries.

6 : INDIAN LAND
AND ITS ALLOTMENT

The principal point of dispute
between white and Indian historically has been land. The
greatest legal gap between the two cultures has been the
respective attitudes toward that commodity. Or should one
say, rather than "commodity," "sacred and inalienable
mother"? The contrast between the two phrases symbolizes,
if it does not fully explain, the basic attitude of the two cultures towards the object which they disputed. In the context
of white America, land was a resource, waiting to be exploited. "In the beginning," wrote John Locke, "all the world
was America." Locke proceeded to shape a theory of the
relationship between the individual and the state in terms of
the assumptions of individual men agreeing to appropriate
the land they desired. European thought had not always pos-
ited man's relation to the earth in this fashion. Indeed, the
"Old World" contained, and contains, many of the same
"communal" assumptions about the earth than mark Indian
society. But when the "New World" was thrown open, like a
providential gift, to the European explorers, the meaning of
land in European culture took on new definition, and so did
the legal attributes of its acquisition and use.

To the Indian, on the other hand, with surprising uniformity throughout the vast reaches of the American continent, the land was "given," not "taken"; it was the mother to be respected, not the wanton daughter to be debauched; it existed prior to each man's brief mortal stay on earth, and would remain after it. It could be used, but not abused. It was to be enjoyed, but not alienated. In the spiritual assumptions of most Indian groups land served the role of source and sustainer of life; "she" played the role of mother to her "children." Ever-bountiful, she provided life, whose conduct and meaning were of central concern. Portions of her bounty often remained "sacred"—free even from activities necessary to sustain the life of her children.

An Indian prophet, Wowoka, who founded a religion which joined Christian and native beliefs, when asked to follow the paths of agriculture (he being of a non-agricultural people) replied:

"You ask me to plow the ground. Shall I take a knife and tear my mother's bosom? Then when I die she will not take me to her bosom to rest.

"You ask me to dig for stones! Shall I dig under her skin for her bones? Then when I die I cannot enter her body to be born again.

"You ask me to cut grass and make hay and sell it, and be rich like white men but how dare I cut my mother's hair?"[42]

The Europeans introduced the assumption that land could be exchanged for money. The land was treated like a commodity in English America as well as in Spanish America.[43] In pre-conquest Peru, to take one example, land and other commodities were controlled by the Inca state. Families or individuals seem only to have had usufructary rights to land. The Spaniards changed all this, introducing the concept of individual purchase of estates. Perhaps because of the similarities of European systems of appropriating the land, the Indian policy of the modern Peruvian state (as well as that of other Latin American states) has resembled that of the United States. From 1824 until 1919 Peruvian Indian policy was based on the forced integration of Indians into Peruvian society as individual land owners who could sell and otherwise alienate their property. The resulting loss of Indian land led to a constitutional recognition, in 1919, of the legal existence of Indian communities, and the establishment of a governmental agency responsible for Indian affairs, including the registering of surviving Indian communities.[44]

The practice in the United States of allotting to individual Indians tracts of tribal land antedates the Dawes Severalty Act of 1887. As early as 1798, such individual allotments were made in accordance with the terms of treaties.[45] But the real impetus to allotment on a general basis came in 1887 with the Dawes Act. At the time the Indian land base amounted to 138,000,000 acres. Between 1887 and 1934, about 60 per cent of this land passed out of Indian hands. The allotted land was to be held in trust for a period of 20 years, after which the Indian had unrestricted power to use and sell. Unallotted lands on the reservation were designated as surplus and ceded to the government, which then sold them to whites, placing the proceeds in trust for the tribes concerned. Sixty million acres were lost through the sale of lands designated "surplus" by the government after the allotments had been made to the Indians. In addition to this tribal land, 27,000,-000 acres or two thirds of the land allotted to individual Indians, was also lost by sale between 1887 and 1934.

Indians to whom land has been allotted, or who have inherited it, possess such land as owners. Families who do not own land may be assigned tracts or leased land by the tribal authorities, where lands remain in tribal ownership. Improvements made on the tribal land by individuals are normally their personal property. Sometimes unallotted tribal lands are used for communal pastures or gardens, or leased to outsiders, the proceeds going to the tribal treasury.[46]

The Indian Reorganization Act of 1933 provided the legislative rationale for the maintenance of Indian tribal land bases. Indeed, the efforts of the Indian Bureau in the 1930's and 1940's was to encourage the Indian to build up the land base of the reservation, his principal resource. The land of the reservations belongs to the Indians—to individuals, tribes, bands, and other groups. The land is held in trust for the Indian by the government, but it is the property of the Indians. Attempts have been made over the years—indeed over all of American history—to raid this land and its resources on the theory that it is merely government land, available for exploitation by anyone clever enough to stake a claim to it. Like parkland, Indian land provides a convenient target for exploitation by individuals and by governmental units, for public and private purposes, because of the political ineffectiveness of the occupants. Though the land of the Indian reservations is generally the poorest land in the country, its value is high.[47]

While the policy of breaking up Indian tribal lands in favor of allotments received its biggest impetus with the Dawes Act of 1887, the drive to encourage and even to force allotments on the Indians has also been evident after both of America's world wars. In keeping with a 1906 law which authorized the Secretary of the Interior to remove trusteeship restrictions and to issue a patent-in-fee "whenever he shall be satisfied that any Indian allottee is competent and capable of managing his or her affairs," a policy of "greater liberalism" was initiated in the period 1917–1921. Special competency commissions were set up to carry out the new policy. As a result, 20,000 fee patents were issued to individual Indians in the period, more than double the number issued prior to 1917 under the authority of the 1906 statute. The inevitable failure of the policy, by which many Indians were quickly separated from their land, helped to create the public concern which led to the 1926 study of the Institute for Government Research (the Meriam Report) and its call for the reform of American Indian policy.[48]

In the period following World War II, land hunger was such that the demand for fee patents and for the removal of restrictions against alienation similarly increased. Secretary of the Interior Ickes had halted the sale of Indian allotments and heirship lands, except in emergencies, by an order of August 14, 1933. The Indian Reorganization Act (adopted June 18, 1934), declared that no lands remaining in tribal ownership should be individually allotted in those reservations which voted to accept the application of the act. The Secretary of the Interior was authorized to issue fee patents and to remove the restriction against sales where such action was in the Indian interest. But the pressure brought to bear on the Secretary in the postwar years by those interested in acquiring Indian lands resulted in a number of private bills and legislation requiring the Secretary to issue fee patents. "Unless the Nation is prepared to pauperize the Indian people," the Acting Commissioner of the Bureau of Indian Affairs reported in his annual report for the year ended June 30, 1948, "discretion must continue to be exercised in issuing patents-in-fee, and that discretion to be effective must be lodged in a responsible official."[49]

The onset of the Eisenhower administration caused an increase in the transfer of Indian land from Indians to non-Indians under the provisions of the programs designed to free the Indian from Federal trusteeship. Five hundred thousand acres, comprising 3,200 tracts, or about $3\frac{1}{2}$ per cent of the acreage held by Indian individuals, were removed from trust or restricted status during the single fiscal year ending June 30, 1954. There were 1,609 sales to non-Indians, while only 88 tracts were purchased from non-Indians for tribes and individuals.[50]

The federal government as well as private individuals have made inroads into the Indian land base. In the Seneca-Kinzua case of the 1960's, the Treaty of Canadaigua of 1794, granting the Senecas a right in perpetuity to their reservation lands in New York State, was ignored when the government sought to build a dam on the site. Although it excited the concern of many white Americans, including Edmund Wilson, the writer, the Indians could not maintain their possession. Compensation in terms of market value was considered, by the values of white society, to be a sufficient exchange for the taking of the lands in violation of the pledged word of the United States.

Three anthropologists—Stanley Diamond of Syracuse University, William C. Sturtevant of the Smithsonian Institution, and William N. Fenton of the New York State Museum and Science Service—pointed out in 1963 in written testimony before the subcommittees on Indian Affairs of the Senate and House of Representatives (Eighty-eighth Congress, First Session) that to the Indian the land of the reservation is "a material segment of an ancient tradition and the basis and focus for his identity as an Indian." No Indian, they noted, had in recent years volunteered to sell his reservation.

> No matter how crude living and other facilities may be in fact, the reservation itself is a home and a shelter, and the most tangible symbol of Indianness, both for those now living there and for many tribe members temporarily living elsewhere. In this, Indians differ from other citizens, including other minority groups, for whom the specific land they occupy is of far less cultural and psychological significance.

Diamond, Sturtevant and Fenton urged that the Senecas be compensated culturally as well as materially, by providing them the resources to construct, in effect, a new reservation. The fundamental criterion in such cases, they pointed out, should be cultural. The measurement of the problem could not be in terms of the prevailing values of white society.[51]

The anthropologists' plea was unavailing. The Senecas were paid off in financial counters, not in cultural security. Although the final financial settlement was "upped" by the United States Government, it was, nevertheless, a financial settlement, an exchange of a community for money. A new "home" has been built in portions of the reservation not affected by the dam, and the ceremonial "long-house" has been rebuilt in the new community, but whether or not the sense of community takes root in the new ground cannot yet be asserted. The new Seneca community is one closely resembling its white neighbors. The Indian is becoming used to the world of mortgage payments, monthly electricity bills, and the like, problems which for the most part did not affect his life before the move. Something has gone out of his life; something has come into it. Just what the new Seneca nation will be has yet to be determined.

7 : LAND AND
ITS DESCENT

An increasingly serious prob-
lem affecting the Indian land base is the fractionation of interests in Indian heirship land. The problem arose with the
General Allotment Act of February 8, 1887 (the Dawes Act)
which provided for the allotment of 160 acres to each Indian
family head residing on a reservation, 80 acres to each unmar-
ried person over 18 years of age and 40 acres to every other
person under 18 years of age. The land was given in a trust
or restricted status, not as an outright gift in fee title. The
purpose of the Act was, of course, to break up tribal holdings
and force the Indian into the individualistic economy of his
white brothers.

Before the policy was discontinued in the 1930's, more than
40 million acres of Indian land were parceled out to be held
in trust for individual Indians. About three-fourths of this
land has passed out of Indian ownership. The government
retains trust responsibility for the remaining 11 million
acres.[52]

Upon the death of the original allottees the allotments, or
portions of them, have descended to heirs or devisees. As
these heirs in turn have died, their holdings have been subdi-

150

vided among their heirs or devisees, and so on through the years. As a result, about half of the allotted Indian lands are in an heirship status. The authors of the original legislation failed to anticipate the problems that would be caused by the partitioning of an individual's land following his death. Thousands of the allotments in an heirship status are subject to so many undivided interests that they can be utilized only with difficulty by their Indian owners, and administered with even more difficulty and expense by the Federal government. Undivided interests in a single allotment can often be expressed by fractions with a common denominator of 1,000,000 or more.

Representative Wayne N. Aspinall, who in 1965 introduced H.R. 11113, a Bill to Reduce the Number of Fractional Interests in Trust and Restricted Allotments of Indian Lands, and for Other Purposes, asserted in his testimony on the bill in 1966 that problems of managing heirship land "will be so acute by the turn of the century that the Federal government will be unable to bear the burden of handling the administration of the land and the Indians will find their lands so fractionated that their utilization will be nearly impossible." Aspinall's bill, introduced after a detailed study of the problem, is the successor to a series of bills introduced in previous Congresses.[53]

State laws instead of tribal laws govern the nature of inheritance of allotted lands, adding to the difficulty of effective use. An Indian may own parts of allotments in his own or other reservations, but to work a single tract, he needs the approval of all his fellow owners. Even Indian superintendents cannot effectively lease or otherwise utilize heirship land except under special circumstances.

The practice of allotments was halted by the Indian Reorganization Act of 1934 on the reservations to which it applied, and executive orders extended the trust period in the case of tribes not accepting the provisions of the Act relating to tribal

organization. But the damage had been done, and the heirship problem continues to plague the Indian and the Bureau
of Indian Affairs. Because of the difficulty of making leases or
otherwise utilizing efficiently Indian land in heirship status,
about one-half million acres of the six million in this status lie
idle. One and one-half million acres are used by non-Indians,
and 45,000 are leased to the tribes.[54]

On the San Carlos and Navajo reservations, where the land
was never allotted, no such problem of idle lands exists, and
organization of the land in efficient units is possible. In contrast, in the Plains States, where allotments are owned individually and inherited according to state law, consolidation
of fractionated holdings involves a complicated and expen-
sive legal effort. The attempt of the tribal council of the Rose-
bud Sioux, beginning in 1943, to purchase and merge land
into economically profitable units was successful in acquiring
land from single owners but virtually a complete failure in
regard to multiple-heirship tracts. The administrative and legal costs of acquiring clear titles was too overwhelming a
burden.

8 : GAMBLING
WITH THE LAND

In the closing years of the John-
son administration a bill was introduced which, if reintro-
duced and passed in a succeeding Congress, poses a threat to
the Indian land base in a fashion reminiscent of the Dawes
Severalty Act. Though initiated in a Democratic administration, and incorporated in the proposed "Indian Resources
Development Act of 1967," (S. 1816), the thinking behind it
is not distinguished by party label. Secretary of the Interior
Stewart L. Udall, in his statement and testimony on the bill
before the Subcommittee on Indian Affairs of the Senate
Committee on Interior and Insular Affairs, July 11, 1967,
strongly supported the proposed act as essential to the effort
to advance the economic welfare of Indians of the United
States. "It will provide new tools for the development of
Indian resources, and make it possible for Indians to take
greater responsibility for the management of their economic
affairs." The problem of Indian poverty was to be attacked by
providing Indians easier access to capital and greater responsibility in its use. The major elements of the proposed act
included the authorization of $500,000,000 of new appropria-
tions for an Indian loan guarantee and insurance fund and for

augmenting the direct revolving loan fund; authority for the issuance of Federal charters to Indian tribes and groups to form corporations for business or quasi-municipal enterprises; authority for Indian corporations to issue tax-exempt bonds for municipal purposes; authority for tribes on their own initiative to invest, mortgage or sell trust property; provision for escheat to the tribe or the United States of undivided interests in tracts of trust or restricted land, the value of which is less than $100 (an attempt to get at the heirship problem of fractionated Indian interests); and authority for tribes to establish a procedure through which non-resident tribal members wishing to relinquish tribal membership and special Federal services to Indians can be compensated by a share of tribal assets.

The increased credit facilities of the bill were designed to encourage the Indian tribal groups to develop industries and services on the reservations which would increase jobs for the Indians. Secretary Udall felt that the Indian must do more than lease land. He must develop the land himself. He must develop economically as a correlative of developing his ability to manage his own affairs. Some Indian tribes, he asserted, are already doing so, particularly in the Colorado River Valley. They are "wheeling and dealing" and the process must continue, in Udall's view, in order to encourage industry and other income-producing agents to enter the reservation. A number of the senators, however, wondered about the risks involved for the Indians. Senator McGovern, the Subcommittee chairman, asked whether it was not possible for groups to alienate and lose their land if they failed in their attempts to raise their economic level. Udall pointed out that the United States is a "risk society." If we do not pay back our debts we lose our property. But, he opined, there is a certain amount of optimism built into American society. We cannot sit back in fear of loss. The Indian too must be put in the "economic mainstream" of American society, risk and all. We should not push the Indian into the water and say "Sink or Swim" but we should get him into the water.

Senator Gruening of Alaska was similarly skeptical about the professed "emancipation" of the Indian by the act. With its constant restrictions upon Indian action "according to the determination of the Secretary of the Interior," Gruening saw little discretionary authority given the Indian. Indeed, he suggested it be called "An Act to perpetuate and enlarge the powers of the Secretary." Mr. Udall pointed out that in a trust land situation, someone had to be vested with authority for the guardianship of the Indian people, and that the Secretary must legally assume that role. But he hoped that the Indian people might in the future assume greater authority for managing their affairs, and he felt this act would provide some of the opportunity.

Though the provisions of the act were developed more fully by Commissioner Robert L. Bennett and supported as an attempt to break down many of the economic barriers surrounding Indians, "closing them off from fullest development and use of their resources," and though presumably drafted "after extended discussions with Indian leaders over a period of several months" in 1965, the bill causes curious reflections concerning the persistent policy of the American government to force the Indian to adopt white values whether he likes it or not. One recalls that the Dawes Severalty Act, which resulted in an enormous loss of the Indian land base, was similarly justified by the philanthropic Senator Dawes and others in the 1880's as the way to provide full economic opportunity for the Indian and to accustom him to white economic values of self-interest, selfishness, and the like. The coincident risks were not emphasized in the testimony concerning the Dawes Act, though Senator Teller of Colorado characterized an early version of the Allotment bill as "a bill to despoil the Indians of their lands and to make them vagabonds on the face of the earth." On another occasion during the debate on the bill, Teller remarked:

> If I stand alone in the Senate, I want to put upon the record my prophecy in this matter, that when thirty or forty years will have passed and these Indians shall have parted with their title, they will curse the hand that was raised professedly in their defense to secure this kind of legislation and if the people who are clamoring for it understood Indian character, and Indian laws, and Indian morals, and Indian religion, they would not be here clamoring for this at all.[55]

The Indian Resources Bill never got to the floor of Senate or House for debate, so that criticism of its provisions was more muted.

One wonders at the extent to which industries in this country, sensing the possibilities for exploitation of the natural resources of the Indian trust lands, have influenced the Indian Resources Development legislation. One wonders at the extent to which the "risk economy," whose praises Mr. Udall sang, would serve a culture oriented to other goals and other methods. One hesitates to think that another land grab is planned, based on the expected inability of the Indian to compete successfully with whites at their own game. Some Indian communities, no doubt, could safely utilize the provisions of the act to borrow capital and create income-producing ski resorts, or job-making industries. There are Indians and Indian communities which wish to join the economic mainstream of American society. But there are many who do not, and one wonders at the threat inherent in the proposed legislation to the integrity of a society which finds its ultimate sanction and security in the undisturbed possession of its homeland.

Only the first act of this modern drama has been played. The pressures will grow greater; the argument will be expressed more loudly. As in so many cases relating to the confrontation of the red man and the white, the white policy is based on the assumption that the red man should play the game the white man's way and give up the slight security and autonomy that he has painfully managed to wrest from his series of unequal contests with his conqueror.

Hearings on the Indian Resources Bill continued in 1968. On May 15, 1968, simultaneously with the advent of the Poor People's March on Washington, a hearing on the bill before the Senate subcommittee on Indian Affairs was marked by the presence of about a hundred of the "poor people" who sat and stood quietly while various Indian representatives testified on the bill (H.R. 10560, S. 1816) giving it, for the most part, qualified approval, or outright disapproval. John Belindo, of the National Congress of American Indians, presented the conclusion of his organization that the Senate version was unacceptable and asked for clarification of the tax status of all Indians living on reservations.

The fireworks began as James Amory, representing the Committee for Traditional Indian Land and Life, of Los Angeles, charged that the bill was falsely represented as having been written with the consultation of the Indian people. Amory denied that significant consultation had, in fact, taken place. The bill, he asserted, was written in the Bureau of Indian Affairs and the consultation that had taken place was perfunctory. Amory charged, furthermore, that the purposes of the bill were misrepresented by those who supported it. He charged that business interests who had formerly viewed the land as worthless, now saw an opportunity to reap profits from the oil shale, timber, oil, recreation, and other purposes to which the land could be put. Amory suggested that much of the impetus for the bill came from such interests and that the subcommittee should investigate this interest.

When Chairman McGovern called upon others in the room to testify, Clifton Hill, a Creek of Oklahoma, testified and introduced his fellow supporters of the Poor People's March. When Senator Jackson of Washington asked him, "Are they with you?" Hill replied, "No, I'm with them." The Poor People, as though on cue, shouted victory slogans and at several other points tested the chairman's nerve. Finally a Negro minister, A. P. Sampson, of Martin Luther King's office, testified and engaged in a diatribe against Senator Jackson and other senators who, he claimed, ignored people in behalf of resources. Cries of "Sock it to him!" resounded in the chamber as the young Negro refused to yield the floor to Senator Jackson when the Chairman attempted to defend himself.

The hearings were finally terminated. But through all the noisy rhetoric and loose argument, the radicals (or perhaps one should call them traditionals) got across their point that the proposed act would threaten the land base of the Indians by attaching that base as collateral for the mortgages that Indian tribes would be authorized to execute to obtain the money they needed for enterprises of one sort or another. Senator Hatfield's words in an earlier hearing, that the ultimate result might be the confiscation of the Indian land, were recalled.

The inspiration for bringing in the Poor People to the Indian hearing had been a last-minute one which seems to have derived from the mind of Clifton Hill. Though its method was crude, it was, I think, effective. It brought an element of threat and defiance to the Indian voice by allying it to the powerful voice of the Negro radicals. It overshadowed the softer voices of the conventional Indian leaders. When the hearing started, one reporter was present. By the time it was through, dozens of television cameramen, reporters, and others crowded into the hearing room and gave the proceedings an air of importance they had totally lacked before and which is customarily lacking in such hearings.[56]

The proposed Indian Resources Bill did not become law during the Johnson administration, in part because of the courageous opposition put up by its opponents, both tutored and untutored. When the bill is re-introduced it will probably omit the mortgage clauses which would put the Indian land base on the altar of risk capital. Former Commissioner Robert Bennett has revealed that the mortgage provisions in the early versions of the bill were inserted over the objections of the Bureau of Indian Affairs, an instructive example of the limited role played by the Bureau in determining Indian policy within the Department of the Interior.[57]

PART *IV*

The People

Who is an Indian?   :   Like everything else concerning the American Indian, the question "who is an Indian?" is fraught with difficulty and uncertainty. An Indian, legally and judicially, is defined in terms of his relationship to the legal system of the United States. All Indians are citizens, but those Indian citizens who are members, ex-members, or descendants of Indians having recognized tribal status have rights and obligations that are distinct from the rights and obligations of non-Indian citizens. A full-blood Indian who has terminated or abandoned his tribal membership and has no claim to allotments or other benefits or obligations deriving from his tribal association is, for legal purposes, not an Indian. On the other hand, a member of a tribal unit, accepted as such by the tribe though his Indian ancestry may be minuscule or tenuous, is, if accepted as an Indian by the tribal authorities and by the governmental agencies dealing with the tribal authorities, legally an Indian. A proposed Wyandotte tribal roll, for example, listed a person of only 1/256 degree of Wyandotte blood.[1] The Alaska Native Claims Settlement bill, which failed of enactment in 1970, defined a native as a citizen of the United States who is of one-fourth or greater Alaska Eskimo,

Indian, or Aleut ancestry, or "who is regarded as an Alaska Native by the Native Village or Native group of which he claims to be a member and those father or mother is (or, if deceased, was) regarded as Native by such village or group."[1a] Thus the legal definition of an Indian in the United States is more closely related to cultural and legal criteria than to biological ones. If the individual looks upon himself as an Indian, and if an Indian social or legal entity accepts him as an Indian, then he is normally regarded as an Indian, whether or not he can prove that some of his ancestors lived in America before its discovery by Europeans.

Beginning in the early 1800's, the United States by treaty and statute conferred citizenship upon Indians, often as the result of the allotment of parcels of tribal lands to individual Indians. The Dawes Act conferred citizenship upon all Indians to whom land allotments had been made, and to all Indians who had left their reservations to become residents of any state or territory. By 1924, when citizenship was conferred upon all non-citizen Indians born in the United States, two-thirds of all Indians had become citizens. Tribal Indians did not lose their standing as "wards of the United States" by acquiring citizenship. They became both wards and citizens. The fact that Indians were citizens, however, did not automatically entitle them to vote. While most states allowed Indians to vote in the years following the passage of the Citizenship Act, some states did not. In Arizona they were disfranchised until 1948 as "persons under guardianship."

In Arizona, indeed, the Attorney General's office ruled as late as 1944 that reservation tribal Indians living outside the reservation, even though subject to state laws and state taxation, were ineligible to vote.[2]

Other states exercised similar restrictions against Indian voting until recently. The phrase "Indians not taxed" was used several times in the United States Constitution to distinguish white citizens from Indians in the count of "free persons" to determine representation of states in Congress and in computing direct taxes to be levied by the United States. The phrase, along with the phrases "persons under guardianship" or "Indians living in tribal relations" provided the basis for their exclusion from voting by several states until recently. A clear-cut case of discrimination occurred in the proceedings of the Constitutional Convention establishing a government for the state of California. Though permitted to vote as residents of California when under Mexican control, the California Indians were disfranchised by the State Constitution enacted after California became a part of the United States. In an attempt to comply with the spirit of the Treaty of Guadalupe Hidalgo of 1848, which formalized the transfer, the new constitution permitted the legislature, by a two-thirds concurrent vote, to admit Indians, or the descendants of Indians, to the privilege "in such special cases as such a proportion of the legislative body may deem just or proper." The first legislature did not exercise this option.[3]

The historical distinction between Indian and white which has marked the relationship between the two groups from the earliest time has been continued in the legislation and administrative decisions affecting the Indian to this day. Congress has almost universally made matters relating to Indians and Indian reservations the subject of acts separate and distinct from those relating to the public lands, and it is well settled that general laws do not include them unless an intention to do so is manifest.[4] Not infrequently, however, confusion has resulted from the fact that it has not always been clear whether Indians were intended to be included or excluded from legislation such as some of the welfare legislation of the 1960's. Federal assistance programs usually provide aid to governments at the state or local level. Should tribal governments be considered local governments if not mentioned specifically in the acts authorizing such programs? Officials in the Bureau of Indian Affairs early in 1969 considered proposing legislation which would clarify the matter, but the possibility that such legislation might lead to a further blurring of the distinction between Indian tribal governments and Federal and State governments (with the consequent threat of induced termination) led them to drop the idea and to work instead (with great success) for the widest possible practical application of general welfare legislation to the Indian population.

By the General Allotment Act of February 8, 1887 (24 Stat. 388) all allottees were made subject to the criminal laws of the states where they resided. By an amendatory act of May 8, 1906 (35 Stat. 182) Congress withheld such jurisdiction until the issuance of fee simple patents to Indians allotted thereunder. Neither of these acts subjected unallotted Indians to the criminal laws of the states for acts committed within the reservation. Where reservations still exist the jurisdiction of the Federal government, state, and Indian authorities must be determined by the location and nature of the offense and by the race and status of the individuals involved.[5]

Although John Marshall used the term "ward" with reference to the Indians, he was referring to the relationship between the national government and the Indian *tribes* which, as he asserted, "resembles that of a ward to his guardian."[6] In time the term "ward" came to be applied to individual Indians, without restriction, while the word "resembles" was interpreted to mean "is." Felix Cohen has noted that there are ten different connotations of the term "wardship" and there are 1,023 possible combinations of these ten.[7]

In the face of the prevalent assumption by whites that the Indian is getting a "free ride" in terms of his liability to taxes, it is important to point out that Indian tax exemptions are not personal to the Indian but are characteristic of certain forms of property, principally property guaranteed to the Indian under such a freedom from taxation by the United States as a part of a bargain by which the Indian surrendered other lands to the government. The government did not give the Indian his land. The Indian gave the government his land. A traditional Indian response to the constant efforts to abolish or modify this bargain has been to say that the Indian will gladly give up the tax exemptions to the land involved if the Federal government will give back the consideration—the land ceded—on which it was based. Because the tax exemption applies to the land involved in the treaty transaction and not to other land or to the Indian as an individual, it is incorrect to say that "the Indian pays no taxes."

The inconsistency of different departments of the executive branch of the government in defining the term "Indian" is illustrated by the attempt of the Justice Department to exclude the non-Indian natives of Alaska from the benefits of the Indians Claims Commission Act. In three cases involving Eskimo and Aleut communities in Alaska heard before the Indian Claims Commission the government sought to exclude such claims on the grounds that the claimants were not American Indians and were, therefore, ineligible under the act. The act makes no specific mention by name of Aleuts and Eskimos, though the Department of the Interior and numerous court decisions have consistently held that all American aborigines are regarded as Indians under general Indian laws, whether or not they are specified by name.

In a decision rendered May 2, 1968 (19 Ind. Cl. Comm. 140), the Indian Claims Commission rejected the contention of the United States that Eskimos and Aleuts could not be included in the concept of "Indians" and that the Indian Claims Commission was therefore without jurisdiction of those plaintiffs. The Commission, in its decision, considered the question of legislative intent of the Congress in creating the Commission (Act of August 13, 1946, #1, 2, 60 Stat. 1049). It noted that when the Acting Solicitor of the Department of the Interior submitted comments on the bill in 1946, he urged the retention of the phrase "other identifiable group

of American Indians" in order that no group, including certain Alaskan Indian and Eskimo groups, should be thought to
be excluded from the provisions of the bill. The phrase was
retained in the final act. The Commission also noted that no
evidence in the legislative history of the act existed to show
that there was an intention to exclude Aleuts and Eskimos
from the provisions of the act and that, considering the humanitarian and remedial purposes of the act, it was hardly
conceivable that Congress intended to do so. The Commission considered other legislation and court interpretations in
which Eskimos and Aleuts were distinguished from Indians,
but concluded that none of these precedents interfered with
the decision rendered, but rather reenforced it. The Justice
Department, with its customary ardor, appealed the case to
the Court of Claims in an effort to get the decision reversed.
The Court of Claims, however, sharply rejected the Justice
Department's argument that Congress meant to exclude the
descendants of any pre-Columbian inhabitants of North
America.[8]

Indian Courts   :   The origin of Indian police and Indian
courts derives not, as might be thought, from an attempt to
allow or to give a measure of self-government to the Indians.
The reverse is true. Indian police and courts were created in
large measure for the purpose of controlling the Indian and
breaking up tribal leadership and tribal government.

In the period when the treaty-making process reflected a
reasonably accurate assessment of Indian power, no thought
was given by the United States to the question of law enforcement within the borders of the Indian nations. The Indian
had his own elaborate, if unwritten code of law, which, indeed, had always proved more effective in achieving justice in

Indian-white disputes than had the elaborate codes of the English and Americans.

In the late nineteenth century, when white power began to overwhelm and to break the autonomy of the Indian nations, and the Indian agent—representing the Great Father in Washington—began to infringe on the prerogatives of the Indian leaders, the internal judicial problems came to the fore. Traditional Indian lawways existed; but whites now wished to exert more control and power. During the 1860's and 1870's several Indian agencies determined on the need for Indian police. The agent for the Pawnees in 1862 appointed six leading warriors, provided them with uniforms, and entrusted them with the suppression of horse stealing and other crimes to which the Pawnees were too much addicted. In 1873 John P. Clum, a twenty-three-year-old Rutgers graduate, arrived in Arizona to become agent for the San Carlos Apaches. Three years later, when he left the agency, after consolidating five agencies into one and moving thousands of Indians hundreds of miles without the loss of a single life or the destruction of property, he had proved his point that the Indian police he had set up could guarantee law and order better than the regiments of soldiers in the area.

The record of the Indian police set up by agents such as Clum caused the Commissioner of Indian Affairs in 1878 to issue instructions to all Indian agents to organize police forces wherever possible. The Commissioner's instruction made no specific mention of trial and punishment of offenders, and until 1883, when the Secretary of the Interior authorized Courts of Indian Offenses, Indian agents tended to act as judges.

The need for formal Courts of Indian Offenses seems to have originated with Secretary of the Interior (formerly Senator from Colorado) H. M. Teller. Appointed Secretary in 1882, Teller wished to eradicate "certain of the old heathenish dances; such as the sundance, scalp-dance, &c." as well as to attack the institution of polygamy, the power of medicine men, and other Indian customs. At Teller's request, Commissioner of Indian Affairs Hiram Price formulated a plan to assign the top three officers of each police force the additional duty of judge of a Court of Indian Offenses. The judges were not to be paid; the Secretary also wished economy. Such courts were thereupon established as the agent and the Commissioner of Indian Affairs thought appropriate. The Five Civilized Tribes, the Indians of New York, the Osage, the Pueblos, and the Eastern Cherokees, all of whom had recognized tribal governments, were excluded. Price formulated a set of rules for such courts which were approved in 1883 and circulated to the agents. The courts were without other legal or judicial sanction, and they applied common sense rather than formal law to the cases heard. Drunkenness was the most frequent type of case heard; family relations next.[9]

The development of Indian courts suffered a setback in the 1880's largely as a result of congressional reaction to the decision of the Supreme Court *In re Crow Dog* (109 U.S. 556, 1883).

Crow Dog had killed Spotted Tail after the latter had appropriated the wife of a friend on the Sioux reservation. The case was handled by the Indians with satisfaction made in the Indian manner, but Crow Dog was arrested by federal agents. He appealed for a writ of habeas corpus claiming that federal courts lacked jurisdiction under the 1817 act which extended federal criminal jurisdiction over the Indian country except for offenses committed by one Indian against another. The Supreme Court freed Crow Dog and said that any prosecution must be pressed within the judicial system of the tribe.

Congress found the decision outrageous and by a provision of the Indian Appropriation Act of 1885 extended the federal criminal jurisdiction to the seven major offenses of murder, manslaughter, rape, assault with intent to kill, arson, burglary and larceny (23 Stat. 385, 1885). In 1932 the Congress raised the total from seven to ten crimes. Another was added in 1956. The Seven Major Crimes Act of 1885, as it was known, did not abrogate existing treaties, but it illustrated the persistent congressional attempt to eliminate by legislation the legal distinctions between the Indians and the non-Indian population of the United States.

Eventually Indian police and courts were able to acquire more prestige and the meager salaries allotted were increased. But the Dawes Act of 1887 reduced the importance of the courts by allotting land individually to Indians and placing Indians receiving such allotments under the civil and criminal jurisdiction of the state or territory where they resided. The Curtis Act of 1898, moreover, specifically dissolved the courts and police of the Five Civilized Tribes and placed the Indians under the jurisdiction of the federal courts. The sale of surplus land to whites within the former reservations made the maintenance of a clear-cut Indian judicial system that much more difficult.

The Wheeler-Howard Act of 1934 provided for a new form of "tribal courts" functioning under Department of the Interior regulations. Fifty-one such courts were in operation in 1964, along with eleven of the older Courts of Indian Offenses.[10]

The relatively great success of Indian courts and police in the face of the disadvantages of ridiculously low pay, the stigma of serving as an agent of the white conqueror against one's own people, and the like, call for some explanation. It may well be that the chance to play a role of prestige and power, the right to bear arms among fellow warriors deprived of their arms, the privilege of wearing formal uniforms expressing that authority, and the frequent scouting and tracking missions against renegades, gave back to the Indian something he thought he had lost forever. Though he served as an agent of those who had destroyed the autonomy of his tribe his role demanded more individual physical courage, resourcefulness, and fidelity than did the role of chief of a people no longer able to make war or exercise an independent policy. Though the new role was provided by the conqueror, it served as a substitute for some of the values that the conqueror had destroyed.

The status of tribal courts and the validity of their judgments have been subject to conflicting court decisions, some of which will be discussed in the next section. Although the "internal sovereignty" of the tribes as "separate political communities" has frequently been upheld by the courts, the independence and range of their decisions—administrative and judicial—have frequently been challenged in other court decisions. In part the confusion arises from the steadily diminishing power of the tribes from the nineteenth century to the present day. Even though a 1959 decision (*Native American Church* v. *Navajo Tribal Council,* 272 F.2d 131, 134, 10th Cir.) could assert that Indian tribes were not states but occupied a "status higher than that of States," other courts have implied that tribal autonomy and the tribal court system represent a status less than that of States, and have attempted to diminish their independence and authority by asserting that tribal courts serve merely an educational and disciplinary role. In part the confusion stems from the intricate problem of jurisdiction. Federal, state and tribal courts may all have jurisdiction over the same subject matter. Depending upon who performed a particular action, where he performed it, and who brought the matter to judicial notice, the legal results can vary considerably.

In *Williams* v. *Lee,* 1959 (358 U.S. 217), the Supreme Court denied jurisdiction to a state court in a suit brought by a non-Indian in an Arizona court against a Navajo Reservation Indian for goods sold the Indian on the reservation. The court averred that "[T]o allow the exercise of state jurisdiction here would undermine the authority of the tribal courts over Reservation affairs and hence would infringe on the right of the Indians to govern themselves." Other cases—particularly in lower courts—have chipped away at the strong support given the tribal courts by this decision and by others of like nature. The subject is liable to remain confused because of the complex jurisdictional problems and because of the conflicting interpretations of the extent of federal, state and tribal authority. [10a]

Constitutional Rights : Until the passage of Public Law 90–284, April 11, 1968 (82 Stat. 77) the federal courts traditionally held that constitutional guarantees of freedom of worship, speech, the press, the right to assemble and petition the government, the privilege against self-incrimination, the guarantee against double jeopardy, and the prohibition against loss of life, liberty or property without due process of law, were not intended to apply to Indians in their tribal capacity. Indians were regarded, at the time of the formation of the Constitution, not—with some exceptions—as individual citizens of the Union, but as members of distinct political communities with whom numerous treaty relationships, inherited by the United Staes from colonial days, existed. The peculiar traditions of the Indian nations were well known to the Founding Fathers and to later statesmen, and no attempt was made to equate these traditions with the traditions of English common law or to force the Indians, in their internal judicial procedure, to follow English models. That one should take specific traditions evolving out of the particular heritage of English law and try to apply them in a totally different situation would have seemed improper to English and Indians alike. The applicability of such provisions, in all their complexity, even to the *English* colonists in America can, indeed, be questioned.

The history of the interpretation of such rights in English

and American law has a special fascination and interest. The evolution of the privilege against self-incrimination from an informal rule to prevent extorted confessions into an elaborate formal right permitting an accused to remain silent if he thinks an answer might tend to incriminate him, is an example of the evolution of these constitutional rights in Anglo-American law.[11] The tendency of recent court decisions to strengthen and elaborate these individual rights has had a disputed effect on law and order in the society as a whole. Such rights express the values of a society consciously based on the idea that governments are instituted by individual men to serve their particular interests. The democratic traditions of England and America, based as they are on assumptions about human nature and human history drawn from John Locke and other libertarians, are not universal, or even European. They certainly are not predominant within the Asian, African or pre-European American systems. Most systems of government have given the state great leeway in exercising power against the particular interests of individual citizens. Those citizens, or members of a society, are not normally conceived to have come together as individuals to form a state to fit their individual conveniences. Rather, most states—including most Indian nations—have been founded on the assumption of a preexisting unity of the race, however it may have been created. The nation or group exists as the embodiment of the collective wills of its members, both past, present and future, and their roles are set down in highly elaborate codes of behavior. The strong communal aspect to such groupings, the absence of European concepts of exclusive and absolute individual possession of the land, has been noted. Many of the individual rights accorded to those brought up in the English tradition are, or were, alien to Indian assumptions of right.

Individual rights so zealously and formally guarded by a

system evolving in the English tradition, therefore, may not be transferable to a different environment. Only to the extent that the Indian system is based on similar values will the application of such constitutional guarantees be appropriate. In fact, the procedures of the two systems have a considerable degree of overlap. Even before the passage of Public Law 90–284, one-fifth of the tribal constitutions contained a bill of rights, patterned on the American bill of rights, guaranteeing rights of worship, association and even trial by jury for serious cases.

It is important to keep in mind that there are no offenses over which Indian tribal courts have jurisdiction which carry a penalty of more than six months in jail. Tribal courts are thus, in fact, effectively barred from considering (in most jurisdictions) cases more significant than misdemeanors. Though constitutional rights can be involved in such cases, the incidence of important issues arising in such circumstances is liable to be low.[12]

Nevertheless, despite such guarantees of individual liberties within the Indian legal structure, and despite the habitual Indian respect for individual viewpoints, complaints have arisen from Indians and non-Indians of denials of constitutional safeguards traditionally assumed to be the privilege of American citizenship. The Task Force appointed by President John F. Kennedy heard many such complaints and recommended that the Secretary of the Interior and the tribes require adequate protection of such rights in the Indian courts. It is inevitable that in a cultural situation where some Indians live according to one set of values and others according to another, and in a context in which the Indian law must function in close relationship to white law, that there will be conflicts of law. What is surprising is how few such conflicts have arisen among the thousands of cases tried and how infrequently tribal statutes have infringed upon such "rights." In part this situation derives from the strong influence exercised by the Secretary of the Interior on the passage of tribal laws, but it also derives from the innate fairness of the Indian legal system which, while it may differ in form and procedure from our own system, seeks the good of the society in terms that are not totally foreign to our own conceptions.

Though some of the concern with the Indian's constitutional rights originated with individual Indians, more of the impetus seems to have come from the white man. Commentators in legal journals who dealt with the problem in the 1960's were almost universally critical of the failure of Indian courts to meet outside standards of professional legal practice, or to accord the same constitutional protections known in white courts. Belittling references to the "fiction" of Indian sovereignty were frequently coupled with assertions that the system of tribal courts was established "to educate Indians gradually to the ways of American justice," as though they were some form of high school student council. [13] Indeed, one senses a greater cultural blindness on the part of the custodians of Anglo-Saxon law than on the part of the legislators who, while also antipathetic to variant legal systems in the American commonwealth, were more worried about the organizational confusion stemming from that variance than about the quality of Indian justice. In any event, the clamor over the alleged denial of individual rights by Indian tribal governments encouraged the subcommittee on Constitutional Rights (Senator Sam J. Ervin, Jr., of North Carolina, Chairman) of the Senate Committee on the Judiciary (Senator James O. Eastland, of Mississippi, Chairman) to hold hearings and conduct investigations in 1961, in 1964 and in 1965 (Eighty-eighth and Eighty-ninth Congressses), the heralded purpose of which was "the protection of the constitutional rights of the American Indian." Draft legislation was prepared by the committee to meet the problem, and extensive testimony taken.[14]

How problems can arise in the attempt to apply the Bill of
Rights enacted by American descendants of English colonists
to the Indians whom they conquered is seen in the very first
guarantee: that "Congress shall make no law respecting an
establishment of religion, or prohibiting the free exercise
thereof; . . ." Frank J. Barry, Solicitor of the Department of
the Interior, in testimony before the subcommittee in 1965,
recommended against the attempt to prohibit an Indian tribal
government from making laws respecting the establishment
of religion. The Indian political system, he pointed out, is
frequently "deeply rooted in their religious system" and the
prohibition, "while it might be a desirable long-term objective, would result in the probable destruction of tribal government in some cases." The religious provision included in the
act (P.L. 90–284) that was passed in 1968 prohibits tribes
from making or enforcing any law prohibiting the free exercise of religion, but makes no mention of the establishment
of religion.[15]

An example of the difficulty of applying the religious guarantee of the First Amendment to the American Indian is illustrated in the 1959 case of the *Native American Church* v. *the
Navajo Tribal Council* (272 F. 2d 131). In 1940 the Navajo
Tribal Council adopted a resolution prohibiting the use of
peyote on the Navajo reservation, on the grounds that the
religious use of peyote was not in keeping with the orthodox
religious traditions of the Navajo tribe. The resolution was
approved by the Secretary of the Interior and became law on
the reservation. The Native American Church, whose members use peyote, a cactus product, as an element in their
religious observance, brought an action against the tribal
council to have the resolution declared invalid. The Court of
Appeals for the 10th Circuit rejected the action, noting that
the First Amendment applies only to Congress and, by means
of the Fourteenth Amendment, to the states. But, the judgment noted,

Indian tribes are not States. They are subordinate and dependent nations possessed of all powers as such only to the extent that they have expressly been required to surrender them by the superior sovereign, the United States. . . . No provision in the Constitution makes the first amendment applicable to Indian nations nor is there any law of Congress doing so. It follows that neither under the Constitution or the laws of Congress, do the Federal courts have jurisdiction of tribal laws or regulations, even though they may have an impact to some extent on forms of religious worship.[16]

Representatives of the church fought the decision by attempting to obtain relief through legislation that would sustain what they regarded as their constitutional right to practice their religion as they saw fit. Earlier, in 1937, the church had fought a desperate battle against a bill to prohibit the interstate shipment of peyote, which was regarded by many as a habit-forming drug having orgiastic and hallucinating effects on those who used it. Such effects were vigorously denied and refuted by the leading anthropologists of the day, who pointed out that the use of the root (which is chewed) is similar to the use of sacramental wine in Christian ceremonies. Such wine had been excluded from the Prohibition enactment. So, also, said the anthropologist A. L. Kroeber, should peyote.

It is of interest to note the ambiguous position of the Secretary of the Interior concerning the peyote problem. While giving his assent to the anti-peyote ordinance, he prohibited the use of federal money or personnel in enforcing it, in order to avoid charges of violating the First Amendment guarantee of religious freedom.[17]

Another landmark case in the history leading to the Indian Civil Rights Bill of 1968 was that of *Madeline Colliflower* v. *John Garland, Sheriff of County of Blaine, Montana.* Madeline Colliflower, a member of the Gros Ventre tribe, part of the Fort

Belknap Indian community located on the Fort Belknap reservation in Blaine County, was arrested by the chief of police of the reservation, Joe Plumage, on a warrant issued by a judge of the Court of Indian Offenses, Fort Belknap Jurisdiction, United States Indian Service, for failing to obey a lawful order of the court to remove her cattle from land leased by another person. On June 25, 1963, she was found guilty and sentenced to a fine of $25.00 or five days in jail. Mrs. Colliflower elected to take the jail sentence. She then sought a writ of habeas corpus in the district court, claiming that her confinement was illegal and in violation of her constitutional rights because she was not afforded the right to counsel, was not afforded any trial, was not confronted by any witnesses against her, and because the action of the court was taken summarily and arbitrarily, and without just cause. Her claim was based on the due process clause of the Fifth Amendment to the Constitution of the United States, and on the Fourteenth Amendment.

The district court did not pass on the merits of the question because it decided that it did not have jurisdiction to issue a writ of habeas corpus since the Indian was committed by a tribal court. The decision was appealed and the court of appeals for the 9th Circuit, on February 4, 1965, reversed the order and remanded the matter for further proceedings.

In considering the early history of U.S. relations with the Gros Ventres and Blackfoot Indians, the court examined the Fort Laramie Treaty of September 17, 1851, and a second treaty of October 17, 1855, both of which dealt with definition of boundaries, payment of annuities and the like. No mention is made of self-government by the Indians or of tribal courts in the treaties, though it is clear that there is recognition of the Blackfoot nation as a nation. Following the Act of March 3, 1871, which terminated the practice of making treaties with Indians, though recognizing all treaties previously made and ratified, a Blackfoot Indian reservation was established in what is now the state of Montana by an executive order of July 5, 1873. Subsequent acts of Congress and executive orders in 1874, 1875, 1880, and 1888, more closely defined the boundaries of the reservation and divided it into three parts, one of which was the Fort Belknap reservation.

The first reference to tribal courts noted by the Court of Appeals in its decision was in the annual report of the Commissioner of Indian Affairs for 1885, which spoke of rules prepared in the office of the Secretary of the Interior dated April 10, 1883, for the establishment of a court of Indian offenses at each of the Indian agencies, except that for the Five Civilized Tribes in the Indian Territory. The Commissioner conceded that no special law authorized the establishment of such courts, but claimed authority for their establishment under the general provisions of law giving the Interior Department supervision of the Indians. The establishment of the courts was specifically related to the implementation of the policy to suppress certain "old heathen and barbarous customs, such as the sundance, scalp-dance, polygamy, etc." with the avowed purpose "to destroy the tribal relations as fast as possible and to use every endeavor to bring the Indians under the influence of law." Congress took cognizance of these courts in 1888, by appropriations for their support, both at Fort Belknap and elsewhere.[18]

In 1889 the Commissioner noted that these courts of Indian offenses, established since 1882 as "a tentative and somewhat crude attempt to break up superstitious practices, brutalizing dances, plural marriages and kindred evils, and to provide an Indian tribunal which, under the guidance of the agent, could take cognizance of crimes, misdemeanors and disputes among Indians, and by which they could be taught to respect law and obtain some rudimentary knowledge of legal processes," had been of "great benefit to the Indians and of material assistance to the agents."

The existence of tribal courts at Fort Belknap was

confirmed by the Wheeler-Howard Indian Reorganization Act of 1934 which allowed Indian tribes to adopt constitutions and by-laws when ratified by the members of the tribe and approved by the Secretary of the Interior. Under the powers of the act, a Law and Order Court was established as part of the Gros Ventres government. The Code of Indian tribal offenses adopted by the Fort Belknap Indian community was taken almost verbatim from the regulations of the Bureau of Indian Affairs whose purpose was stated to be "to provide adequate machinery of law enforcement for those Indian tribes in which traditional agencies for the enforcement of tribal law and custom have broken down and for which no adequate substitute has been provided under Federal or State law." The regulations also indicated that such a court of Indian offenses should not be established on reservations where justice was effectively administered under state laws and by state law enforcement agencies.

Judges of the tribal court, the Court of Appeals noted, are appointed by the Commissioner of Indian Affairs subject to confirmation by two-thirds vote of the tribal council. A judge may be removed by the Commissioner, for cause, upon recommendation of the tribal council.

The Court of Appeals, in laying the basis for asserting federal involvement in the tribal judicial process had, nevertheless, to recognize the series of decisions establishing the separateness of the Indian nations. Foremost among the decisions establishing such autonomy was Chief Justice Marshall's opinion in *Worcester* v. *Georgia,* 1832, which has been discussed in Part II of this book. Marshall asserted in his 1832 decision that "The Indian nations had always been considered as distinct, independent, political communities, retaining their original natural rights, as the undisputed possessors of the soil, from time immemorial. . . ." He went on to conclude that the Cherokee nation was "a distinct community, occupying its own territory, with boundaries accurately described, in which the laws of Georgia have no force, and which the citizens of Georgia can have no right to enter, but with the consent of the Cherokees themselves, or in conformity with treaties, and with the acts of congress."

The Court of Appeals, in *Colliflower,* had similarly to consider the decision of the Supreme Court in *United States* v. *Kagama,* 1886 (118 U.S. 373, 381–85), in which the court pointed out that the Indian tribes

> . . . were, and always have been regarded as having a semi-independent position when they preserved their tribal relations; not as States, not as nations, not as possessed of the full attributes of sovereignty, but as a separate people, with the power of regulating their internal and social relations, and thus far not brought under the laws of the Union or of the State within whose limits they resided.
>
> . . . These Indian tribes *are* the wards of the nation. They are communities *dependent* on the United States. Dependent largely for their daily food. Dependent for their political rights. They owe no allegiance to the States, and receive from them no protection. Because of the local ill feeling, the people of the States where they are found are often their deadliest enemies. From their very weakness and helplessness, so largely due to the course of dealing of the Federal Government with them and the treaties in which it has been promised, there arises the duty of protection, and with it the power. This has always been recognized by the Executive and by Congress, and by this court, whenever the question has arisen.

Yet the Court of Appeals in *Colliflower* noted that since the time of John Marshall the " 'independence' of the Indian tribes and their resemblance to nations, has decreased, and their dependency has increased." The court noted, moreover, that "As the United States has expanded, it has repeatedly broken its treaties, has taken the Indians' land by force, has repeatedly imposed new and more restrictive treaties upon them, has confined them in ever smaller reservations, often far from their original homes, and has reduced them to the status of dependent wards of the government."

The Court of Appeals, citing more recent cases, noted the increasing influence of state law and the growing tendency to apply congressional legislation to Indians. It asserted the basic proposition, stated in *Winton* v. *Ames,* 1921 (255 U.S. 373, 392), that "It is thoroughly established that Congress has plenary powers over the Indians and over their tribal relations" and, by *United States* v. *Kagama,* 1886 (118 U.S. at 379), that the Indian reservations are a part of the territory of the United States. Yet the court conceded that the notion of sovereignty still barred the way of one who wishes to sue an Indian tribe, and that an Indian tribe has the power, if no act of Congress or treaty provision forbids it, to enact its own laws for the government of its people and to establish courts to enforce them. It also conceded that the fact that all Indians are now citizens does not affect the jurisdiction of tribal courts. But the court did "doubt the present validity" of the proposition, expressed in *Native American Church* v. *Navajo Council* and in Felix Cohen's *Handbook of Federal Indian Law,* 1942 (pp. 124, 181), that the Constitution applies to the Indians, in the conduct of tribal affairs, only when it expressly binds them, or is made binding by treaty or act of Congress. The court attempted to "explain" the decisions in *Native American Church* v. *Navajo Tribal Council* and in *Talton* v. *Mayes,* 1896 (163 U.S. 376), in other terms.

The Court of Appeals concluded that "In spite of the theory that for some purposes an Indian tribe is an independent sovereignty, we think that, in the light of their history, it is pure fiction to say that the Indian courts functioning in the Fort Belknap Indian community are not in part, at least, arms of the federal government." The court went on to conclude that,

Under these circumstances, we think that these courts function in part as a federal agency and in part as a tribal agency, and that consequently it is competent for a federal court in a habeas corpus proceeding to inquire into the legality of the detention of an Indian pursuant to an order of an Indian court. . . .

It may well be that one hundred years ago it would have been held that a federal court lacked jurisdiction to issue a writ of habeas corpus at the instance of an Indian imprisoned in a tribal jail, pursuant to the judgment of a tribal court. We think, however, that the status of the Indians today is such, and particularly that the history and status of the tribal court at the Fort Belknap Reservation is such, that we should uphold the jurisdiction of a federal court in this habeas corpus proceeding.

The court specifically disclaimed the intention of requiring the tribal court to comply with every constitutional restriction that was applicable to federal or state courts, and also denied the conclusion that the Fourteenth Amendment applied to tribal courts at all; nevertheless, it reversed the order of the district court in the Colliflower case and upheld the jurisdiction of a federal court in such a proceeding.

It is of interest to note that the United States filed a memorandum as *amicus curiae* when the appeal was heard fully agreeing with Mrs. Colliflower that the constitutional guarantee of "due process of law" is applicable to Indian tribal court proceedings and that a district court of the United States accordingly has jurisdiction to inquire by habeas corpus whether a tribal prisoner in custody is held "in violation of the Constitution" because the proceedings which led to his incarceration were fundamentally unfair.

The memorandum, submitted by Ramsey Clark, then Assistant Attorney General and Roger P. Marquis, Attorney, Department of Justice, sidestepped the question of whether all the specific procedural rules prescribed by the Bill of Rights applied to Indian court proceedings. The memorandum asserted, as did the Court of Appeals, that such a position was not inconsistent with previous cases such as *Talton* v. *Mayes,* 1896 (163 U.S. 376).

The memorandum concluded that "Today, when Congress has expressly confirmed the citizenship of Indians (43 Stat. 253) and the old notions of autonomous Indian 'nations' have been modified to a significant degree (*Kake Village* v. *Egan,* 369 U.S. 60, 72 [1962]), it is all the more appropriate to recognize the operation of constitutional guarantees in Indian affairs."

Cases such as the Colliflower case indicate the degree to which courts will condition their decisions on the basis of non-legal assumptions about the relative power and independence of the Indian people of the continent. Laws, treaties, judicial decisions and other instruments recognizing the distinct and separate status of Indian political units are modified on the basis of the erosion of that independence occasioned by violation of those instruments by later representatives of the United States. It is sad to see decisions overturned by reference to later violation of those decisions; it is even sadder to see such reversals cloaked in the robes of fundamental rights. The history of American legal actions toward the American Indian is replete with instances of violations of earlier rules of law (devised in the context of a particular power equilibrium) to take advantage of the declining bargaining position of the Indian tribes. The white man of today has largely forgotten the Indian nations which his great grandfather knew. Now all he sees are individual Indians possessing rights different from his own, rights he would rather destroy than understand or respect. That the attitude can dominate court decisions as it has too often dominated legislative halls and executive agencies, and that it can be phrased in terms of a moral duty, constitutes another of the tragic elements in American Indian policy.

Arthur Lazarus, Jr., one of the most active Indian lawyers

and representative of the Hualapai of Arizona, the Metlakatla of Alaska, Nez Perce of Idaho, Oglala Sioux of South Dakota, the Salt River Pima-Maricopa, and the San Carlos Apache of Arizona, in testimony before the House Committee on Interior and Insular Affairs, hailed the ruling of the Court of Appeals in overturning the decision of the district court in denying Mrs. Colliflower her petition for a writ of habeas corpus. "That is a landmark case," Lazarus asserted. "In my opinion, that is the way the courts will go in the future, when they are faced with deprivations of constitutional rights."[19]

On April 11, 1968, after seven years of hearings and discussion, Public Law 90–284 (82 Stat. 77), an Act dealing with the Constitutional Rights of the Indians—sometimes called the Indian Civil Rights (or Bill of Rights) Act—became law. The act declares that

No Indian tribe in exercising powers of self-government shall—
(1) make or enforce any law prohibiting the free exercise of religion, or abridging the freedom of speech, or of the press, or the right of the people peaceably to assemble and to petition for a redress of grievances;
(2) violate the right of the people to be secure in their persons, houses, papers, and effects against unreasonable search and seizures, nor issue warrants, but upon probable cause, supported by oath or affirmation, and particularly describing the place to be searched and the person or thing to be seized;
(3) subject any person for the same offense to be twice put in jeopardy;
(4) compel any person in any criminal case to be a witness against himself;
(5) take any private property for a public use without just compensation;
(6) deny to any person in a criminal proceeding the right to a speedy and public trial, to be informed of the nature and cause of the accusation, to be confronted with the witnesses against him, to have compulsory process for obtaining witnesses in his

favor, and at his own expense to have the assistance of counsel for his defense;

(7) require excessive bail, impose excessive fines, inflict cruel and unusual punishments, and in no event impose for conviction of any one offense any penalty or punishment greater than imprisonment for a term of six months or a fine of $500, or both;

(8) deny to any person within its jurisdiction the equal protection of its laws or deprive any person of liberty or property without due process of law;

(9) pass any bill of attainder or ex post facto law; or

(10) deny to any person accused of an offense punishable by imprisonment the right, upon request, to a trial by jury of not less than six persons.[20]

The privilege of the writ of habeas corpus was also declared to be available to any person, in a court of the United States, to test the legality of his detention by order of an Indian tribe. In addition the act authorized and directed the Secretary of the Interior to recommend to the Congress a model code to govern the administration of justice by courts of Indian offenses on Indian reservations. The code was to assure that Indian court procedure was as close as possible to the procedure in non-Indian courts, particularly in so far as the constitutional rights of the accused were concerned.

The act also authorized states to assume jurisdiction—both criminal and civil—over offenses committed by or against Indians in the areas of Indian country situated within such states, but only with the consent of the Indian tribe affected. Partial assumption of jurisdiction by states over certain geographical areas and particular offenses was authorized. Retrocession of jurisdiction—either criminal or civil—by a state to the United States over Indian areas or offenses previously assumed—without consent—by some states under the provision of Public Law 280, August 15, 1953, was authorized.

The Indian Constitutional Rights Act of 1968 was swallowed by most of the Indian communities in part because it provided for Indian consent before a state could assume jurisdiction over offenses committed within its territory. The Indians had almost unanimously opposed the mandatory provision of the 1953 act (even President Eisenhower had criticized it in signing the act) and asked for its repeal. The new act, while not affecting the actions taken under the 1953 act, provided that further assumption of jurisdiction be conditional upon Indian consent. Hence the Indian support.

The provisions for guaranteeing constitutional rights to individual Indians in their tribal proceedings were, in general, unobjectionable, since most tribes followed such rules in practice. Moreover, the high-sounding nature of these rights made objection difficult. Nevertheless, valid objections to such provisions existed and were expressed, most effectively by the representatives of the Pueblos of New Mexico. Domingo Montoya, Chairman of the All Indian Pueblo Council of New Mexico, in his testimony on the bill on March 29, 1968, pointed out that the Pueblo Indians of New Mexico had been following their own forms of government, with the approval and acquiescence of their successive conquerors, for centuries. While losing "some of their independence . . . they did not lose their language, their religion, their form of social organization or the other essential features of their way of life." Why the Pueblo way of life did not break down and disappear like that of many other tribal groups, Montoya suggested, may have been related to the ability of their system of government to hold the people together in justice. Indeed, Montoya suggested, "We are, perhaps, more like a large family in each pueblo than we are like a nation."

"We do not object to the principles set forth in S. 1843 [one of the predecessor bills] because these same principles are part and parcel of our own traditional concepts of justice and our way of life; the procedures required by the proposed legislation are, however, highly objectionable to us because they tend to eliminate our traditional ways of attaining the basic objectives of justice and equity." Montoya pointed out that the introduction of a jury system was superfluous in the Pueblo system where the tribal councils administer justice and are, in their very composition, in the nature of a jury. Moreover, the expense of a jury trial, and of the other formal legal guarantees of white courts, could not be supported by the Pueblo communities. As for the proposal for a model code, Montoya pointed out that the New Mexican pueblos have their own code of justice which seeks to make the injured party whole. "For example, if one of our members should injure another to the extent that the injured party for a period of time could not work his fields or provide for his family, our system traditionally requires the aggressor to substitute his services in providing for the injured and his family," Montoya noted. "Since such an offense," Montoya went on, "is against the tribe as well, we sometimes exact an additional penalty for the tribe in the form of community work." Montoya wondered whether the Pueblo system was not, indeed, superior to the white system. When it was revealed, in the testimony of another Indian, Governor Pat Calabaza, of the Santo Domingo Pueblo, New Mexico, that the pueblo did not have and did not need a jail, the intermittently hostile questioner, Congressman Lloyd Meeds of the State of Washington, was somewhat nonplussed.[21]

It is difficult for whites to understand that the Indian culture may require different procedures to attain the same end. When the Department of the Interior was asked by Lewis A. Sigler, Consultant on Indian Affairs of the Committee on Interior and Insular Affairs of the House of Representatives, whether the jury trial requirement was compatible with present tribal customs and procedure, Harry R. Anderson, Assistant Secretary of the Interior, responded by pointing out that, "with the possible exception of the traditional court system of the pueblos in New Mexico, whose laws are based on custom

and tradition, all tribal codes have provision for jury trials."
Anderson noted that for the years 1960 and 1961, the latest
period for which information was available, 80,000 cases, civil
and criminal, were heard, and in only 58 cases were jury trials
requested. "We do not know," the Assistant Secretary continued, "why the use of juries has been so minimal."[22]

The inability of the white man to comprehend the Indian
reaction to white legal processes is also evident in the Indian
practice of pleading to a charge. As John S. Boyden, a lawyer
of Salt Lake City, Utah, pointed out in a letter, concerning the
prohibition against compelling any person in a criminal case
to be a witness against himself:

> The defendants' standard of integrity in many Indian courts is
> much higher than in the State and Federal Courts of the United
> States. When requested to enter a plea to a charge the Indian
> defendant, standing before respected tribal judicial leaders, with
> complete candor usually discloses the facts. With mutual honesty
> and through the dictates of experience, the Indian judge often
> takes a statement of innocence at face value, discharging the
> defendant who has indeed, according to tribal custom, been
> placed in jeopardy. The same Indian defendants in off-reserva-
> tion courts soon learn to play the game of "white man's justice,"
> guilty persons entering pleas of not guilty merely to throw the
> burden of proof upon the prosecution. From their viewpoint it
> is not an elevating experience. We are indeed fearful that the
> decisions of Federal and State Courts, in the light of non-Indian
> experience, interpreting "testifying against oneself" would
> stulify [sic] an honorable Indian practice while the constructions
> of the same courts as to what is "double jeopardy" would open
> an inverted loophole to in fact try a defendant twice.[23]

The Indian Constitutional Rights Act does not provide constitutional protections for individual Indians in their relations
with the federal government, or with its branches, or with the
state governments. These guarantees already exist. What the

act does is to move into the areas where the existence of such protections is not clear, that is to say, in the relationship between the individual Indian and his tribal government (where one exists) in order to prescribe that the legal culture evolving in Anglo-Saxon law shall be applied to the legal culture of the Indian communities whether or not they retain a distinct point of view after hundreds of years of similar assaults on their legal, moral, social, economic, political, and military culture. Though the recent assault is couched in terms of altruism on the part of the whites, and though considerable native support—particularly by acculturated individuals—is evident, it is a cultural assault nevertheless, and one in the tradition of virtually every white policy imposed on the Indian. It is the tradition that somehow the Indian should conform, aspire or submit to the dominant white culture of the United States.[24]

The first suit entered under the Indian Constitutional Rights Act of 1968 was filed by a group of Navajo tribesmen, against the chairman of the Navajo Tribal Council, in behalf of a white man, Theodore Mitchell, the director of a non-profit corporation (funded by Office of Economic Opportunity funds) operating on the reservation. The case arose as an outgrowth of an exclusion order issued against Mitchell by the Advisory Council of the Navajo Tribal Council on August 8, 1968. The offense committed by Mitchell, whose organization is designed to provide non-profit legal services to the Navajo, was to guffaw loudly during a meeting of the Advisory Council when one member of the Council asked the Acting Associate Solicitor of the Department of the Interior about the legality of excluding individuals from the Navajo country. When the solicitor asked Mrs. Annie Wauneka (the Council member involved) whether she had anyone in mind, several persons present laughed, most loudly Mitchell, about whom the inquiry seemed to be directed. Mrs. Wauneka interpreted the laugh as an insult to the dignity of the Council and the following day walked over to Mitchell, struck him and ordered him to leave. Mitchell was formally expelled from the reservation, though allowed to come back under guard to defend himself before the Navajo Council. Failing to obtain a reversal of the ruling from the Navajo Tribal Council, Mitchell and his friends sued Raymond Nakai, the head of the tribal council, in the U.S. District Court for the District of Arizona. In its decision, the court held the exclusion order against Mitchell unlawful under the Indian Civil Rights Act [25 U.S.C. #1302 (8) and (1)] as lacking in due process and as abridging freedom of speech. The court, on February 28, 1969, ruled that the attempt to remove Mitchell constituted "punishment" not for being in contempt of the legislative or judicial process of the Navajo Tribal Council but for opposing the Council on a matter unrelated to the supposed affront to the dignity of the tribal government. The Navajo Tribal Council was permanently enjoined from threatening to enforce the order of removal against Mitchell.

The Mitchell case illustrates several significant aspects of current Indian policy. First of all it derives from the creation of an organization on the Navajo Reservation which, according to its critics, has openly boasted of running the tribal council and the Bureau of Indian Affairs out of the Navajo country in two years' time. In other words, the new organization, known by the letters DNA (for Dinebeiina Nahiilna Be Agaditahe, Inc.) is perceived as a threat by the existing tribal leadership, as indeed it is. Secondly, the case and its outcome illustrate the ability of the new Constitutional Rights Act to protect constitutionally sanctioned activity (by Indians and others on the reservation) directed against the existing tribal government. The case is, therefore, doubly important. It weakens the authority of the existing tribal government (which its critics assert is dictatorial and undemocratic) and upholds the right of the dissenters to use the basic privileges of the first ten amendments to the Constitution (as incorporated in the Indian Civil Rights Act) to oppose that leadership.[25]

The legal historian, Monroe E. Price, Professor of Law at the University of California at Los Angeles, while acknowledging the threat to the tribal government caused by the activities of DNA lawyers, has nevertheless asserted that the DNA program "in far more important ways [is] a buttress to sovereignty, a reinforcer of the tribal structure." While this theory—also espoused by Theodore Mitchell—is plausible, one also detects more than a little wishful thinking in it.[25a]

No cases have yet been brought under the Civil Rights Act in the Pueblo area, but already the rumblings of discontent can be heard. The New Mexico State Board of the American Civil Liberties Union in 1970 adopted the minority report of its Indian Rights Committee, rejecting the request of New Mexico's Pueblo Indians, made on religious grounds, for support for their plea for exemption from immediate compliance with certain provisions of the Indian Civil Rights Act. The action caused at least one member of the ACLU, Frances L. Swadesh, an anthropologist, to drop out of that organization in protest.[25b] The inability of white liberals to understand that a cultural pattern different from their own might still have social value and moral validity continues to be a stumbling block in our relations with the Indians.

Hunting, Fishing and Water Rights   :   The interpretations of rights of hunting and fishing guaranteed to Indian tribes by treaty or statute are complex and uncertain. Such rights are in some respects treated as property rights and in some respects as individual rights. When the Klamath Indians were "terminated," the Solicitor of the Department of the Interior ruled that withdrawing members were to receive no pay for hunting and fishing rights because such rights were incident to tribal membership and terminated on withdrawal of federal supervision.[26]

Administrative decisions in the 1950's prohibited states from enforcing their criminal laws, including their fish and game laws, against the Indians on Indian reservations or on lands purchased by the federal government for Indian use and set apart under the superintendence of the government, whether or not declared to be an Indian reservation.

By a 1958 administrative decision of the Department of the Interior, Indians allotted prior to the effective date of the Act of May 8, 1906 (34 Stat. 182) amending the General Allotment Act might be prosecuted for violations of the state game laws within the reservation. Unallotted Indians and Indians allotted after 1906 might not, however, be so prosecuted.[27]

The ambiguous Indian legislation of the Eisenhower administration threw to the courts the determination of the extent to which the Indians retained many of their traditional privileges of hunting and fishing.

In 1963 the Wisconsin Supreme Court held that the exclusive hunting and fishing rights on their reservation claimed by the Menominee tribe by virtue of the Treaty of Wolf River in 1854 (10 Stat. 1064) were in fact abrogated by the Congress in the Termination Act of 1954, to which the Menominees were subject. The Court of Claims, however, ruled that the Menominee Termination Act of 1954 did not abrogate or cut off the exclusive hunting or fishing rights which the treaty granted. Because of the conflict between the two courts, the Supreme Court of the United States agreed to hear the case in 1968. Both the Menominees and the United States urged that the judgment of the Court of Claims be affirmed. The state of Wisconsin urged that the judgment of the Court of Claims be reversed. The Supreme Court (391 U.S. 404) upheld the judgment of the Court of Claims. The court noted that Public Law 280, granting jurisdiction to certain states over Indians within their territories, was amended to apply to the Menominees two months after the Termination Act became law in 1961, but that the law says nothing about depriving Indian tribes of hunting, trapping or fishing rights under federal treaties. Public Law 280 says that all *statutes* of the United States which affect Indians because of their status as Indians shall no longer apply to Indians but, as the court noted, the word "statutes" is evidence that the Congress did not intend to void rights granted under *treaties.* Despite the decision of the majority of the court, Justices Stewart and Black dissented, asserting that the Termination Act did in fact take away treaty rights. Otherwise, Stewart noted in his dissent, Wisconsin could not tax property owned by the Menominees, a right which could also be claimed under the Treaty of Wolf River.

In *Puyallup Tribe* v. *Department of Game of Washington et al.* (391 U.S. 392), decided May 27, 1968, the Supreme Court further clarified the hunting and fishing rights retained by the American Indians. In the Puyallup case, the "right of taking fish at all usual and accustomed grounds and stations" was "secured," in the Treaty of Medicine Creek made by the United States with the Puyallup and Nisqually Indians in 1854 (10 Stat. 1132), "to said Indians, in common with all citizens of the Territory. . . ." The court noted that it had several times in the past upheld the right of Indians to fish at accustomed places, even after loss of ownership of the places in question. But it pointed out that the *manner* in which fishing might be done, and the *purpose*—whether or not commercial—were not mentioned in the Treaty of Medicine Creek. The court placed great weight on the absence of any phrase implying the right of the Indians to fish in the "usual and accustomed" manner. It also noted that the treaty granted the Indians the right to fish "in common with all citizens of the Territory." Certainly, the court concluded, the right of the latter could be regulated, and it therefore saw no reason why the right of the Indians could not also be regulated by the police power of the state as to the manner and size of the take, and the restriction of commercial fishing, etc., provided such regulations were appropriate and non-discriminatory.

The court left unanswered the exact nature of the types of regulatory measures that would be considered appropriate and nondiscriminatory, but recalled its 1942 decision in *Tulee* v. *Washington* (315 U.S. 681) reversing the state court which convicted Tulee, a Yakima Indian, for fishing without a license off the Yakima reservation. Whether a license or other regulation would be considered "reasonable and necessary" for the legitimate conservation interest of the state the court left undetermined.

Numerous other court battles are now being fought by Indians in an attempt to uphold their traditional hunting and fishing rights. At stake is not only a property right and sometimes a treaty right, but a cultural and psychological support as well. Hunting, fishing, and trapping have always loomed large in Indian culture, even among those tribes whose primary subsistence has derived from agriculture. To some extent the activity serves as a substitute for war, and develops skills and attitudes highly honored in most Indian societies.

Along with hunting and fishing rights, Indian water rights are coming increasingly at issue. This is particularly true in the western United States where rainfall is scarce. Because the land is valueless without water, water rights may be more valuable than the land itself. The character of such rights are in dispute. Do they derive, like aboriginal title to the land, from the fact that the Indians used or controlled the water? Are Indian rights prior and superior to those of other claimants, whether federal, state or local? Do treaties which specify Indian rights to the water reflect a gift from the government to the Indians or from the Indians to the government?

A case which established basic principles in this field was that of *Winters* v. *U.S.* (1906–1907). Winters and other non-Indian defendants had diverted water from the Milk River used to irrigate the lands of the Fort Belknap Indian Reservation in the State of Montana. The Blackfeet Indians obtained an injunction to restrain Winters and his group. On appeal the injunction was sustained by the Court of Appeals for the Ninth Circuit and by the Supreme Court. The Circuit Court upheld the ruling of the district court that when the Indians made the Treaty of October 17, 1855, with the government, they reserved the right to use the waters of Milk River, at least to the extent reasonably necessary to irrigate their lands, *even* though no mention was made of those rights in the treaty or in a subsequent act of Congress and in a federal agreement with the Indians. The Supreme Court upheld the ruling and pointed out that to believe otherwise—to believe that the Indians would give up the water that made their arid lands livable—would be impossible.

Despite the Winters decision, Indian water rights have been diminished by action of states, localities, individuals, companies, and the Federal government itself. Indeed, the history of Indian water rights suggests, in the opinion of one expert, that while by "sound logic, legal precedent, and expressed language upon which the States were admitted to the Union, the states and those claiming under them may not interfere with the rights of the American Indians, [i]n practice the converse has prevailed."[28]

That the Federal government has been a party to the increasing appropriation of waters to which the Indians by specific treaty provision or by general legal theory can lay a claim, has been too evident. As more and more reclamation and power projects have been instituted to increase water flow to white agricultural and commercial users, the Indian has seen his rights evaporate. The most dramatic case is the threat to Pyramid Lake in Nevada which is presently threatened by the Washoe Reclamation Project. If the project is carried through, the level of the lake will be reduced and the recreation and fishing values that accrued in the past to the Northern Paiute Indians of the Pyramid Lake Indian Reservation will be lost or diminished. The glare of publicity and the concern of the general public may yet result in an alteration of the present course by which the lake seems fated to change its traditional character.[28a]

*The Status of Canadian Indians   :   The status of the Indians in Canada is of interest not only because it shows how a nation deriving from English roots dealt with a problem similar to that facing its brother to the south, but because some of the Indians of North America live, or have lived on both sides of the border.

In the evolution of the English judicial system in Canada and the United States one of the most striking differences has been the authority claimed by the courts of each nation to decide on the validity of statute law. In the United States, the courts early assumed the power of judicial review, by which justices—or more particularly the justices of the Supreme Court—asserted the right to declare a law passed by the Congress of the United States to be unconstitutional. In Canada, the courts have followed a tradition of greater respect for the will of Parliament. The Canadian courts have not presumed to declare that an Act of the Canadian Parliament is illegal and unconstitutional. It has, rather, attempted to apply the law made by the Parliament and, in cases of conflict of laws, to assert a narrowly judicial interpretation of the conflict. That this distinction in the roles assumed by the court systems of the two countries is not without significance is seen in the rulings made by Canadian courts in cases involving conflicts between rights granted Indians under international treaties and restrictions imposed by legislation enacted by the Canadian Parliament. In the Canadian system, where there is a clear conflict between an international treaty and a statute, the courts are bound to apply the latter against the former. To cite one example: by the terms of the Jay Treaty of 1794 between the United States and Great Britain Indians "passing or repassing [the border] with their own proper Goods and Effects of whatever nature" were exempt from the payment of "any Impost or Duty whatever." In *Francis* v. *The Queen* (1956), the Supreme Court of Canada unanimously held that the treaty could not be pleaded as a defense to exempt an Indian from the duties imposed by the Customs Act enacted by Parliament. The decision in effect held that the Parliament of Canada had legislated so as to violate the Jay Treaty.[28b] The St. Regis Mohawk Indians, who live on both sides of the Canadian-United States border in upstate New York, have continued to protest this ruling as a clear-cut violation of their treaty rights. They have engaged in "confrontation politics" —stopping traffic over an international bridge that passes through their reservation—but so far without impact upon Canadian customs practice. Canadian authorities have arrested or dispersed the St. Regis Mohawks whenever they have attempted to interfere with such traffic in order to call attention to their demands.

Just as the Canadian Parliament has, in effect, violated an international treaty insofar as the rights of the Indians are concerned, so have Canadian courts ruled that Indians may not plead the provisions of an Indian treaty as a defense against the charge of violating a federal statute. Most often the issue has been precipitated by a "violation" of an act prohibiting hunting or fishing under certain conditions. Thus, in the case of *Sikyea* v. *The Queen,* an Indian was accused of shooting a wild duck out of season contrary to regulations established under the Migratory Birds Convention Act (1952). The Indian's defense was that he was entitled to hunt for food at any time of the year, notwithstanding any regulations or legislation to the contrary, in accordance with an Indian treaty. The decision of the Northwest Territories

Court of Appeal, with which the Supreme Court of Canada agreed, held that the Migratory Birds Act took away the rights guaranteed the Indians in their treaties. The justice delivering the reasons of the Court of Appeal, however, refused to believe that the Government of Canada realized that in implementing the Migratory Birds convention it was breaching the treaties formerly made with the Indians. "It is much more likely that these obligations under the treaties were overlooked—a case of the left hand having forgotten what the right hand had done."[28c]

The existence of an Indian treaty or agreement guaranteeing hunting rights has been found effective against provincial (as opposed to Dominion) legislation. In the case of *Regina* v. *Prince* (1964), an Indian was accused of violating a Manitoba statute prohibiting the use of night lights in hunting big game. Although convicted by the Manitoba Court of Appeal the Supreme Court of Canada reversed the decision, agreeing with the dissenting opinion of the Court of Appeal of Manitoba. In that dissent, Justice J. A. Freedman pointed out that

> To hunt game with the aid of a night light is clearly unsportsmanlike. Here, however, the accused Indians were not engaged in sport. They were engaged in a quest for food. Once that quest was satisfied they would then be subject to the restrictions of the Act.[28d]

Regina v. *Prince* turned on the question of the method of hunting; other cases of a similar nature have turned on the question of whether the Indian was hunting for food or for sport or commerce. If the former, and if he is protected in this right by prior agreement or treaty, his right so to do has been upheld, notwithstanding the provisions of provincial game laws prohibiting or limiting to certain seasons such activities.

The British North American Act of 1867 gave exclusive

jurisdiction over "Indians, and lands reserved for Indians" to the Parliament of Canada. Note that the Act did not say Indians *on* lands reserved for the Indians but Indians *and* lands reserved for the Indians. The Parliament has exercised that right in many ways, among them by the enactment of the Indian Act (1952) by which various regulations applicable to Indians as distinct from non-Indians have been codified. Recently, as in the United States, a number of cases alleging denial of "constitutional" rights of Indians have been heard. In the cases north of the border a conflict has been alleged between the Indian Act and the Canadian Bill of Rights (1960) which declares that "the right of the individual to equality before the law and the protection of the law" shall exist without discrimination by reason of "race, national origin, colour, religion or sex."

In *Her Majesty the Queen* v. *Joseph Drybones,* decided November 20, 1969, the Supreme Court of Canada sought to resolve the conflict. The Court heard the case on appeal from a judgment of the Court of Appeal for the Northwest Territories. That court had previously dismissed an appeal by the Crown from a judgment of the Territorial Court of the Northwest Territories acquitting Joseph Drybones of being "unlawfully intoxicated off a reserve" contrary to the provisions of the Indian Act. The facts were not in dispute. Drybones was drunk on the evening of April 8, 1967, in the Old Stope Hotel in Yellowknife in the Northwest Territories which is not on an Indian reserve. While the Liquor Ordinance applicable to the Northwest Territories forbids anyone from being in an intoxicated condition in a public place, it provides no fine for the act and the maximum term of imprisonment is thirty days. Under the Indian Act, however, the same offense may be punishable by a fine of not less than ten dollars or more than fifty and/or imprisonment not to exceed three months.

The argument successfully advanced in the two lower courts was that Drybones, by reason of his race, was denied "equality before the law" with his fellow non-Indian Canadians and that the applicable provision of the Indian Act was an abridgment of one of the human rights declared to be existing in Canada by the Canadian Bill of Rights. That law declares that

> Every law of Canada shall, unless it is expressly declared by an Act of the Parliament of Canada that it shall operate notwithstanding the Canadian Bill of Rights, be so construed and applied as not to abrogate, abridge or infringe, or to authorize the abrogation, abridgement or infringement of any of the rights or freedoms herein recognized and declared.

The Supreme Court was called upon to decide whether the applicable section of the Indian Act was rendered inoperative by reason of the Canadian Bill of Rights. The decision hinged on whether the Bill of Rights should be considered as a statutory declaration of fundamental human rights or merely a rule of interpretation for construing legislation existing at the time it was enacted. The Court upheld the former contention, ruling 6 to 3 that the appeal should be dismissed and the lower court ruling upheld, thus declaring the applicable section of the Indian Act to be inoperative.

In dissenting opinions of great persuasiveness, however, the three dissenters, including the Chief Justice, rejected the assumptions of their brothers, pointing out, first of all, that concepts such as "due process of law," "equality before the law," "freedom of religion," "freedom of speech"—all rights guaranteed by the Canadian Bill of Rights—were "largely unlimited and undefined" and "apt to expand and to vary [in their definition] as is strikingly apparent in other countries." The dissenters asserted that the ruling would call into question any federal attempt to legislate especially for the Indians, including attempts to benefit them by providing special health or educational facilities. More importantly, the dissenters charged that the decision of the majority altered the fundamental principle of Canadian and British law that the responsibility for updating statutes in a changing world rests exclusively with Parliament. Instead, the minority in effect charged, the majority was introducing the practice of judicial review developed south of the border which would mean that "henceforth the courts are to declare inoperative all enactments that are considered as not in conformity with some legal principles stated in very general language, or rather merely enumerated without any definition."[28e]

On both sides of the border the problem of reconciling the individual rights of all citizens, including Indians as individuals, with the special relationship that has grown up between the Indian communities as communities and the sovereign remains. That problem must be illuminated by a knowledge of history and a comprehension of cultural differences, as well as by a devotion to justice and a feeling of good will towards those one does not understand.

The status of the Canadian Indian is presently in doubt. The Canadian government, in the 1960's, initiated a restudy of the entire matter, culminating in the publication of a "white paper" in 1970. The thrust of the proposed Canadian government policy seems to be in the direction of terminating the special legal status of the Indian as it derives from treaties. The Indian would, in this scheme, look to the provinces—like other Canadian citizens—for health, education and housing services. The Canadian government, early in 1970, designated an Indian Claims Commissioner to make recommendations to the government. No case has been submitted to the commissioner, largely because his mandate does not extend to claims based upon aboriginal rights.

To this emerging government Indian policy, the increasingly aware and active Indian population—250,000 "registered Indians" and 100,000 not included in the census, organized in groups such as the National Indian Brotherhood—

responded in June 1970 with their own "red paper" entitled *Citizens Plus*. The Canadian Indians have found an eloquent spokesman in Harold Cardinal, president of the Indian Association of Alberta, whose book *The Unjust Society: The Tragedy of Canada's Indians* (Edmonton, Alberta, 1969) uncompromisingly throws down the gauntlet to Prime Minister Trudeau's government. In an emotional confrontation between the Prime Minister and representatives of the Indian Association of Alberta and the National Indian Brotherhood, in Ottawa, June 4, 1970, Mr. Trudeau conceded that the government's "white paper," developed by a young, inexperienced Indian Affairs Minister, Jean Chrétien, may have been naive in some of its statements. Trudeau insisted on the sincerity of the government's desire to achieve an equitable solution, however, and promised to restudy the matter. The Indians insist upon the preservation of their treaty rights and on the special status which they possess under those treaties. At the same time, where Indians are without special treaty rights, they demand compensation for the taking of their aboriginal rights. The scene has been set for a resolution of Canada's Indian problem but the outcome cannot yet be foreseen.

*On the Reservation   :   *Of the half million Indians now in the United States, approximately 60 per cent are still on reservations.[29] Anthropologists see the reservation serving as a refuge from the fierce competition of the white world which is also open to the Indian. Though the land may have been the least valuable of that which he originally possessed, or land upon which he was forced, and though it may have few past ties to his nation the reservation is an island of stability in a sea of troubles. The Indian has made it his "home" in the Frostian sense that it is the place where, when you have to go there, they have to take you in. The communal character of

Indian society—so strikingly revealed in the Indian's willingness to share the fruits of the land and the land itself, and in
the kinship and clan ties linking closely individuals beyond
the nuclear family—is preserved in these oases where the law
of the individual, and white values generally, do not rule
supreme.

The white stereotype of the American Indian—etched in
hate and contempt, sees the reservation as an island of privilege or a refuge for incompetence. Since the white—be he
reformer or Indian-hater—sees the elimination of differences
between white and Indian as the proper solution of the Indian
problem (of course the elimination of the differences means
that the Indian must become like the white—not vice versa)
the reservation stands as an anomaly in American society.
Indeed, the image of the reservation reenforces the contempt
often held by the self-reliant white for the Indian, and reduces
the pity he might be expected to show for an impoverished
Indian in comparison with a derelict member of his "own"
society. Often the white assumes that the reservation is an
unmerited gift to the Indian from a welfare-minded government. The white rarely recalls (except in a different context)
that the reservations are for the most part the remnants of the
homelands of these Indians, or are the areas allocated to them
in exchange for more desirable lands farther East from which
they were removed—not always voluntarily. The Indian has
been most successful where he has existed in greatest numbers and where the land was least attractive to white settlers.
Hence, most reservations are west of the Mississippi, with
heavy concentrations in the dry Southwest. The largest reservations are in Arizona where over 21 million acres of Indian
land—tribal and allotted—are held under government trust.
Of these the largest is the Navajo reservation, which is about
the size of West Virginia, occupying portions of New Mexico
and Utah as well as of Arizona, and containing approximately
80,000 Navahos.[30]

A reservation is a tract of land owned by a tribe, the land being held in trust by the federal government for the use and benefit of the tribe. Land within a reservation can include land covered by exclusive titles, dependent Indian communities, and Indian allotments where the title has not been extinguished. There exist approximately 300 separate Indian land units (reservations, pueblos, colonies, rancherias, and communities) under the administrative jurisdiction of the Bureau of Indian Affairs, along with scattered allotments in the public domain.[31]

While some white men think of the reservation as a refuge, others—particularly Europeans—think of it as a concentration camp. In fact, an Indian can live or not live on the reservation as he chooses, may go and come as he chooses, may educate his children as he chooses, and may determine his other activities as he pleases. What an individual living on the reservation cannot do is to alienate the land he lives on. Depending on the precise legal status of the land, he or the tribal authority may lease reservation land or allotments, but he cannot buy and sell land as he might outside of a reservation. Reservation land cannot be sold without an act of Congress, while certain other Indian-occupied lands require the consent of the Secretary of the Interior.

The Bureau of Indian Affairs : In a study he called "The Erosion of Indian Rights, 1950–1953: A Case Study in Bureaucracy," the late Felix S. Cohen, a leading student of Indian law, pointed out that the Indians were the only racial group in the United States whose rights were more limited in 1953, when his article was written, than they were in 1950.[32] The period 1934–1950 was marked by steadily increasing self-government and autonomy under the impetus given Indian rights by the New Deal. Administrative restrictions upon

Indian freedom of religion were removed, orders forbidding use of Indian languages by Indian school children were repealed, an Indian arts and crafts board was set up, and numerous other administrative actions indicating respect for Indian culture were taken.

In May, 1950, however, when Dillon S. Myer was appointed Commissioner of Indian Affairs, the clock was turned back to an earlier era. Myer, like some of his predecessors, particularly in the nineteenth century, assumed that the Bureau had the unquestioned right to manage the affairs of the Indians. The authority for Bureau management, by which 2,200 regulations issued by the Commissioner of Indian Affairs (in force in 1950) were justified, was Section 1 of the Act of July 9, 1832, which established the office of Commissioner of Indian Affairs and vested in the office "the management of all Indian Affairs." Similar statutes vest responsibility for "matters respecting foreign affairs" in the State Department, and the like. Though Cohen's interpretation of the statute suggested that it merely granted "the management of all Indian Affairs (of the Federal Government)" he noted that it had come to be read as "the management of all the affairs of the Indians." The trend was particularly evident in the nineteenth century when many former army officers were taken into the Indian Bureau. Similarly the Indian agent, from being a commercial agent or consul of the United States in the country of an alien people—his original function—had developed into an office with power to direct the affairs of the Indians, a transformation that puzzled even the Commissioner of Indian Affairs, as expressed in his annual report for 1892.

As a result, instances of intimidation, pressure and coercion by Bureau employees directed against Indians refusing to submit to its arbitrary government are not hard to find in the Bureau's past. In addition to the arbitrary and often illegal procedure of the Bureau its officials often showed their anti-Indian sentiment in their interpretation of existing regulations. For example, although the Secretary of the Interior was authorized by Congress in 1934 to appoint Indians to positions in the Indian Office without regard to civil service laws, the Bureau ignored the direction and continued to fill most Bureau positions with whites. An appearance of compliance was given by the Bureau's policy of giving preference to an Indian applicant who scored the same grade as a white on a civil service examination. But the precise direction of Congress was ignored as was the peculiar Indian cultural background which put all non-acculturated Indians at a disadvantage in competing with whites on civil service tests.

In a host of ways the Indian Bureau, when governed by a spirit hostile to Indian culture, can frustrate the Indian will. The power of the Bureau as surrogate for the Indian in matters of land ownership, leasing arrangements, tribal income, tribal property, tribal credits, and the like, has been such that in periods of unsympathetic administrators, such as that of Dillon Myer in the 1950's, the Indian has been reduced to insignificance and despair.

The Bureau, except for the period of New Deal influence, has tended to hoard up power to itself even while rhetorically talking about terminating Bureau supervision of Indian economic and social life. According to the indictment by Felix Cohen, its tendency to self-aggrandizement has not only been carried on by deceiving or ignoring the Indian, but, on occasion, also by flouting the will of the Secretary of the Interior and of the Department's Solicitor who reviews Indian Bureau rulings. In part, the history of the Bureau of Indian Affairs reflects the normal process of bureaucratic growth; in part it reflects the antipathy or ignorance of the dominant white majority concerning the Indian minority. The combination of these two attributes has caused the Bureau to have achieved the unenviable reputation of being either hopeless or hateful. Few government bureaus have a less savory record.

In recent years the phenomenon of strong Indian Commissioners, operating with some independence of the Secretary of the Interior, has disappeared. Strong Secretaries of the Interior, such as Stewart Udall, have taken the lead in formulating Indian policy. Because the Secretary of the Interior is primarily concerned with the public lands and their exploitation, Indian policy has tended to be seen in relation to this goal.

On vital matters relating to Indian policy, the Secretary of the Interior takes center stage. The Commissioner of Indian Affairs plays a supporting role. The roles are demonstrated in testimony before Senate and House subcommittees on Indian affairs. In the absence of the Secretary, the General Counsel of the Interior Department or the Assistant Secretary for Public Land Management will often be the spokesman on Indian policy with the Commissioner of Indian Affairs sitting quietly at his elbow.

Just prior to leaving the government, Secretary of the Interior Stewart L. Udall, discussing his eight-year term as Secretary, noted that if there was any area in which he failed, it was "that I didn't do enough for the American Indian."[33] Udall's plaint is reminiscent of Secretary of Defense Robert McNamara's similar observation that he regretted waiting until nearly the end of his term before requiring non-discriminatory housing practices in areas adjacent to military bases. Human rights tend to take a back seat to other forces. In departments as large as Interior or Defense the manipulation of resources tends to obscure the demands of justice. The voice of conscience is heard, but often not until the action is done and reflection has begun.

Because of the influence exerted by white society, and specifically the Bureau of Indian Affairs, on tribal government, the Indian representatives who tend to emerge are those most like the whites, most amenable to white interests, or most capable of dealing with whites. These are the "responsible" people in white eyes. They may be "marginal" men in their own society, sometimes welcomed as a link to white society, sometimes tolerated as a buffer between white society and Indian values, and sometimes despised as a "white man's Indian," a willing representative of a colonial regime. The administration of tribal property—for example, the sale of reservation timber, or the introduction of industry (as, for example, the building of a fishhook plant on the Pine Ridge Sioux reservation)—is too often structured in terms of white administrative assumptions. When Indian cultural values clash with white economic assumptions, the white assumptions prevail. That is where the power lies.[34]

Indian representatives, such as the late Clyde Warrior, a full-blood Ponca Indian from Oklahoma, a leader of the Indian youth movement in the Southwest, have challenged the honesty and significance of so-called tribal governments. "If these sovereign entities have self-government," Warrior asks, "why are their acts subject to approval by the Secretary of the Interior?" Warrior, taking Kay County, Oklahoma, as a political community, noted that it is not really a community in the Indian sense. The Ponca tribe which lives in Kay County is a community but lacks any real power. A white community controls the institutional and economic structure of the county. "We only live there. There is no Ponca tribal government. It is only named that. We are among the poor, the powerless, the inexperienced and the inarticulate." Warrior, and others like him, look back to the vision of the days when the Ponca people hunted buffalo and made their own decisions. "White businessmen and bureaucrats did not make the Ponca decisions, the Poncas made these decisions and carried them out." From the depths of powerlessness, some Indians cry out for recognition.[35]

The inability of white Bureau employees to see the Indian point of view is captured in the reaction of a Mississippi Choctaw a few years ago to the complaint of an education specialist from the Bureau that his community was not taking full advantage of the schools the government provided for them. The Choctaw leader asked the Bureau employee: "Tell me, if Khrushchev took over this country, how long would it be before you turned Communist?" The education specialist missed the Indian's logic and sarcasm. "Why, I don't think I ever would," he replied.[36] Perhaps the greatest failing of Bureau employees after their inability to understand cultural differences is their inability to laugh at themselves when they play the role of "authority" or "expert".

While the Bureau of Indian Affairs has shown itself over the years to be insensitive and unimaginative, its reputation is not entirely deserved. A cluster of myths has gathered around the Bureau, and it has become the whipping boy for critics of American Indian policy. It is accused of running a concentration camp system and dictating every move of the Indian, a view which ignores the freedom of any Indian to leave the reservation and the autonomy still possessed by tribal organizations in certain areas. It faces the crushing indictment that after more than a hundred years of Bureau management the Indian is the poorest, least healthy and least educated segment of American society. The charge is true, but the blame must rest more on the sources of white policy toward the Indian than on the bureau charged with carrying out that policy.

Commissioner Robert L. Bennett, the full-blooded Indian Commissioner appointed by President Johnson, moved slowly towards a less paternalistic role for the Bureau. Anxious to avoid a serious split within the Bureau should he radically overturn past policy, trained in the caution of a career Bureau servant, personally disinclined to the flamboyant, showy approach, Bennett went along with approaches and programs in his early years of office with which he was not entirely happy. As he sensed his growing acceptance among both the white governmental establishment and the Indian people themselves, Bennett charted a course designed to delegate more responsibilities to the Indian communities themselves. Bennett foresaw the development of the Bureau as an increasingly professional body, with reduced numbers of personnel, gradually contracting out its operational responsibilies for running schools, repairing roads, and the like, to Indian communities willing and anxious to manage their affairs for themselves. Bennett also envisaged the possibility that title to schools, and other federally owned property held in trust for the Indians, would eventually be turned over to the Indian communities which showed the ability to cherish and to nourish them.[37]

As the Johnson administration came to a close and the Nixon administration began, Bennett moved to head off aggressive critics—"part of the anti-establishment syndrome of some so-called bright and sometimes angry young men—who equate anger with intelligence," as Bennett put it in testimony before the subcommittee on the Interior of the Senate Appropriations Committee, March 12, 1969. These "new discoverers of Indians" who, Bennett asserted, "find their way into high positions in Government and then seek to impose their will on Indian people from their positions of vantage as staff officers in the Government or in the Congress," had attacked the Bureau frontally in its most sensitive spot: education. The importance of the educational function of the Bureau cannot be denied. Commissioner Bennett had himself asserted that "It is my view that the entire Bureau is basically an educational instrumentality. . . ." The fact that the young men of the Indian Education subcommittee of the Senate Labor and Public Welfare Committee published in 1969 six hefty volumes condemning the Bureau's record in Indian education was a personal affront to Bennett. Though the subcomittee's study had few immediate practical results it put the Bureau still further on the defensive and laid the groundwork for possible change.

A further blow to the embattled Bureau was the publication

on November 5, 1969, of *Our Brother's Keeper: The Indian in White America,* edited by Edgar S. Cahn of the Citizens' Advocate Center, an organization dedicated to community change and supported by various foundations. The report depicted The Bureau as "A Terminal Case of Bureaucracy" though it carefully avoided recommendations that would terminate the existence of an organization to which the Indian is bound in a love-hate relationship.

Other attacks on the efficiency of the Bureau of Indian Affairs have added to its woes. Senator Proxmire of Wisconsin asked Commissioner Bennett, on March 12, 1969, to explain the fact that the Congress appropriates for the Indian, through the channels of the several departments concerned with the Indian, an amount (roughly $500,000,000) equivalent to $1,000 per Indian. Since the amount appropriated is greater than the per capita income of the Indian, Proxmire, a member of the Joint Economic Committee, asked how one could meet the objection that most of the money appropriated does not reach the Indian. Would the money not be better spent, Proxmire asked, as a direct grant to the individual Indian? Bennett was unable effectively to answer the Senator in open hearing.

Though anxious to stay on under the new administration, Bennett soon realized that President Nixon wanted his own man in charge of the Bureau. He found his man, after a long search, in Louis R. Bruce, a St. Regis Mohawk and a Republican, who worked as an executive in New York City. Bruce is a quiet dedicated individual, comparatively advanced in years, comparatively inexperienced in Indian affairs despite his Indian ancestry, though he had distinguished himself in fighting the termination legislation of the 1950's. What legacy he will leave in the controversy-ridden Bureau cannot yet be foretold. The first years of his administration, however, have been impressive. Old-line white administrators have been eased out of the top policy jobs and replaced by Indians so that the

Bureau is now strongly Indian oriented and staffed at top and bottom levels, with a white filling in between. Bruce, with the effective backing first of Secretary of the Interior Walter Hickel and then of his successor Rogers Morton, as well as the Vice President and the President, has moved to carry into effect some of the plans for greater Indian control of Indian affairs which remained only cautious hopes in previous administrations. The powers of the Area Directors and Agency Superintendents have, in particular, been, reduced.[37a] Candidate Nixon's promise that the Indian point of view would be sought and would be heeded has been fulfilled by President Nixon.

Congress and the Indian : The Congress has always felt a traditional interest in Indian affairs deriving from the authority given it in the Constitution "to regulate Commerce with foreign Nations, and among the several States, and with the Indian Tribes." This control has been exercised through the several committees of the House and Senate concerned with Indian affairs. Principal among them have been the subcommittees on Indian Affairs of the parent Committees on Interior and Insular Affairs of both the Senate and House of Representatives. Membership on these committees is traditionally held by senators and representatives from states having large Indian populations, such as Arizona, New Mexico, Alaska, Montana, and Washington. Subcommittee members often show a great deal of sympathy for the Indians, but their concern must often be modified by the larger framework of the regulation and utilization of the land resources of the nation that is the principal concern of the parent committees. Moreover, all members reflect the white cultural assumptions which place a higher value on economic efficiency, full utilization of resources, self-sufficiency, and the like, than on the preservation of tribal cultural attitudes and values.

Staff members of the traditional committees concerned with Indian affairs tend to be more committed to white values and less tolerant of Indian views than their bosses. In the past —though less frequently today—one heard expressed among this group impatience and annoyance with the Indian attempt to hold on to the legal rights and cultural values he has inherited from the past. The white staffer (and often his boss) tends to discount the weight of past decisions and attitudes. Rights accorded or wrongs committed in the distant past have little meaning to him. Insistence on relating the past to the present seems to him querulous and ungracious. The present-day Indian should, like himself, take things as they are and make his own way in the world. The past was a long time ago, and who thinks about his ancestors?

Late in the Johnson administration the dominant role of the Interior and Insular Affairs committee of the Senate in Indian matters was challenged by a new Senate subcommittee. The subcommittee, a Special Subcommittee on Indian Education of the parent Labor and Public Welfare Committee, conducted hearings on the inadequacies of Indian education throughout 1967 and 1968. The light that the committee brought to bear on the subject was automatically strong because of the personality and standing of Robert F. Kennedy of New York, chairman of the subcommittee. The new Indian subcommittee reflected the social conscience of those Americans particularly concerned with racial and social discrimination. That concern is not usually shared to the same degree by members of the traditional subcommittees on Indian Affairs of the Interior and Insular Affairs committees of the two houses. A symbolic confrontation between the "new" and "old" approaches occurred on March 5, 1968, when, just prior to declaring himself a candidate for the Presidency in

1968, Robert F. Kennedy testified before the Senate subcommittee on Indian Affairs of the Interior and Insular Affairs Committee on the subject of Senate Concurrent Resolution 11 which recommended a new national Indian policy. In a statement read with conviction and sincerity, Kennedy recounted the appalling conditions that his special subcommittee of the Labor and Public Welfare Committee had discovered in the course of investigating the quality and effectiveness of educational programs for Indian children in the United States. Kennedy reiterated the proposition contained in the resolution that the "first American" is still the last American in terms of income, employment, health and education. Kennedy pointed out, furthermore, that just because Indians are not on reservations, which they are not in many states, does not mean that they are assimilated. "Termination of federal responsibility," Kennedy asserted, "does not solve the problem. It is merely a transfer of responsibility to government units which have a less adequate financial base to cope with it."

In recounting the sad story of lack of effective education for the Indian, Kennedy noted that "out of ideological fervor for 'state responsibility,' out of a concern for lowering federal expenditures and demanding 'rapid assimilation whatever the cost,' we have forgotten or simply overlooked the fate of the Indian child." Kennedy pointed out that the passage of Concurrent Resolution 11 would restate and "in essence" repudiate the policy that characterized the 1950's. The tragedies of the Menominee and Klamath Indians under termination should, Kennedy asserted, serve as sufficient warning that termination of federal responsibilities is not the answer. No action was taken on the resolution at the time.

The fond hopes of those who believed that Kennedy's subcommittee would create a real revolution in Indian life were dashed by the assassination of the New York senator in June

1968. The strong voice was stilled. Whether the impetus given by Senator Kennedy to a general reform of American Indian policy can be sustained remains to be seen. Senator Edward Kennedy of Massachusetts, early in 1969, took up his brother's work on the Indian education subcommittee, finished its work and since its dissolution has made the American Indian an object of his special concern.

To a lesser extent other committees of Congress have challenged the exclusive right of the Indian affairs subcommittees of both houses to the overseeing of America's Indian problem. Senator Ervin's special subcommittee on Indian rights of the Judiciary Committee usurped what some Indian committee members regarded as their role by pushing through Congress the Indian Constitutional Rights Act without "clearing" the matter through the traditional committees. Though Ervin's subcommittee held numerous hearings over the years on the subject, the Indian subcommittees of the Senate and House did not. The passage of the bill, as a rider to a fair housing bill, without full consideration by the Indian Affairs subcommittees, created some annoyance among members of the traditional committees.

There is a distinct possibility that the unsuccessful attempts of Senate liberals to reform Indian policy during the Johnson administration may succeed during the Nixon administration by and with the help of the Republican president and vice president. President Nixon's statement of July 7, 1970, renewed the call, sounded by Robert Kennedy in 1968, for a formal congressional repudiation of the termination policy. That concern has been echoed by Vice President Spiro Agnew in his capacity as chairman of the National Council on Indian Opportunity, established by an Executive Order of President Johnson on March 6, 1968. President Nixon's statement of July 7, 1970, drew high praise from Senate liberals, including Senator Harris of Oklahoma, former Democratic

National Committee chairman. With support from such diverse figures as Richard Nixon, Spiro Agnew, Edward Kennedy and Fred Harris, the possibility of reversing, in the 1970's, the traditional congressional approach to Indian affairs, seems more likely than ever before.

Education and the Indian : "Tradition is the enemy of progress." This was the motto of an Indian school in the Southwest that I passed in 1952. The school was a boarding school, the form of schooling most favored by white administrators in the nineteenth and early twentieth century specifically because it tore the Indian child from his cultural matrix and dragged him into an alien world. It was a world marked by punctuality, discipline, competition, study and punishment; a cold and friendless passage to the culture that counted. I have often thought about the lone Indian who succeeded in graduating from Harvard in the seventeenth century. Many others entered, but despaired. Imagine the cultural shock of leaving the bosom of an Indian village for the sterile intricacies of Puritan theology at Harvard College in the seventeenth century! The shock would probably be fatal for most twentieth-century whites. The problem, it should be unnecessary to point out, is not intelligence, but culture. Similarly, the Indian boy of the Western United States, confronted with an equally confusing American culture of the twentieth century, must have been torn to the depths of his soul as he weighed the unfortunate choices open to him either by acceptance or rejection.

The most famous Indian boarding school was the Carlisle Indian School at Carlisle, Pennsylvania Military Barracks, which a dedicated Army captain, Richard Henry Pratt, set up after the Civil War.[38] Perhaps it is appropriate, in the light of the similar experience undergone by other minorities in

America, that it was sports, and particularly football, that helped the Indians of Carlisle to gain respect in white society. In any event, with the shift in sentiment brought about during the administration of Franklin D. Roosevelt, the emphasis was increasingly placed on day schools, and increasingly American Indians have been educated in such schools, remaining in touch with their cultural origins at home, while being taught the alien culture of their conquerors during school hours. Nothing is liable to shake the assumptions of white society in the virtues of a white education for Indians, but this attitude is no longer expressed in the crude form in which it has been previously couched. Moreover, the Indian is increasingly accepting the educational system provided him as the only way in which he can prepare himself for competition in the white world, a competition to which he has increasingly resigned himself.

In the years following World War II the American public was shocked to learn that the Navajo reservation, in part because of its unwillingness to accept white education, lacked schools for almost three-fourths of its school-age population. Legislation was introduced in the Eighty-first Congress to remedy this "oversight" but little hope was expressed of being able to provide seats for all the children who needed seats. Indeed, the problem of Navajo children without educational opportunities was still a problem nearly a decade later. In the year ending June 30, 1955, as a result of an emergency educational program which started in the fall of 1954, the total enrollment of Navajo children in federal, public, and mission schools both on and off the reservation was increased from 16,215 at the beginning of the year to 23,679 at the close.[39]

Under the commissionership of Phileo Nash, an anthropologist, the predecessor of Robert Bennett, the role of the Bureau of Indian Affairs in education and in economic development was emphasized, but Nash's inability to control the destiny of the Bureau was patently obvious and differences of opinion with those determining Indian policy led to his resignation. Nash emphasized that the Bureau's role was not to govern, but to assist the Indian in finding his way in modern American society. He found sentiment, both inside and outside the Bureau, too frequently at odds with his conception. Bureau employees were inclined to peremptory and uncompromising attitudes, attitudes stimulated by what they regard as the uncooperativeness of their Indian "charges." A mutual disinclination to accept the attitudes and assumptions of the other side leads to strained relations despite the best will in the world.

On the other side, Congress and the American people generally find it hard to sympathize with educational programs designed to teach English as a second language to Indian school children. Their assumption often is that the Indian should long since have been utilizing English as his principal language. Perhaps the urban riots of the late 1960's and the growing emphasis upon teaching English as a second language to Negro youths will have a sobering effect on those who long believed that both Negro and Indian needed merely to be prodded to cause them to "catch up" with the dominant whites.

Experiments with Indian school children have indicated that the less influenced the Indian society is by white values, the less likely are the children to compete with one another or to strive to excel in terms of their standing with one another. The competitive thrust of white society is a concommitant of white economic, social and psychological values. Where it has not triumphed, the more common Indian value of cooperativeness has persisted. The Indian child in his more traditional role is liable to cooperate with his mates and to strive *not* to exceed his fellows in visible terms. To excel, yes. But not in the cold rating system of the white world where the measurement is made not internally by one's peers but externally by one's alien superiors.[40]

While the Bureau of Indian Affairs talked complacently about progress in education, testimony heard before the Robert Kennedy subcommittee on Indian education in 1968 painted a different picture. A clinical psychologist, Harry Saslow, of the Albuquerque Boarding School, Albuquerque, New Mexico, emphasized the depersonalization and impersonalization of Indian boarding schools. Depression, he found, was the most pervasive problem among students. Taking the Indian child at six or eight away from his parents and putting him in boarding school was, in the psychologist's eyes (as in those of Senator Kennedy) productive of unhappiness and discontent. The majority of the students at boarding school go home at Christmas, but some stay twelve months of the year. The problem is not so much in errors of commission as of omission. The student is not so much hurt as not helped. He is lonely. He feels his destiny is not in his hands. He knows that things are controlled by whites and he is educated to make his way in a white world that often has no attractions or provision for him. Yet his education deprives him of an understanding of his own culture so that he has no full comprehension of a tradition which might sustain him as an alternative. He is caught between two cultures and knows not enough about either.[41]

Though the boarding school has been the focus of attacks by the new critics of Indian policy, former Commissioner Bennett, himself a product of an Indian boarding school, upheld the validity of the system. The process of education requires isolation from too frequent contacts with parents and home, the Commissioner felt. Bennett also discounted the figures of suicides and the evidence of alienation cited by critics of the schools. Yet, because of the vehemence of the attack, the Bureau of Indian Affairs has tended to move in the direction urged by its critics.

One of the principal problems facing the Indian off the reservation is the eligibility problem. If he goes to a social welfare agency, to a school board, or the like, he is often, by virtue of his Indian race, assumed to be a responsibility of the Bureau of Indian Affairs and sent to the nearest office of the Bureau. The Bureau, however, is responsible for the Indian only so long as he is on the reservation, not when he is exercising his right to go off it and make his way in the white world. The failure of the white world to understand that when he is in that world he is entitled to the rights accorded citizens in that world is a cause of great hardship and despair to Indians. The neglect of the Indian off the reservation is particularly acute in the supportive services—such as school counseling—which are required by the Indian away from home. Despite state responsibility for meeting such needs the responsibility is often ignored or assumed to be the province of the Bureau of Indian affairs.

The growing importance of education in the thinking of those concerned with the Indian was reflected in the creation of an assistant commissionership for Indian education in the Bureau of Indian Affairs late in 1966. The new position was to make possible, according to the Bureau, an enlargement of its activities in such fields as curriculum development, especially that concerned with teaching English as a second language and in counseling and guidance. Time will determine whether the change was meaningful. Taken in conjunction with the renewed interest in Indian education in Congress, however, it indicated that Americans of the 1960's were beginning to think of education as a key to Indian development in much the same way that Americans of the nineteenth century thought of allotment of land to individuals as a remedy for Indian backwardness.

Despite the effort of the Bureau to pay increased attention to education, its critics say that it has failed miserably to achieve the goal of sound education for the Indian. In a blistering statement before the Special Subcommittee on Indian Education of the Labor and Public Welfare Committee, February 18, 1969, Ralph Nader spoke of the "legacy of failure" bequeathed by the Bureau of Indian Affairs to the Indian. Nader attributed the inadequate educational achievement of Indians to insensitivity, cultural blindness, bureaucratic arrogance, and sheer stupidity on the part of Bureau employees and on the part of some public school employees handling Indian children. Nader pointed out that the Indian's knowledge of his own heritage, and his awareness of his own special relationship with government was lacking because of an education designed to "make a white man" out of him. The failure to take the Indian's own language into consideration in the teaching process was also attacked by Nader. "A more intelligent mixture of native languages and English," Nader asserted, "would not only improve the student's eventual language proficiency, but would also serve to ease the culture conflict faced by the child."

Nader also asserted that despite the greater emphasis placed on education in the central office, the real control of Indian education was lodged in the area directors, who control budget requests, the allocation of funds, and the hiring and firing of personnel. The area director is, in Nader's view, "the school board."

The first serious experimentation in involving Indian parents directly in the school process did not take place until 1966. In that year a contract was signed with a group of Navajo parents to operate a combined day and boarding school—called the Rough Rock Demonstration School—on the Navajo reservation. Control of school policy, including the handling of a budget of nearly a million dollars, was placed firmly in the hands of Indians most of whom were without formal education and some of whom were illiterate. The experiment, in the eyes of those concerned with reforming Indian education, including executives of foundations, like the Donner Foundation (which, with the Office of Economic Opportunity and the Bureau of Indian Affairs provided the money to support the program) has been a resounding success. Although Commissioner of Indian Affairs Bennett was more reserved about the success of the school, and questioned the wisdom of paying a school board instead of relying upon its uncompensated interest, he encouraged the involvement of other Indian communities in school boards during 1969–1970.[42]

In 1969 there were 178,476 Indian students, ages 5 to 18, enrolled in public, Federal, private and mission schools. Approximately 12,000 children of this age group were not in school. Of the total in school, 119,000 were in public schools, 36,263 in boarding schools operated by the Bureau of Indian Affairs, 16,100 in Bureau day schools, 108 in Bureau hosiptal schools, and 4,089 in dormitories maintained by the Bureau for children attending public schools. The Bureau operated 77 boarding schools, 144 day schools, 2 hospital schools and 18 dormitories. The number of Indian children being educated in public schools has steadily increased, aided by the financial assistance provided local school districts under the Johnson-O'Malley Act of 1934 (which provides financial support to 14 states and four separate school districts with large Indian populations) and under Public Law 874 (which provided financial support, in cooperation with the Department of Health, Education and Welfare, to aid federally affected areas). The closer relationship between state school systems and the Indian system has been welcomed by many Indian groups. Sixty-one tribes have established compulsory education regulations that conform with those of the states where they live.

On the other hand, some more traditional Indian groups have rebelled at efforts to close down reservation schools. The attempt of the Bureau of Indian Affairs to close down, on July 1, 1968, a small grade school at Tama, Iowa, created an instant reaction. Forty-five Mesquakie Indian children were attending school there on the reservation purchased by their ancestors, a separate body of the Sac tribe which, with the Fox, had a hundred years earlier been pushed out of Iowa into Kansas. The Mesquakie Indians, who had not been consulted about the closing of the school, promptly sought judicial relief. They got it in September, 1968, in the Federal District Court at Cedar Rapids, when U.S. District Court Judge Edward J. McManus ordered the school reopened in the fall. The Mesquakie were able to call upon a number of influential white friends in their attempt to retain their Indian school. The validity of integration into a white school system that is often both distant from and cold toward Indian values can be questioned, as the Mesquakie questioned it.[43]

A similar reaction occurred in Ramah, New Mexico, where until June 1968 there was a state public school in which Navajo children constituted a majority. The parent Gallup-McKinley County School Board (60% of whose 12,000 students are Indians yet which had in 1970 only one Indian school board member) decided to close the Ramah school and to force the children to attend a consolidated high school at Zuni, New Mexico, twenty miles away, or Bureau of Indian Affairs boarding schools off the reservation. The 1500 Indian residents of the area, however, decided to resist the decision. They elected their own five-member school board on February 6, 1970. None of the five members had a high school diploma but all were rich in natural good sense. With the aid of the DNA—a Navajo legal services organization—they got Bureau funds for a contract under which they would operate the first locally controlled Indian high school in the country. Whether the experiment will succeed or fail will be known later. But the action illustrates the point made by Peterson Zah, Deputy Director of DNA, that "There can be no alternative to local education of Indians." The possibility of local education of Indians under the Johnson-O'Malley Act has not been realized because the large school districts—often con-

trolled by whites even in Indian areas—have tended to perpetuate the impersonal education familiar to the Indian student in the old Bureau schools. The involvement of Indian
parents in the educational process is—in the eyes of some
Indian reformers—vital.[44] That involvement received a dramatic boost late in July 1970 when President Nixon issued a
policy statement in Indian affairs in which such control was
encouraged and recommended.

As Indian education on the elementary and secondary level
achieves increasing Indian involvement, the number of Indians going on to college has increased dramatically. In 1966,
120 Indians graduated from four-year colleges and universities, double the number graduating five years before that. In
1970, 4,500 Indians were estimated to be in attendance at
institutions of higher education. The Bureau of Indian Affairs
provided financial support to 3,432 students in 1969 (with
grants totaling more than $3,000,000) of which number 241
graduated from college. The Bureau also assists Indians engaged in adult educational programs in more than 300 communities.

As part of the attempt to remove areas of difference between Indians and non-Indians, a bill was introduced in the
House of Representatives (90th Congress, 1st Session, H.R.
9397, April 27, 1967) to remove the prohibition on the attendance of Indian scholarship students at sectarian colleges and
universities. A similar bill in the Senate (S. 876, November 2,
1967) sought the same objective. At the time the act of March
2, 1917, prohibiting appropriations from the Treasury of the
United States for education of Indian children in any sectarian
school, was passed, there was no federal higher education
program, and the restriction applied only to elementary and
secondary pupils. Repeal of the provision in 1968 brought
Indians into the same status as non-Indians with regard to the
1958 National Defense Education Act, and the Higher Education Act of 1967.[44a]

Anthropologists and the Indian   :   Anthropologists have in many ways been the best friend of the Indian because of their attempt to approach him without value assumptions. Anthropologists have traditionally taken a more relativistic point of view with regard to values than other scholars. They have sought to understand the values of the peoples they have chosen to study, and have not interpreted their culture solely in terms of the values of white European civilization. While there is a growing interest among anthropologists in isolating universal values from the welter of cultures they study, this interest has tended to emerge from the data assembled about countless cultures and not to have been imposed in a theoretical way.

Anthropology has had a particularly strong tradition in the United States. The country itself has provided a laboratory for study, with hundreds of Indian nations, tribes, bands, and groups continuing to occupy their ancient territories, or the reservations to which the dominant white culture confined them in the nineteenth century. Study of the Indian in a scientific fashion was commenced early. The first publication of the Smithsonian Institution, founded in 1846 for the increase and diffusion of knowledge among men, concerned prehistoric mounds of the Midwest. The first secretary of the Smithsonian, Joseph Henry, encouraged such research and eventually a Bureau of American Ethnology was created within the Smithsonian Institution to support such work. The bureau published approximately 275 scholarly studies of the Indian before its amalgation in 1964 with other anthropologically oriented activities of the Smithsonian. As universities burgeoned in the late nineteenth and early twentieth centuries, anthropology as a discipline developed rapidly. The American Anthropological Association, an outgrowth of the Anthropological Society of Washington, founded in 1879, had grown to 7000 members and 1500 fellows in 1970.

Graduate degrees in anthropology are offered by more than a hundred universities in the United States.[45]

But despite their relatively value-free approach, anthropologists have tended to use the Indian in an exploitative way. Knowledge rather than furs or land has been the product sought by the anthropologist. Personal commitment to Indian welfare has rarely accompanied a professional interest in Indian life. The Indian, deprived of so much of his material wealth, has often been reluctant to convey the innermost secrets of his spiritual life. The most outspoken expression of Indian annoyance with the anthropologist is contained in Vine Deloria, Jr.'s book, *Custer Died for Your Sins* (New York: Macmillan, 1969). "We should not be objects of observation for those who do nothing to help us," Deloria, a Standing Rock Sioux and former executive secretary of the National Congress of American Indians, asserts. Where were the anthropologists when the Indian was fighting termination policy? he asks. "Why should we continue to be the private zoos for anthropologists?" Deloria's attack on the anthropological profession, while reflecting a basic rage, is also, one suspects, not entirely believed by the author himself but is rather designed to stimulate white anthropologists to greater consideration of the Indian as a human being.[45a]

Despite his growing irritation at the anthropologist, the Indian has generally found him a friend because of his willingness to listen and to record, rather than to lay down the law or to insist upon the truth of an alien culture. Anthropologists have increasingly rallied to the defense of Indian groups threatened with loss of land or other values. The participation of anthropologists in behalf of Indian nations bringing cases under the Indian Claims Commission Act has been based on more than economic or professional interest. There has been a strong moral sentiment that now is the time for the anthropologist to repay his debts to his informants.

Anthropologists, particularly Sol Tax of the University of

Chicago, and Nancy Lurie, now with the University of Wisconsin, Milwaukee, played key roles in getting different Indian groups together during the week of June 13–20, 1961, at the American Indian Chicago Conference. Four hundred and sixty Indians from ninety tribes met at Chicago and issued a "Declaration of Indian Purpose" which sought to preserve traditional values and rights in the face of the steady encroachment of white economic power and law. The unity of Indian interests vis-a-vis the whites has led to an increasing emphasis among Indian groups upon those elements in their history and culture that give them a common bond. The signs of a Pan Indian movement are clear. Long identified as a single entity in terms of the white view and interest, the different Indian groups are finding that a unified presentation of their problems and consolidated application of their power can be more productive than separate efforts. Anthropologists, despite their concern with cultural differences among Indian groups, have encouraged this united front as they have accepted the responsibility for helping the Indian in his present-day quest for recognition and respect.

The Indian's New-Found White Friends   :   As American youth have become alienated from their own culture, there has been a remarkable awakening of interest in American Indian cultures on the part of those most disaffected with conventional white values. "Hippie" communities have found the Indian. Indian dress, Indian habits, Indian posters are a distinguishing mark of many hippie communities. The attraction of a culture which never wanted "in" to white society to those who now want "out" is a great one. Historical traits of the Indian are exalted by the new generation: passivity in behavior, refusal to heap up material goods, willingness to share what one has, deliberation in debate (aided by the smoking of a

pipe), search for spiritual vision, unconcern with the "rat
race" of existence, these and other characteristics long identified with the Indian have emerged in the hippie culture.
Some of these attitudes are, of course, not specifically Indian,
and models for such behavior can be found in the Orient and
in other cultures, but the American hippie can rejoice in
finding a native culture that upholds (or used to uphold) these
values and which was abused and crucified by an unthinking,
unsympathetic white culture. Evidence seems to indicate that
the hippie is identifying increasingly with the red man and
decreasingly with the black man who was formerly the object
of his concern and admiration as one rejected by the world
and by white values.

Will the fascination of the hippie culture with the red man
continue? Odds are that it will, because of the near identity
of fundamental values. This is not to say that the two cultures
will appreciate each other or co-exist. The evidence from the
Southwestern United States, where many of the new "com-
munes" and "families" of hippies are congregating because
of the pleasant outdoor living conditions and nearness to the
awesome beauty of the natural environment of the region,
suggests that the Indians are more bothered than flattered by
their imitative white brothers. While the values of the two
communities may show parallels, the speech, the dress, and
the "style" of the two groups show marked differences which
make fraternization difficult. Nevertheless, America now has
a communally oriented, non-competitively organized nature-
worshipping culture not derived from the native inhabitants
of the country. The two cultures will probably co-exist better
than have the more traditional forms of white culture coexisted with Indian cultures in the past.

Charitable foundations have also turned their faces toward
the American Indian. In 1966 Miss Doris Duke made grants
to support an American Indian History Study in seven universities in the Western states. The projects seek to obtain the

Indian viewpoint about his history and to develop methods by which the Indian can more effectively communicate that history to himself and to the American public. A number of conferences have been supported by Miss Duke to facilitate that purpose. The Ford Foundation has established a massive program of scholarships to Indian students designed to produce an educated elite in the presently maturing generation of Indians. In addition, the Ford Foundation funds efforts to encourage Indians to organize in educational, economic and artistic endeavors. The William H. Donner Foundation, Inc., of New York, is another charitable trust that began in the late 1960s to support projects pertaining to the American Indian. Among the projects it has supported is the Rough Rock Elementary School on the Navajo reservation.

Friends of the Indian are emerging from the civil rights movement. As the white man finds himself superfluous or unwanted among Negro civil rights workers, he has sometimes turned his benevolence to the Indian. Although Indians are suspicious of whites (with good reason) they tend to be more willing than blacks to accept help from this quarter. The Indian does not have to seek to regain his identity as the Negro does. He has always cherished and maintained it. Hence it is easier for him to accept disinterested and competent white help, even while maintaining his skepticism and distrust of white motives. Some extremists of the "Red Power" movement, however, like their brothers in the "Black Power" movement, believe that no white man can legitimately know or write about the Indian. Irritation at Stan Steiner, whose book *The New Indians* (New York: Harper & Row, 1968) sought to speak for Indians who refused to speak for themselves, has been no less intense because he did in fact what the Indians could not or would not do. Books such as Steiner's book, billed as the first full-scale report of the "Red Power" movement, have helped to erode the stereotype of the Indian as either picturesque or passive.

Social Life : The autonomy of the Indians has been recognized in various ways by the United States, not the least in upholding the validity of marriage and divorce by so-called "Indian custom"—that is, marriage without benefit of clergy and divorce by unilateral action of one party. The courts, both state and federal, have almost uniformly upheld such Indian practices on the theory that the national government has recognized the autonomy of the Indians in such matters and has removed them from the realm of state law in this respect. Marriages under Indian custom are not to be regarded as common-law marriages, but as possessing the legal force of a ceremonial marriage between whites.[46] The rulings of the courts and the decisions of the Department of the Interior on such matters apply to the natives of Alaska as they do to those of the continental United States. The validity of marriages among Indians in Alaska by native custom is thus protected.[47]

Wherever whites and Indians have met, they have interbred. Sometimes the unions have been elevated, as in the case of the marriage of John Rolfe of Virginia and the Princess Pocahontas. Sometimes the unions have been merely expedient, as they often were with the wide-ranging fur trappers. Sometimes the liaisons have been debased and unfeeling. Too often the intercourse between white and Indian has resulted in the corruption of native values. A typical recent example occurred when the "DEW Line" early warning system was constructed in the Arctic "wastes" of Alaska and Canada. American servicemen manning the system were attracted to Eskimo women. Liaisons, some in the form of permanent marriages but more in the form of concubinage or prostitution were the inevitable by-product. Sometimes these liaisons were tolerated by base commanders; sometimes they were prohibited or discouraged. The high pay of the Americans, and the imported luxuries that accompanied that pay— hamburgers, for example—began to influence and modify the preexisting culture. Eskimo men, as well as the Eskimo women, could obtain employment on a day-labor basis at the installations. No discrimination in pay was authorized. An Eskimo could live in a money economy, be employed as a laborer at the base, eat hamburgers, drink Coke, and in other ways "assimilate" the alien culture. For many the impact has been decisive. Traditional activities, such as seal hunting or ivory carving, were abandoned by many.

Anthropologists have studied Indian culture intensively, and from the earliest times have delved deeply into kinship systems as fundamental indicators of social structure. Such systems vary widely among the Indian cultures, and have been modified by contact with other groups, and by technological, economic, and ecological changes. One of the most influential factors in changing Indian kinship patterns has been Indian-white marriage. Orientation to white values and to white kinship patterns has often been generated by such marriages which, in turn, stimulate larger differences between the "acculturated" or "progressive" families of an Indian community and the "unacculturated" and "conservative" families. Restrictions and modifications of "cross-cousin" marriage patterns have stemmed, in part, from such influences.[48]

On some reservations the male Indian has become dispirited and ineffective for lack of a meaningful role in society. The old roles are denied him. New ones have not been acquired in the surrounding white community and few opportunities present themselves on the reservation. The Indian female, on the other hand, is often concerned with finding ways to let her children develop meaningful roles in white society. Her efforts are often groping, but she frequently senses—more readily than the male—the practical value of an outside education and an outside accommodation to the dominant society.

Meaning in the life of many Indian groups was supplied in large measure by the attainment of virtues often associated with war: bravery, strength, perseverance, cunning, contempt for death. Other virtues—such as wisdom and experience among the old, industry and frugality among the women—

were, of course, cherished, but Indian life to a remarkable degree (considering the incredible diversity of Indian nations and the enormous range of cultural traits) elevated these war-like virtues. Even in a losing cause, against the constant crushing weight of white numbers and weapons, these virtues could be demonstrated, and Indian self-respect maintained.

The removal of war as a legitimate activity of Indian life had, as a consequence, a significant impact on Indian life. No substitution of economic, aesthetic or political virtues could fill the void or achieve the status of the more demanding virtues of war. Though the debilitating effects of this shift of role were most pronounced in the nineteenth century, their impact still lingers.

World War II provided an opportunity for the partial recapture of the historic Indian military virtues, even in the service of an alien conqueror and across vast oceans in the territory of alien nations. The Office of Indian Affairs reported in 1944 that the war had brought about the greatest exodus of Indians from reservations that had ever taken place. Out of 65,000 able-bodied men from 18 to 50 years of age, 30 per cent had joined the armed forces and 25 per cent had entered war industries and other war services. Ten thousand more men, women and children left the reservations to work on farms and ranches for varying periods of time.

The record of Indian fighting men in the service of the United States was impressive. Numerous decorations were won by Indians, including the Medal of Honor. The Indian, probably to a greater degree than his white comrades-in-arms, did not fight an ideological war, a war to make the world safe for a democracy which he knew only as a victim rather than as a participant. Rather the Indian found a personal sense of achievement in recapturing traditional Indian virtues in the military service of his erstwhile oppressor. Bravery is a soldierly virtue, and a soldier of any nation can demonstrate it.[49]

One of the most serious problems facing the Indian today is drunkenness. Though obviously widespread and disruptive, Indian drunkenness has rarely been analyzed in print by anthropologists. A recent observer, Theodore D. Graves, comments that "There appears to be an unspoken taboo against exposing a behavioral pattern that is so manifestly disfunctional, perhaps because it challenges our set notions about the nature of culture and reflects with discredit upon Indian friends with whom we sympathetically identify." Graves notes that this is neither a service to them nor to science, and points out that the Indians of the community he studied have been sufficiently concerned by the problem to establish a permanent "Alcoholism Committee" as part of its governmental structure and to sponsor "alcoholism work-shops" in an attempt to deal with the problem.

Graves' study noted that acculturation in the Southwestern United States community studied had a different effect on the Spanish minority and on the Indian minority. The Spanish-American group showed higher rates of drinking and deviant behavior among the acculturated group, while the opposite was the case with the Indian minority. In attempting to deter-mine how access to the economic rewards of the dominant Anglo-American society influenced this behavior, Graves found that high rates of both drinking and deviant behavior occurred among the Spanish-American group only for rela-tively acculturated subjects with low economic access to the new goals they had adopted. For the Indians relatively low rates of both drinking and deviant behavior occurred only among those who both were acculturated and had a job that provided them with the opportunity to achieve their new goals. High rates of drinking and deviant behavior were found among unacculturated Indians regardless of their degree of economic access. The explanation of these findings required an analysis of social and psychological controls among both groups. Spanish-Americans displayed strong social and psy-chological controls through such institutions (often internal-ized) as the family and church. The Indian showed weak social and psychological controls, perhaps deriving from the tradition of independent thought and action characteristic of a semi-nomadic hunting and gathering economy of the past.[50]

The revolutionary effect of loss of traditional controls and inability to share in the economic rewards of the new society has been particularly destructive to the Indian. Drink introduced by Europeans has allowed him at least temporarily to obliterate the consciousness of his loss of self-respect and of his inability to share in the economic rewards of the society to which he has been "acculturated." Consciousness that drink itself impedes his economic access and degrades his nature has proved less compelling than the pleasure of obliterating the memory of the problem itself. Indian leaders, from the earliest time, attempted to keep liquor away from their people, knowing its seductive and destructive power. Invariably they failed both because of the attraction of the grape to the tribesmen and the profit and advantage of the trade to the white.

So persistent has the problem of Indian drunkenness been that the possibility of physiological explanation should not be completely ignored in favor of a cultural explanation. But evidence to establish a physiological basis for Indian drunkenness is not available. It is conceivable, however, that Indian cultural patterns of food ingestion, in terms of amount, regularity, and social context may throw some light on the differential effects of alcohol on the white man and on the red. Indian religion and mystical visions, in which one tries to "get out of himself," may also help to explain the attractions of an agent which can dissociate one's imagined self from one's real self. The extent to which alcohol has served or can serve the Indian as a mind-expanding or mind-annihilating drug needs also to be considered.

The ease with which Indians in the armed services in World War II could obtain liquor made the then existing prohibition against the sale of liquor to Indians seem discriminatory, particularly to Indian veterans. In 1946, therefore, a bill sponsored by the Bureau of Indian Affairs was introduced to permit the sale or gift of liquor to Indians outside the Indian reservations. The bill—never enacted into law—maintained the prohibition against the possession or use of intoxicating beverages on the reservations where neither Indian nor non-Indian could possess them legally.[51] The Eisenhower administration achieved the goal of the Bureau of Indian Affairs with the enactment of Public Law 277, approved August 15, 1953, which removed the prohibition against sales of alcoholic beverages to Indians outside the Indian country and provided for legalizing the introduction of alcoholic beverages within the Indian country on a local option basis under the authority of tribal governments. This was another step in "freeing" the Indian from the restrictions placed upon him, whatever the nature of those restrictions might be.[52]

By 1968, fifty-five Indian tribal groups had exercised the local option to legalize intoxicants on the reservation. Although welcoming the removal of restrictions outside the Indian country, the Indians have been generally slow in authorizing sale of liquor within the reservations.

The Indian of the Future   :   The American Indian of the future cannot fully revert to a past culture nor can he completely retain his present culture. Cultures do not remain static and isolated. They evolve. Paul Radin, in his *The Story of the American Indian* (revised edition, 1944), pointed out that many European innovations, such as the use of iron and the adoption of the horse, have been accepted by the Indians as legitimate extensions and growths of their own civilizations. The three major traits normally associated with the Navajos: sheep-herding, silverwork and blankets—he notes—represent borrowings from the Spaniards. Moreover, "practically all" of their great rituals derive from other Indian groups with whom they came into contact indirectly through the media-

tion of their conquerors. No Navajo, he asserts, would understand what an anthropologist or historian meant if told that
most of what he possessed today had come to him from non-
Navajo sources.[53]

Radin looked to Mexico to provide a center for an Indian
renaissance, with which the Indians of the United States, a
large proportion of whom are in physical proximity to Mexico, would ideally be associated, if given autonomy. Radin did
not see the white man conceding that autonomy to the red
man, but hinted at a future possibility of such a change.

The crushing burden upon the American Indian is that the
one option most natural to him—to be an Indian—is the one
that is denied him in white America. Even the Report of the
Commission on the Rights, Liberties, and Responsibilities of
the American Indian, established by the Fund for the Republic, Inc., in March, 1957, and whose final report was issued by
the University of Oklahoma Press in 1966, illustrates the
point. Though asserting that "the Indian himself should be
the focus of all public policy affecting him," though encourag-
ing the retention by the Indian of his pride in being an Indian,
though recognizing that "no program imposed from outside
can serve as a substitute for one willed by Indians themselves," the committee defined the future of the Indian in
terms of white values and policy. The Indian must be made
"a self-respecting and useful American citizen. . . ." His
"desire to share in the advantages of modern civilization"
must be aroused. "He must devote his energy, ability, and
perseverance wholeheartedly to the effort to improve his education, political participation, health practices, and standard
of living." It may well be that these goals are valid for the
Indian in 1970. But, be it remembered, a similar spirit motivated earlier reformers, such as Senator Dawes. What the
Indian is not allowed to be is what he was or is; he must
change, say his friends and enemies. With such friends and
enemies, who needs an Indian?[54]

Recent trends in minority attitudes suggest that the assumptions of the "melting pot"—of the inevitability and desirability of the integration of minority groups into the body of American life—are increasingly irrelevant. The bland, homogenized middleclass white America that used to be assumed to be the desirable form of the mix is increasingly rejected by minority groups. The Negro has come to recognize as a prime mistake his rejection of his blackness. In reaction to years of humiliating attempts to convince his white model of his identity to that model, the Negro has developed both extreme forms of racial separatism, as in the case of the black Muslims, and more moderate assertions of the validity of black values, black culture, black community. The Indian, who more than any other minority group resisted integration from the start, is now being emulated by those groups which made the attempt and failed. Still, the pressures placed upon him are such that after years of holding out against insuperable odds, the Indian is gradually losing his separateness and his identity. At the same time, and after years of trying, without success, to abandon his separate identity, the Negro has begun to search for an identity separate from the race with which his language, culture, and values are mixed.

When Senator Robert F. Kennedy and Senator Fannin of Arizona held hearings on Indian education in Eastern Oklahoma early in 1968, Mr. Andrew Dreadfulwater, Chairman of the Original Cherokee Community Organization, testified before the subcommittee to say that there were two kinds of Cherokee but that these classes were not based on the degree of Indian blood. Rather, Dreadfulwater asserted, one kind of Cherokee identifies himself as a Cherokee; the other thinks of himself as white. The concern of the new Indian radical movement is to reestablish its Indian identity. For the purpose, the memories of the past are vital, not only to call up the image of Indian identity and achievement, but to maintain the fire. As Scott McLemore, Secretary of the Original Cherokee Community Organization, put it, "We are in what one might call a 'Cold War.' It is the 'War of the Velvet Gloved People.'

You must realize that the war against us has never ended. Why do you think we are still an uneducated people? Why do you think we are still a poverty stricken people?" [55]

The danger of the policy of assimilation, so fondly hoped for by friends and enemies of the Indian alike, is that once conceded as a fundamental principle underlying the Indian-white relationship, it cuts the ground out from under the maintenance of any right, organizational structure, or value that is distinctively Indian. Assimilation is the ally of termination, whether its proponents realize it or not. The insistence upon assimilation—albeit for the Indian's benefit—undercuts the recognition of the distinct nature and distinct rights of the Indian as Indian. How can separate tribal governments, separate reservations, separate rights and obligations be countenanced among a population which is assimilated to the life, law, and values of the dominant power? It is hard to see how the Indian can retain his lands and his culture once the validity of assimilation is conceded.

It is strange that white America now seems almost more inclined to admit a policy of racial separation for its black minority, descendants of imported slaves, than to recognize that desire on the part of the former possessors of the continent.

The ultimate hope of the traditionalists is to establish the full sovereignty of the Indian over the lands he occupies. Though seemingly quixotic, the attitude is regarded as logical and even necessary by some Indians, not so much because of the possibility of obtaining white assent to the doctrine but as a way of maintaining their own integrity. Too frequently they have seen their fellow Indians acquiesce to overwhelming power and attempt to salvage something from the confrontation. The new radical Indian, who often has nothing to lose but the ragged scraps of real or imagined traditions, finds it more satisfying to insist on complete Indian sovereignty even while realizing the unlikelihood of achieving it. A lost cause is better than none at all.

EPILOGUE

The expansion of one people into the territory of another has rarely been distinguished by the application of legal or moral theories which safeguard the rights of the original inhabitants. A student of expansion in Japan, Russia, India and a host of other countries will discover that hypocrisy and greed are not monopolies of Western Europe or of the United States. Indeed, one is impressed by the extent to which the application of legal and moral principles, weak though they may have been, have preserved for the American Indian a more favorable status than has been achieved by the original peoples of many other lands overrun by more powerful outsiders.

The discoverers and administrators who came to the New World carried in their minds the intellectual attitudes of the Greeks toward the "barbarians" and the moral assumptions of medieval Christians toward the "heathen." The actions of the European colonists toward the Indians reflect the faults and virtues of that heritage. Because of the virtues of that heritage the Indians have maintained significant portions of their original power and authority. To the extent that an Indian wishes to remain an Indian, or an Indian community, tribe, or nation wishes to remain Indian, he or it must guard the reserved rights hammered out in the centuries long relationship with the white man.

The status of the Indian is varied and complex. Of primary importance to both Indian and white man is the land which each can claim. While asserting grandiose and theoretical titles to the entire continent by virtue of "discovery," the English colonists and their American successors recognized the natives' "original title" to the lands they possessed. Exactly how much land the Indian could claim, sell or retain was the subject of much debate and many treaties. The nature of the Indian title to that land was the subject of even greater debate. Indian title lacked the security and power of English title in fee simple. Yet the colonial authorities at first and the American courts later normally agreed that the Indian should be paid for his title. Sometimes, it is true, this recognition of Indian right was made belatedly, after the Indian had in fact been despoiled or cheated of the land by immigrant Americans in search of their destiny.

What of the status of the Indian as an individual? The whites at first recognized and accepted the tribal and national character of the Indian collectivities with which they dealt. It could hardly have been otherwise. The very future of the colonies and the security of many of the states depended upon a satisfactory accommodation to the power that could be marshaled by these Indian political units. With the decline of that power and the growth of the power of the intruders, the individual Indian became more and more subject to white codes of law and white regulation of his activities. The "Indian country" came gradually to be delimited by white surveyors rather than by Indian warriors. The Indian "homelands" were converted into "reservations." Indian law and Indian custom, which tolerated the trader and government envoy of colonial times, were gradually supplanted by Anglo-American law and custom communicated by a superintendent or agent who could call upon irresistible power to enforce his "advice." Indian law and custom survived, but in an attenuated form. Constant pressure has characteristically been exerted by the Congress, and often by the Executive, to harry the Indian until he will conform to white standards of value and behavior.

All cultures change. No one can absolutely bar such change. But one can preserve values. This is what the Indian now seeks to do after passing through the valley of despair and hopelessness. Drunkenness, poverty and ignorance are the measures of what the Indian has lost. But the Indian has another measure, that of the things he has retained: his language, his land, his rights as an Indian. The shock of what was lost is a shock that will never be forgotten, but the retention of Indian values by the Indian young means that the Indian point of view will never be extinguished. Agencies of government are more than ever conscious of the rights due the American Indian. Whether it is in debate in the Congress over the settlement of the Indian claims in Alaska, or in the adjudication of an ancient claim for damages in the Indian Claims Commission, the Indian can now claim the respect and attention hitherto denied him. In large measure that respect derives from and can be comprehended only by a study of the history of the relationship between the white man and the red.

On July 8, 1970, President Nixon sent a message to the Congress which, if implemented, may mark a new deal for the American Indian comparable to the change effected by the Wheeler-Howard Act and related legislation in the presidency of Franklin D. Roosevelt. The sincerity of the message was questioned by some, who saw in it the same old meaningless "pontification" (the word is that of Senator Gravel of Alaska on the floor of the Senate on July 14, 1970). But on the part of many, including liberal Democrats like Senator Harris of Oklahoma, the message was a sincere declaration of a turnabout in American Indian policy. The message unilaterally renounced and repudiated for the executive branch the termination policy of the past, and affirmed for the executive branch that the United States government would honor the treaty and trusteeship obligations to the Indians so long as the Indian groups themselves believed such a policy desirable. The President affirmed, for the executive branch, that the historic relationship between the Federal government and the Indian communities "cannot be abridged without the consent of the Indians." The President's message was lofty in tone and precise in its implications. In addition to denouncing the policy of forced termination, it also rejected its opposite: excessive dependence upon the Federal government. It called instead for self-determination without the threat of eventual termination. In order to encourage self-determination it urged that any Indian community be allowed to assume administrative responsibility for any service program presently administered by a federal agency. Determination of whether the service would or would not be taken over would rest ultimately with the Indian community, not with the government. The "right of retrocession" would also be guaranteed: if the local community decided, after taking over a program, that it wished to give it back to the government, it could do so.

The President also urged the restoration of 48,000 acres of sacred land near Blue Lake in New Mexico to the Taos Indians from whom it had been taken by the Federal government in 1906 and made into a national forest. The religious implications of the lake in its pristine and unpolluted form was recognized by the message.

The message also called for Indian control of Indian schools and for other measures to foster self-determination within the Indian communities. It called, moreover, for an end to the subordination of the Bureau of Indian Affairs under the Assistant Secretary of the Interior for Public Land

Management, proposing instead an Assistant Secretary of the Interior for Indian and Territorial Affairs. It also proposed an Indian Trust Counsel Authority to assure independent legal representation for the Indians' natural resource rights, a measure which would alter the present situation in which the government lawyers for the Department of the Interior and the Department of Justice who provide services to the Indians argue against the larger interests of their own departments.

Whether the Nixon program will be implemented by Congress or not remains to be seen. Forty-eight thousand acres of land surrounding Blue Lake were returned to the Taos Indians by an act signed by President Nixon on December 15, 1970. The proposals for reorganizing the Department of the Interior, on the other hand, were thrown in doubt by a more comprehensive reorganization scheme for the entire executive branch proposed by President Nixon in 1971. Some Indians, pleased by the original proposal, were worried that they might be "lost" in the larger scheme. Despite the uncertainty over the reorganization of the executive branch the proposals of the new administration have a coherence and logic lacking in the many highly publicized initiatives of the previous administration. No one can blame the Indians if they continue to disbelieve in the word of the white man, but the growing nation-wide comprehension of the historical background to, and recognition of the moral consequences of, the Federal relationship with the Indian tribes gives hope that at long last an equitable solution to the Indian problem may be within reach.

FOOTNOTES

PART I

1. St. Augustine, *Opera Omnia,* ed. J. P. Migne (Paris, 1841–1861), III, 781; *The Letters of Saint Augustine,* trans. Rev. J. G. Cunningham, (Edinburgh, 1872), I, 409–410, Vol. VI of *The Works of Aurelius Augustine, Bishop of Hippo,* ed. Rev. Marcus Dods.

2. Didymus Beaufort, *La guerre comme instrument de secours ou de punition* (The Hague, 1933), pp. 11, 23, 28, 30, and 50. See also John Eppstein, *The Catholic Tradition of the Law of Nations* (London, 1935), p. 59.

3. Paraphrase of St. Augustine quoted by St. Thomas Aquinas, *The "Summa Theologica,"* trans. by Fathers of the English Dominican Province, Part II of Second Part, First Number (London, 1917), Qu. 40, Art. 1, p. 503. James Brown Scott, *Law, the State, and the International Community* (New York, 1939), I, 221 n.

4. Frances Gardiner Davenport, *European Treaties bearing on the History of the United States and its Dependencies to 1648* (Washington, 1917), pp. 58–62.

5. Lewis U. Hanke, *The Spanish Struggle for Justice in the Conquest of America* (Philadelphia, 1949), p. 34.

6. Quoted in Lewis U. Hanke, "The *Requerimiento* and its interpreters," *Revista de Historia de America,* Year I, No. 1 (1938), pp. 2–5.

7. Bartolomé de las Casas, *Historia de las Indias,* ed. Augustin

Millares Carlo (Mexico City, 1951), III, 31 (Bk. III, Ch. LVIII). Silvio Zavala, *New Viewpoints on the Spanish Colonization of America* (Philadelphia, 1943), p. 11.

8. Hanke, *op. cit.*, pp. 23–24.

9. *Ibid.*, p. 63. See also Lewis U. Hanke, *Bartolomé de las Casas* (Gainesville, Florida, 1952), p. 98, and Ernest Nys, *Le droit de la guerre et les precurseurs de Grotius* (Brussels, 1882), p. 227.

10. Quoted in Hanke, *Spanish Struggle for Justice*, pp. 51–52.

11. Franciscus de Victoria, *De Indis et de iure belli relectiones*, ed. Ernest Nys (Washington, 1917), pp. 127–8 (Sec. 1, Nos. 23–24).

12. Quoted in Lewis U. Hanke, "Pope Paul III and the American Indians," *Harvard Theological Review*, Vol. 30, No. 2 (April 1937), 77.

13. Victoria, *op. cit.*, pp. 144–5 (Sec. 2, Nos. 14–15).

14. *Ibid.*, pp. 152–5 (Sec. 3, Nos, 3, 6, 7).

15. *Ibid.*, p. 156 (Sec. 3, No. 9).

16. Gilbert Chinard, *L'Exotisme Américain dans la littérature francaise au XVIe siècle* (Paris, 1911), pp. 181–2.

17. Related in Beaufort, *op. cit.*, Introduction, viii.

18. James Brown Scott, *The Spanish Origin of International Law: Francisco de Vitoria and his Law of Nations* (Oxford, 1934), pp. 282–3. Scott is less positive in this view in his *Law, the State, and the International Community* (New York, 1939), I, 319, 322.

19. Beaufort, *op. cit.*, pp. 127, 131; Eppstein, *op. cit.*, pp. 113, 250–1.

20. An example of how Vitoria wrestled with this problem is seen in his 1534 letter to Father Miguel de Arcos concerning the justness of the Peruvian conquest; quoted in full in Father Vicente Beltrán de Heredia, *Francisco de Vitoria* (Barcelona, 1939), pp. 121–4.

21. Hanke, "Pope Paul III and the American Indians," p. 83.

22. *Ibid.*, p. 72.

23. *Ibid.*, p. 76.

24. Quoted in Hanke, *Spanish Struggle for Justice*, p. 118.

25. *Ibid.*, pp. 153–7.

26. Juan Ginés de Sepúlveda, *Democrates alter, sive de justis belli causis apud Indos*, in *Tratado sobre las justas causas de la guerra contra los Indios* (Latin text and Spanish translation) ed. Marcelino Menendez

y Pelayo (Mexico City, 1941), pp. 104–5. *Democrates alter* (so called because Sepúlveda had written a "first" *Democrates* in 1535) was written in 1548 but not published because the authorities at the universities of Salamanca and Alcala, at the insistence of Las Casas, determined that its doctrine was not sound. The English translation of the passage quoted is by Hanke, in his *Spanish Struggle for Justice*, p. 122.

27. Aristotle, *Politics*, trans. Benjamin Jowett, in *The Works of Aristotle*, ed. W. D. Ross (Oxford, 1921), 1254a (Bk. I, Ch. 5), 1256b (Bk. I, Ch. 8), 1327b (Bk. VII, Ch. 7), 1252b (Bk. I, Ch. 2). Sepúlveda, op. cit., pp. 108–111.

28. Robert O. Schlaifer, *Greek Theories of Slavery from Homer to Aristotle* (Cambridge, Mass., 1936), pp. 165–9, 182, 201–2. See also E. E. Sikes, *The Anthropology of the Greeks* (London, 1914), pp. 69–71; J. A. K. Thomson, *Greeks and Barbarians* (London, 1921), pp. 60, 84; Scott, *Law, the State, and the International Community*, I, 51–2.

29. Quoted in Hanke, *Spanish Struggle for Justice*, p. 125.

30. Ernest Nys, *Etudes de droit international et de droit politique* (Brussels, 1896), pp. 234–5.

31. Quoted in Hanke, *Spanish Struggle for Justice*, p. 127.

32. Hanke, *Bartolomé de las Casas*, p. 73.

33. F. G. Bell, *Juan Ginés de Sepúlveda* (Oxford, 1925), p. 38.

34. Davenport, *op. cit.*, pp. 58, 61.

35. Quoted in Hanke, *Spanish Struggle for Justice*, p. 167.

36. Hugo Grotius, *De jure belli ac pacis libri tres* [1625] trans. Francis W. Kelsey (Oxford, 1925), II, 506 (Bk. II, Ch. XX, Sec. xl).

37. Hanke, *Spanish Struggle for Justice*, p. 172.

38. Francisco Suarez, *Selections from Three Works: De legibus, ac Deo legislatore, 1612; Defensio fidei Catholicae, et Apostolicae adversus Anglicanae sectae errores, 1613; De triplici virtute theologica, fide, spe, et charitate, 1621*, trans. Gladys L. Williams, Ammi Brown and John Waldron (London, 1944), II, 771 (Disp. XVIII, Sec. IV, No. 5), II, 825–6 (Disp. XIII, Sec. V, No. 5).

39. *Ibid.*, II, 679 (*Defensio fidei Catholicae*, Bk. III, Ch. V, Sec. 19); II, 133 (*De legibus, ac Deo legislatore*, Bk. I, Ch. XVIII, Sec. 4).

40. *Ibid.*, II, 757–67 (*De triplici virtute*, Disp. XVIII, Sec. III); II, 741–2 (*De triplici virtute*, Disp. XVIII, Sec. 1).

41. *Ibid.*, II, 746 (*De triplici virtute*, Disp. XVIII, Sec. 1).

42. *Ibid.*

43. Alberico Gentili, *De jure belli libri tres*, trans. John C. Rolfe (London, 1933), II, 38–41 (Bk. I, Ch. IX).

44. *Ibid.*, II, 53–54 (Bk. I, Ch. XII).

45. Ibid., II, 89, 123 (Bk. I, Ch. XIX; Bk. I, Ch. XXV).

46. Grotius, *op. cit.*, II, 517 (Bk. II, Ch. XX, Sec. xlix); II, 201 (Bk. II, Ch. II, Sec. xv).

47. The justification is present in H. Noldin, *Summa Theologiae Moralis,* Editio XVII by A. Schmitt (Innsbruck, 1945), II, 339 (Quaestio Septima: De bello, No. 353), but is dropped in the 1955 edition revised by G. Heinzel. See also Eppstein, *op. cit.*, pp. 82–83, and Scott, *The Spanish Origin of International Law,* p. 153, and Rev. Raymond de Martini, O.F.M., *The Right of Nations to Expand by Conquest,* Catholic University of America Studies in Sacred Theology, Second Series, No. 1 (Washington, 1947), pp. 48–49. The author was told by the Very Reverend Francis J. Connell, Dean of the School of Theology, Catholic University of America, in response to a question during a lecture on "Moral Problems of Modern Warfare" at Harvard University, March 24, 1953, that the right to preach the Gospel remained a justifiable reason for war but that "practically" one should go about correcting the wrong in another way.

48. José de Acosta, *Historia Natural y Moral de las Indias,* ed. Edmundo O'Gorman (Mexico City, 1940), pp. 447–8 (Bk. VI, Ch. I).

49. José de Acosta, *De Natura novi orbis libri duo et de promulgatione evangelii, apud barbaros, sive de procuranda Indorum salute libri sex* (Salamanca, 1589), pp. 118–22.

PART II

1. Preface to the second edition (1598) of Hakluyt's *Principall Navigations.*

1ª. Edward P. Cheyney, "International Law under Queen Elizabeth," *English Historical Review,* XX (1905), 660, quoting from Camden, *Annales* (1605 edn.), 309, about the reply to Spain, ca. 1580, either in the form of a paper drawn by the Privy Council and afterwards lost or suppressed, or in the form of the substance of a verbal statement made to the Spanish ambassador or some later commissioners. The following discussion is derived largely from Wilcomb E. Washburn, "The Moral and Legal Justifications for Dispossessing the Indians," in James Morton Smith, ed., *Seventeenth-Century America: Essays in Colonial History* (Chapel Hill, 1959), 16–25.

2. Letters Patent to John Cabot, March 5, 1496, in Henry Steele Commager, ed., *Documents of American History (New York, 1944)*, 5. *My italics.*

3. William W. Bishop, Jr., *International Law: Cases and Materials* (New York, 1953), 272.

4. Arthur S. Keller, Oliver J. Lissitzyn, and Frederick J. Mann, *Creation of Rights of Sovereignty through Symbolic Acts, 1400–1800* (New York, 1938), 148. For an admirable and detailed analysis of this complex subject see John Thomas Juricek, English Claims in North America to 1660: A Study in Legal and Constitutional History, Ph.D. Dissertation, University of Chicago, June 1970.

5. "And to bring in the title of *First-discovery,* to me it seems as little reason, that the sailing of a Spanish Ship upon the coast of *India,* should intitle the King of Spain to that Countrey, as the sayling of an Indian or English Ship upon the coast of *Spain,* should intitle either the *Indians* or *English* unto the Dominion thereof. No question but the just right or title to those Countries appertains to the Natives themselves; who, if they shall willingly and freely invite the *English* to their protection, what title soever they have in them, no doubt but they may legally transferr it or communicate it to others." Thomas Gage, *The English-American his Travail by Sea and Land: Or a New Survey of the West-Indies, containing a Journall of Three thousand and Three hundred Miles within the main Land of America* (London, 1648), Epistle Dedicatory. J. Eric S. Thompson has edited a new edition of Gage's *Travels* (Norman, Oklahoma, 1958).

6. "A Discourse of the Original and Fundamental Cause of Natural, Arbitrary, Necessary, and Unnatural War," in *The Works of Sir Walter Ralegh, Kt.* (Oxford, 1829), VIII, 277.

7. [Samuel de Champlain?], "Abstract of the Discoveries in New France," 1631, in E. B. O'Callaghan, ed., *Documents Relative to*

the Colonial History of the State of New York (Albany, New York, 1855), IX, 2.

8. Thomas Salmon, *Modern History; or, the Present State of All Nations,* Vol. XXXI, Being the Fourth Volume of *America* (London, 1738), 557.

9. See, for example, Arthur Percival Newton, *The Colonising Activities of the English Puritans* (New Haven, Conn., 1914), 96.

10. Roger Clap's "Memoirs" [London, 1731], in Alexander Young, ed., *Chronicles of the First Planters of the Colony of Massachusetts, from 1623 to 1636* (Boston, 1846), 350.

11. "Description of the Now-Discovered River and Country of Virginia," June 21, 1607, in *Virginia Magazine of History and Biography,* XIV (1907), 377.

12. In Edward Arber and A. G. Bradley, eds., *Travels and Works of Captain John Smith* (Edinburgh, 1910), I, 65.

13. Alexander Brown, *The First Republic in America* (Boston, 1898), 41–42.

14. Captain John Smith quoted in Philip L. Barbour, *Pocahontas and Her World* (Boston, 1970), pp. 48, 54.

15. George Thorpe to Sir Edwin Sandys, Mary 15, 1621, in Susan M. Kingsbury, ed., *The Records of the Virginia Company of London* (4 Vols., Washington, 1906–35), III, 446.

16. "A Declaration of the State of the Colony and . . . a Relation of the Barbarous Massacre . . ." (London, 1622), reprinted, *ibid.,* 556–57.

17. Treasurer and Council for Virginia to Governor and Council in Virginia, August 1, 1622, *ibid.,* 672; see also John Martin, "The Manner howe to bringe in the Indians into subjection without makinge an utter exterpation of them together with the reasons," December 15, 1622, *ibid.,* 704–7.

18. Council in Virginia to Virginia Company of London, January 20, 1622/23, *ibid.,* IV, 9.

19. See, for example, Council in Virginia to Virginia Company of London, April 3 and 4, 1623, *ibid.,* 99, 102.

20. Robert Bennett to Edward Bennett, June 9, 1623, *ibid.,* 221–22; also printed in *American Historical Review,* XXVII (1922), 505–8.

21. Virginia Company of London to Governor and Council in Virginia, August 6, 1623, in Kingsbury, ed., *Records of the Virginia Company*, IV, 269–70; Council in Virginia to Virginia Company of London, January 30, 1623/24, *ibid.*, 451.

22. John Daly Burk, *The History of Virginia from its first Settlement to the Commencement of the Revolution* (Petersburg, Virginia, 1804–5), I, 308–9.

23. See Washburn, Wilcomb E. "A Moral History of Indian-White Relations," *Ethnohistory*, IV (1957), 47–61.

24. England, in Elizabeth's day, had a population variously estimated between two and five million people. J. B. Black, *The Reign of Elizabeth, 1558–1603* (Oxford, 1945), 195; Carl Bridenbaugh, *Vexed and Troubled Englishmen, 1590–1642* (New York, 1968), 15.

25. John Locke, *An Essay Concerning the True Original, Extent and End of Civil Government* (1690), Chap. V, "Of Property." Immanuel Kant in *The Science of Right* (1796), Pt. I. Chap. II, sec. i, no. 15, writing as the representative of a nation which did not participate in the profitable overseas voyages, denounced the doctrine as impious and championed the right of the American Indian to hold his land in whatever way he pleased. Representatives of the expanding maritime nations, however, found no difficulty in justifying their nations' claims.

26. Theodore Roosevelt, *The Winning of the West* (New York, 1889–96), I, 90.

27. See, for example, Harold Underwood Faulkner, *American Economic History*, 5th edn. (New York, 1943), 58–60, and Roy Harvey Pearce, *The Savages of America: A Study of the Indian and the Idea of Civilization* (Baltimore, 1953), 66. An example of the inability to see the Indians as other than hunters is evident in Roger Burlingame's chapter "Mission in Virginia" in *The American Conscience* (New York, 1957). Burlingame quotes the passage of Edward Waterhouse cited above that "now their cleared lands [*sic*] . . . shall be inhabited by us" and immediately comments that "the policy hitherto observed of keeping hands off the Indian hunting would be ended. . . ." (p. 68).

28. *Utopia*, Robinson trans. of 1551; new edn. by Rev. T. F. Didbin (London, 1808), Bk. II, Chap. V, 191–92.

29. "A Discourse of the Original and Fundamental Cause of Natural, Arbitrary, Necessary, and Unnatural War," in *Works of Sir Walter Ralegh, Kt.,*—VIII, 291.

30. *Ibid.,* 255.

31. Massachusetts Historical Society, *Proceedings, 1871–1873,* XII (Boston, 1873), 348, 351.

32. Charles McLean Andrews, *The Colonial Period in American History* (New Haven, Conn., 1934–1938), II, 4–5, 24–25.

33. Thucydides, *The Peloponnesian War,* trans. Rex Warner (London, 1954), p. 360 (Bk. V, Ch. 7).

34. Quoted in Wilcomb E. Washburn, *The Governor and the Rebel: A History of Bacon's Rebellion in Virginia* (Chapel Hill, 1957), 71–72.

34ᵃ. Yasu Kawashima, "Legal Origins of the Indian Reservation in Colonial Massachusetts," *New England Quarterly,* Vol. 13 (1969), 42–56. The quotation is from p. 53.

35. Benjamin Franklin to James Parker, March 20, 1751, in Leonard W. Labaree, et. al., eds., *The Papers of Benjamin Franklin,* IV (New Haven, Conn., 1961), 117–21.

36. See the extended discussion of the Proclamation of 1763 in Jack M. Sosin, *Whitehall and the Wilderness: The Middle West in British Colonial Policy, 1760–1775* (Lincoln, Nebraska, 1961).

37. Quoted and discussed in George Dewey Harmon, *Sixty Years of Indian Affairs: Political, Economic, and Diplomatic, 1789–1850* (Chapel Hill, 1941), 2 ff.

38. For a detailed discussion of the matter see Stephen H. Coe, Indian-White Relations on the Pennsylvania-New York Frontier, 1783–1794, Ph.D. Dissertation, American University, Washington, D.C. 1968.

39. Quoted in Francis Paul Prucha, *American Indian Policy in the Formative Years: The Indian Trade and Intercourse Acts, 1790–1834* (Cambridge, Mass.: 1962), 34–35.

40. *Ibid.,* 37.

41. Quoted in *ibid.,* 37. Quoted and discussed in U. S. Department of the Interior, *Federal Indian Law* (Washington, 1958), 94–95. *Federal Indian Law* is a revision and updating through 1956 of the *Handbook of Federal Indian Law* prepared by Felix S. Cohen and first printed in 1940.

42. Prucha, *op. cit.*, 39.

43. Harmon, *op. cit.*, 30–40.

44. Quoted in Harmon, *op. cit.*, 16–17.

45. Quoted in Prucha, *op. cit.*, 140–41. Jefferson expressed this concept clearly in an opinion dated May 3, 1790, on the validity of a grant made by the state of Georgia to certain companies of individuals of a tract of land of which the Indian right had never been extinguished. H. A. Washington, ed., *Writings of Thomas Jefferson*, VII (New York, 1854), 467–69.

46. Prucha, *op. cit.*, 141

46ª. Johnson to Roger Morris, Aug. 26, 1765, quoted in Georgiana C. Nammack, *Fraud, Politics, and the Dispossession of the Indians: The Iroquois Land Frontier in the Colonial Period* (Norman, Okla., 1969), p. 77.

47. Prucha, *op. cit.*, 57, 92.

48. Quoted in "Indian Title to Land, 1800–1825," a paper presented before the Western History Association, Tucson, Arizona, October 18, 1968, by Professor Robert W. McCluggage, Loyola University of Chicago, mimeographed, p. 1.

49. Quoted in *ibid.*, 2.

50. *Ibid.*, 3.

51. *Ibid.*, 5.

52. *Ibid.*, 7.

53. *Ibid.*, 9–10.

54. *Ibid.*, 12.

55. 8 Wheaton 574, 591. The following discussion follows Washburn, "The Moral and Legal Justifications for Dispossessing the Indians," in Smith, *op. cit.*, 27–29.

56. William Wirt to James Madison, October 5, 1830, quoted in John P. Kennedy, *Memoirs of the Life of William Wirt, Attorney-General of the United States*, rev. edn. (Philadelphia, 1850–54), II, 262.

57. Quoted in Charles Warren, *The Supreme Court in United States History*, rev. edn. (Boston, 1937), I, 731.

58. Wirt to Judge Dabney Carr, June 21, 1830, quoted in Kennedy, *op. cit.*, II, 255.

59. Marshall to Judge Carr, n.d., quoted in Kennedy, *op. cit.*, II, 258; Warren, *op. cit.*, I, 751; Albert J. Beveridge, *The Life of John Marshall* (Boston, 1916–19); IV, 546.

60. 5 Peters 15–18; entire report, 1–80.

61. Beveridge, *op. cit.,* IV, 546.

62. 6 Peters 515–97.

63. Massachusetts Historical Society, *Proceedings, 1900–1901,* 2nd ser., XIV (Boston, 1901), 352.

64. Harmon, *op. cit.,* 172–73.

65. Henry E. Fritz, *The Movement for Indian Assimilation, 1860–1890* (Philadelphia, 1963), 62, 65, 68, 69.

66. *Ibid.,* 73, 75.

67. Art. 7, 12 Stat. 1163, quoted in N. D. Houghton, " 'Wards of the United States'—Arizona Applications: A Study of the Legal Status of the Indians," University of Arizona, *Social Science Bulletin,* XVI, no. 3 (Tucson, July 1, 1945), 8.

67ᵃ. William A. Brophy and Sophie D. Aberle, comp., *The Indian: America's Unfinished Business: Report of the Commission on the Rights, Liberties, and Responsibilities of the American Indian* (Norman, Okla., 1966), p. 20.

68. Brookings Institution, Washington, D. C., Institute for Government Research, *The Problem of Indian Administration,* Lewis Meriam, Technical Director of Survey Staff (Baltimore, 1928), esp. 87, 88.

69. Entry for April 11–12, 1933, in *The Secret Diary of Harold L. Ickes: The First Thousand Days, 1933–1936* (New York, 1954), 19–20.

70. Entry for June 8, 1933, *ibid.,* 51.

71. Commissioner of Indian Affairs, *Annual Report, 1949,* 364.

72. Commissioner of Indian Affairs, *Annual Report, 1948,* 372–73.

73. Commissioner of Indian Affairs, *Annual Report, 1946,* 1.

74. Commissioner of Indian Affairs, *Annual Report, 1947,* 348–50.

75. Brophy and Aberle, *op. cit.,* 181. See also Department of the Interior, *Federal Indian Law, op. cit.,* 996–99.

76. Commissioner of Indian Affairs, *Annual Report, 1947,* 351.

77. U.S. Congress. House of Representatives. Committee on Interior and Insular Affairs. 82d Congress, 2d Session. *Report with respect to the House Resolution authorizing the Committee on Interior and Insular Affairs to conduct an investigation of the Bureau of Indian Affairs* (Washington, 1953), 1–2.

78. *Ibid.*, 3.

79. Commissioner of Indian Affairs, *Annual Report, 1954*, 227.

80. *Ibid.* House Concurrent Resolution No. 108 is reprinted in Wilcomb E. Washburn, ed., *The Indian and the White Man* (New York, 1964), 397–98.

81. Commissioner of Indian Affairs, *Annual Report, 1954*, 243–44.

82. Commissioner of Indian Affairs, *Annual Report, 1955*, 248; *Annual Report, 1956*, 215.

83. U.S. Congress. Senate. Subcommittee on Indian Affairs. 85th Congress, 1st Session. *Hearings before the Subcommittee on Indian Affairs of the Committee on Interior and Insular Affairs . . . on Bills pertaining to Federal Indian Policy* (Washington, 1957), 164.

84. *Ibid.*, 266, 275, 277.

85. Gary Orfield, *A Study of the Termination Policy* (Denver: National Congress of American Indians, no date), Chap. I, 2. Multilithed.

86. *Ibid.*, 6.

86ª. Orfield's study has been reprinted in *The Education of American Indians: The Organization Question*, prepared for the Subcommittee on Indian Education of the Committee on Labor and Public Welfare of the United States Senate, 91st Congress, 1st Session, November 1969, Vol. 4 (Washington, 1970), 673–816.

87. Orfield, *op. cit.*, 7.

88. *Ibid.*, 11, 13, 16.

89. Commissioner of Indian Affairs, *Annual Report, 1954*, 228, 232.

90. Commissioner of Indian Affairs, *Annual Report, 1955*, 231.

91. *Ibid.*, 231–32.

92. Orfield, *op. cit.*, Chap. II, 6–7.

93. *Ibid.*, 9.

94. *Ibid.*, Chap. III, 21.

95. *Ibid.*, Chap. VI, 15, 23.

96. *Ibid.*, 18.

97. *Ibid.*, 23.

PART III

1. 324 U.S. 335. See also Glen A. Wilkinson, "Indian Tribal Claims before the Court of Claims," *Georgetown Law Journal*, LV (1966–67), 514–15.

2. Commissioner of Indian Affairs, *Annual Report, 1946,*

3. 25 U.S.C.A. #70a. Claims were to be filed by August 13, 1951.

4. Memo of November 13, 1968, from John Vance to members of the Indian Claims Commission; the argument, in somewhat modified form, is made in John T. Vance, "The Congressional Mandate and the Indian Claims Commission," *North Dakota Law Review*, Vol. 45, No. 3 (Spring, 1969), 325–36.

5. Wilkinson, *op. cit.*, 521–22.

6. Vance, *op. cit.* (footnote 4 above).

7. *Hearing before the Committee on Interior and Insular Affairs, United States Senate, Ninety-First Congress, Second Session, on the status of Indian claims litigation, April 10, 1970* (Washington, 1970), esp. letter of Glen A. Wilkinson, March 4, 1970, pp. 23–25, and letter of Bruce A. Wilkie, April 27, 1970, pp. 30–32.

8. William Peden, ed. (Chapel Hill, 1955), 96.

9. "Original Indian Title," *Minnesota Law Review*, XXXII (1947–48), 34.

10. *Ibid.*, 45–46.

11. Quoted in *ibid.*, 32.

12. *Ibid.*, 29.

13. 329 U.S. 40.

14. Ibid., pp. 2, 5, 7, 8 of slip opinion. The 1935 statute is at 49 Stat. 388.

15. 341 U.S. 48.

16. 348 U.S. 272. That fiscal considerations rather than moral or legal considerations have shaped the denial of a Fifth Amendment protection to Indian tribes suing for compensation for aboriginal title lands unjustly taken from them has been documented at considerable length by a young legal scholar, Howard M. Friedman, in an article entitled "Interest on Indian Claims: Judicial Protection of the Fisc", published in the *Valparaiso Law Journal*, Vol. 5, No. 1 (Fall, 1970), 26–47. As Friedman puts it: "The allowance of interest on only small classes of claims eliminated politically

unacceptable judgments while paying lip-service to the Fifth Amendment." Judicial fear of allowing any Fifth Amendment protection is evident in such recent rulings as that by the Court of Claims in *U.S.* v. *The Delaware Tribe of Indians* (Appeal No. 6–69, decided June 12, 1970), rejecting a procedural rule established by the Indian Claims Commission—the so-called"5% rule"—concerning gratuity offsets allowed the government in Indian claims cases.

17. 348 U.S. 272.

18. 180 Ct. Cl. 375, at 384–87.

19. 177 Ct. Cl. 184; 25 U.S.C.A. #70a, note 15.

20. 147 Ct. Cl. 315; 182 Ct. Cl. 130, slip opinion at 9, 20.

21. 180 Ct. Cl. 487, slip opinion at 3, 6, 8.

21ª. 19 Ind. Cl. Comm. 385.

22. Statement of July 12, 1968, in U. S. Congress. Senate. Committee on Interior and Insular Affairs. 90th Congress, 2d Session. *Hearings . . . on a bill to authorize the Secretary of the Interior to grant certain lands to Alaska Natives, Settle Alaska Native land claims, and for other purposes,* Part 2 (Washington, 1968), 534.

23. U.S. Department of the Interior. *Decisions of the U. S. Department of the Interior.* LXXI (Washington, 1965), 340. Cited as 71 I.D. 340.

24. *Report to the Secretary of the Interior by the Task Force on Alaska Affairs,* December 28, 1962, W. W. Keeler, Chairman, mimeographed, 60.

25. Letter to Hon. Henry M. Jackson, Chairman, Committee on Interior and Insular Affairs, U.S. Senate, April 30, 1968, printed in Appendix C of U.S. Congress. Senate. Committee on Interior and Insular Affairs. 90th Congress. 2d Session. *Hearings . . . on . . . Alaska Native land claims, op. cit.,* [Part 1] (Washington, 1968), 499.

26. Letter of June 15, 1967, to Hon. Hubert H. Humphrey, in *ibid.,* 20.

26ª. *Report* [to accompany S. 1830] *on the Alaska Native Claims Settlement Act of 1970,* 91st Congress, 2d Session, Senate Report No. 91–925, June 11, 1970, 219 pp., esp. p. 82.

27. *Weekly Compilation of Presidential Documents,* March 11, 1968, Vol. IV, no. 10, 447.

28. Statement of July 12, 1968, in *Hearings* cited in footnote 22 above, 535.

29. *Ibid.,* 536, 538, 555.

30. Testimony of Roger G. Connor, Attorney for the Aleut League, July 12, 1968, *Hearings* cited in footnote 22 above, 590; Udall's statement, 536.

31. In *Hearings* cited in footnote 25 above, 189, 192, 198.

32. Treaty of December 29, 1835, 7 Stat. 478, with Cherokee, cited in U. S. Department of the Interior, *Federal Indian Law* (Washington, 1958), 988. *Federal Indian Law* is a revision and updating through 1956 of the *Handbook of Federal Indian Law* prepared by Felix S. Cohen and first printed in 1940.

33. *Federal Indian Law,* 989.

34. *Ibid.,* 991–93.

35. *Ibid.,* 1007–8.

36. *Ibid.,* 996–97.

36ª. Hearings on H. R. 15866, A Bill "To Repeal the Act of August 25, 1959 with respect to final disposition of the affairs of the Choctaw Tribe," before the Subcommittee of Indian Affairs of the Committee on Interior and Insular Affairs of the U. S. Senate, July 14, 1970.

37. *Federal Indian Law,* 892.

38. *U.S.* v. *Lucero,* decided January 1869, quoted in *ibid.,* 897–98.

39. Quoted in *ibid.,* 899–900.

40. *Ibid.,* 902–3.

41. *Ibid.,* 906.

42. Paul Radin, *The Story of the American Indian* (New York, 1944), 368.

43. See, for example, Wilcomb E. Washburn, "Law and Authority in Colonial Virginia," in George Athan Billias, ed., *Selected Essays: Law and Authority in Colonial America* (Barre, Massachusetts: 1965), 127–128.

44. Henry F. Dobyns, "The Struggle for Land in Peru: The Hacienda Vicos Case," *Ethnohistory,* XIII (1966), 97, 101.

45. *Federal Indian Law, op. cit.,* 773–74.

46. N. D. Houghton, " 'Wards of the United States'—Arizona Applications: A Study of the Legal Status of the Indians," University of Arizona, *Social Science Bulletin,* XVI, No. 3 (Tucson, July 1, 1945),

13. Ward Shepard, "Land Problems of an Expanding Indian Population," and Allan G. Harper, "Salvaging the Wreckage of Indian Land Allotment," in Oliver La Farge, ed., *The Changing Indian* (Norman, Okla., 1943), pp. 72–102, esp. p. 76.

47. For a graphic depiction of Indian land areas, see the map issued by the Bureau of Indian Affairs of the U.S. Department of the Interior entitled "Indian Land Areas." See also, U.S. Department of the Interior, Geological Survey, *The National Atlas of the United States of America* (Washington, 1970), pp. 129–132.

48. Harold E. Fey and D'Arcy McNickle, *Indians and Other Americans: Two Ways of Life Meet* (New York, 1959), 81–83.

49. Commissioner of Indian Affairs, *Annual Report, 1948*, 380.

50. Commissioner of Indian Affairs, *Annual Report, 1954*, 245.

51. *American Anthropologist,* LXVI (1964), 631–33.

52. Statement of Harry R. Anderson, Assistant Secretary, Public Land Management, Department of the Interior, February 24, 1966, in U.S. Congress. House of Representatives. Subcommittee on Indian Affairs. 89th Congress, 2d Session. *Hearings before the Subcommittee on Indian Affairs of the Committee on Interior and Insular Affairs on H. R. 11113 to reduce the number of fractional interests in trust and restricted allotments of Indian lands, and for other purposes* (Washington, 1966), 22.

53. *Ibid.,* 8–10.

54. William A. Brophy and Sophie D. Aberle, comp., *The Indian: America's Unfinished Business: Report of the Commission on the Rights, Liberties, and Responsibilities of the American Indian* (Norman, Oklahoma: 1966), 74. See also U.S. Congress. House of Representatives. Committee on Interior and Insular Affairs. 86th Congress, 2d Session. *Indian Heirship Land Study,* 2 vols. (Washington, 1960–61).

55. Quoted in Fey and McNickle, *op. cit.,* 73. In addition to hearings before the Senate Subcommittee on Indian Affairs, hearings were held before the House Subcommittee on Indian Affairs, July 13 and 14, 1967. The *Hearings* were published in 1967.

56. Personal observation of the hearings, which have never been published.

57. Commissioner of Indian Affairs Robert L. Bennett's answer to question of the author from the floor at International Symposium

on the Legal Rights of Indians, sponsored by the Law Schools of the University of Manitoba and the University of North Dakota, Grand Forks, North Dakota, March 7–8, 1969.

PART IV

1. U. S. Department of the Interior, *Federal Indian Law* (Washington, 1958), 986n. *Federal Indian Law* is a revision and updating through 1956 of the *Handbook of Federal Indian Law* prepared by Felix S. Cohen and first printed in 1940.

1ᵃ. Sec. 3 (f) of S. 1830, 91st Congress, 2d Session.

2. N. D. Houghton, " 'Wards of the United States'—Arizona Applications: A Study of the Legal Status of the Indians," University of Arizona, *Social Science Bulletin*, XVI, no. 3 (Tucson, July 1, 1945), 18–19. See also U. S. Department of the Interior, *Digest of Decisions of the Department of the Interior in Cases Relating to the Public Lands (Indian Matters Included)* Vols. 52 to 61, ed. by Elsie M. Kimball, Part 1 (Washington, 1962), 190 (53–80) notes that the act of June 2, 1924 (43 Stat. 253) which declared all noncitizen Indians born within the territorial limits of the United States to be citizens of the United States, did not contemplate any disturbance of the existing status and relations of the Indians with respect to their property and other recognized rights. See also comments on motivation of act by John Collier in Oliver LaFarge, ed., *The Changing Indian* (Norman, Oklahoma, 1943), 5.

3. Quoted in *Federal Indian Law*, 527–29. See also Robert F. Heizer and Alan J. Almquist, *The Other Californians: Prejudice and Discrimination under Spain, Mexico, and the United States to 1920* (Berkeley, California, 1971), pp. 60, 95–104, 115–17.

4. U. S. Department of the Interior, *Digest of Decisions, op. cit.*, 189 (53–680), (53–78).

5. U. S. Department of the Interior, *Digest of Decisions, op. cit.*, 191 (58–456), 190 (61–298).

6. Marshall's phrase was expressed in *Cherokee Nation* v. *Georgia*, 30 U.S. (5 Pet.) 1 (1831).

7. Cohen's remark is quoted in Houghton, *op. cit.*, 17.

8. The case was decided June 20, 1969. Appeal No. 2–68, *The United States* v. *The Native Village of Unalakleet*, Appeal No. 3–68. *The United States* v. *The Aleut Community of St. Paul Island*, and Appeal No. 4–68, *The United States* v. *The Aleut Tribe*, Slip opinion, pp. 1–12.

9. William T. Hagan, *Indian Police and Judges: Experiments in Acculturation and Control* (New Haven, Connecticut: 1966), *passim* and 107.

10. *Ibid.*, 151.

10ª. Albert E. Kane, "Jurisdiction over Indians and Indian Reservations," *Arizona Law Review*, VI (1964–65), 237–55, esp. 238, 249.

11. See, for example, Leonard W. Levy, *Origins of the Fifth Amendment: The Right against Self-Incrimination* (New York, 1968).

12. Testimony of Frank J. Barry, Solicitor, Department of the Interior, June 22, 1965, in U. S. Congress. Senate. Subcommittee on Constitutional Rights. 89th Congress, 1st Session. *Hearings before the Subcommittee on Constitutional Rights of the Committee on the Judiciary on [bills] . . . to protect the constitutional rights of American Indians* (Washington, 1965), 22.

13. Comment on *Colliflower* v. *Garland* in *Harvard Law Review*, LXXIX (1965–66), 438; also comment on *Littell* v. *Nakai, ibid.*, 852.

14. *Hearings, op. cit.* (footnote 12), 1. See also William A. Brophy and Sophie D. Aberle, comp., *The Indian: America's Unfinished Business: Report of the Commission on the Rights, Liberties, and Responsibilities of the American Indian* (Norman, Oklahoma: 1966), 44.

15. *Hearings*, op. cit. (footnote 12), 21.

16. *Ibid.*, 163.

17. Brophy and Aberle, *op. cit.*, 44n.

18. Quoted in decision of Court of Appeals, 9th Circuit, February 4, 1965, in case of *Colliflower* v. *Garland*, No. 19, 170.

19. U. S. Congress. House of Representatives. Subcommittee on Indian Affairs. 90th Congress. 2d Session. *Hearing before the Subcommittee on Indian Affairs of the Committee on Interior and Insular Affairs . . . on H.R. 15419 and Related Bills to establish rights for individuals in their relations with Indian tribes, and for other purposes* (Washington, 1968), 113.

20. 25 U.S.C.A. # 1302, 1303.

21. *Hearing,* op. cit. (footnote 19). 36, 37, 38, 52.

22. *Ibid.,* 29 (letter of March 28, 1968).

23. *Ibid.,* 127 (letter of March 27, 1968 to Rep. James A. Haley, Chairman of the House subcommittee on Indians Affairs).

24. Reply of Attorney General Robert F. Kennedy to query of Senator Ervin, quoted in *ibid.,* 15.

25. *Dodge, et. al.,* v. *Nakai,* mimeographed Opinion, Findings of Fact, Conclusions of Law and Judgment (No. Civ-1209 Pct.) U.S. District Court for the District of Arizona, February 28, 1969. Harold Mott, General Counsel of the Navajo Tribe, has appealed the decision in the Ninth Circuit.

25[a]. Monroe Price, "Lawyers on the Reservation: Some Implications for the Legal Profession," in *Toward Economic Development for Native American Communities: A Compendium of Papers submitted to the Subcommittee on Economy in Government of the Joint Economic Committee, Congress of the United States,* 91st Congress, 1st Session, 2 vols. (Washington, 1969), I, 200.

25[b]. American Anthropological Association, *Fellow Newsletter,* Vol. 10, no. 10 (December 1969), p. 2.

26. *Federal Indian Law,* op. cit., 495–96.

27. U. S. Department of the Interior, *Digest of Decisions, op. cit.,* 191 (58–456), 190 (57–295).

28. William H. Veeder, "Federal Encroachment on Indian Water Rights and the Impairment of Reservation Development," in *Toward Economic Development for Native American Communities, op. cit.* (footnote 25a), II, 483.

28[a]. *Ibid.,* II, 497–512.

28[b]. Kenneth Lysyk, "The Unique Constitutional Position of the Canadian Indians," *Canadian Bar Review* XLV (September 1967), pp. 513–553, at pp. 527–8.

28[c]. Quoted in *ibid.,* p. 530.

28[d]. Quoted in *ibid.,* p. 551.

28[e]. Dissenting view of Judge Pigeon, p. 7 of mimeographed decision of the Supreme Court of Canada in the case of *Her Majesty the Queen* v. *Joseph Drybones.* For additional studies of Canadian Indian law see A. H. Jakeman, "Indian Rights to Hunt for Food,"

Canadian Bar Journal, VI (1963), 223–27, 241; K. Lysyk, "Indian Hunting Rights: Constitutional Considerations and the Role of Indian Treaties in British Columbia," *University of British Columbia Law Review,* II (1966), 401–21.

29. U. S. Department of the Interior, Bureau of Indian Affairs, *Answers to your questions about American Indians* (Washington, 1968), 2.

30. *Ibid.,* 15; see also Brophy and Aberle, *op. cit.,* 215.

31. Brophy and Aberle, *op. cit.,* 13.

32. *Yale Law Journal,* LII (1952–53), 348, 351–62.

33. *Washington Evening Star,* January 9, 1968; *Washington Post,* January 10, 1968.

34. For a strong view of this position, see Robert K. Thomas, "Colonialism: Classic and Internal," *New University Thought,* IV, no. 4 (Detroit: Winter, 1966/67), 37–44.

35. Clyde Warrior, "Poverty, Community, and Power," *New University Thought,* IV, no. 2 (Detroit: Summer, 1965), 5–10.

36. From review by William C. Sturtevant of *American Heritage Book of the Indians,* in *New York Herald Tribune,* October 29, 1961.

37. Testimony of Commissioner Bennett before Appropriations subcommittee, March 12, 1969.

37ª. U. S. Congress. Senate. Interior and Insular Affairs Committee. 91st Congress, 2d Session. *Hearing before the Committee on Interior and Insular Affairs . . . on Proposed Changes in Structure and Policy of the Bureau of Indian Affairs, December 16, 1970* (Washington, 1970).

38. Richard Henry Pratt, *Battlefield and Classroom: Four Decades with the American Indian, 1867–1904,* edited by Robert M. Utley (New Haven, Connecticut: 1964).

39. Commissioner of Indian Affairs, *Annual Report, 1949,* 353; *Annual Report, 1955,* 233.

40. See, for example, Robert J. Havighurst and Bernice L. Neugarten, *American Indian and White Children: A Sociopsychological Investigation* (Chicago, 1955). Havighurst has recently directed a series of studies of Indian education for the Office of Education of the Department of Health, Education, and Welfare.

41. Saslow's testimony, and that of many others, has been published in six volumes of *Hearings before the Special Subcommittee on Indian Education of the Committee on Labor and Public Welfare, United States Senate, Ninetieth Congress, First and Second Sessions, on the Study of*

the Education of Indian Children (Washington, 1969). In addition, a useful study by Brewton Berry entitled *The Education of American Indians: A Survey of the Literature,* prepared for the Special Subcommittee on Indian Education of the Committee on Labor and Public Welfare of the Senate has been published for the use of the Committee (Washington, 1969, 91st Congress, 1st Session). Saslow's statement appears in Part 1, 195–99.

42. Commissioner's Bennett's testimony before Appropriations subcommittee, March 12, 1969.

43. *Washington Post,* December 15, 1968, E4; *Des Moines Register,* October 1, 1968, 3; editorial, October 6; July 21, 6–L.

44. Mimeographed statement by Peterson Zah, prepared for testimony before congressional committee, June 1970.

44ª. Commissioner Bennett's testimony before Appropriations subcommittee, March 12, 1969.

45. *Guide to Graduate Departments of Anthropology for the Year 1968–69,* American Anthropological Association, *Bulletin,* I, no. 4 (Washington, 1968). Also, information supplied by American Anthropological Association.

45ª. Pp. 94–95.

46. U.S. Department of the Interior, *Digest of Decisions, op. cit.,* 192 (54–40), 193 (54–39).

47. *Ibid.,* 193 (54–40).

48. Fred Eggan, *The American Indian: Perspectives for the Study of Social Change* (Chicago, 1966), 73–91.

49. Commissioner of Indian Affairs, *Annual Report, 1944,* 237.

50. Theodore D. Graves, "Acculturation, Access, and Alcohol in a Tri-Ethnic Community," *American Anthropologist,* LIX (1967), 306–21.

51. Commissioner of Indian Affairs, *Annual Report, 1946,* 381.

52. Ibid., *Annual Report, 1954,* 244.

53. Paul Radin, *The Story of the American Indian* (New York, 1944), 374.

54. Brophy and Aberle, *op. cit.,* 3, 5.

55. *The Cherokee Report* (Tahlequah, Okla., May 15, 1968), 4.

INDEX

Boyden, John S., 190
Brant, Joseph, 51
British North American Act of 1867, 200–01
Brookings Institution, 76
Brophy, William A., 81
Brown, Alexander, 34
Bruce, Louis, 138, 213–14
Bureau of American Ethnology, 227
Bureau of Indian Affairs, created (1824), 65; office formally established by act of Congress (1832), 207; transferred to Department of the Interior (1849), 69; educational role of emphasized, 219–20, 222–24; educational role of criticized, 221–23; general discussion of, 206–14; specific references to, 65, 69, 81, 84–86, 88–92, 131, 157, 159, 165
Bureau of the Budget, 129
Burk, John Daly, 37
Bursum, Senator Holm O., 142

Cabot, John and Sebastian, 27, 30
The Caddo Tribe of Oklahoma, et al, v. *U. S.* (1968), 122–23
Caddos, 122–23, 134
Cahn, Edgar S., 213
Calabaza, Pat, 189
Calhoun, John C., 65
California, 86, 165
California Indians, 101–02, 165
Canada, authority of Parliament over Indians, 198–200
Canada, Indian Act (1952) of Parliament of, 201–02
Canada, Indian Claims Commissioner designated, 203
Canada, status of Indians in, 198–204

Canadian Bill of Rights (1960), 201–03
Canadian government "white paper" (1970), 203–04
Canadian Indians, population figures, 203
Cano, Melchior, 16
Cardinal, Harold, *The Unjust Society: The Tragedy of Canada's Indians,* 204
Caribs, 22
Carlisle Indian School, 218
Charles I of Spain (Charles V as emperor), 8, 10, 13, 14
The Cherokee Nation v. *The State of Georgia* (1831), 68
Cherokees, 47, 48, 51, 54, 62–69, 82, 134, 136, 170, 181–83, 239
Cherokee cases, 62, 181–83
Cherry Valley raid, November 11, 1778, 51
Cheyennes, 73, 134
Chickasaws, 48, 134, 137–38
Chinard, Gilbert, on Vitoria, 11
Choctaw Termination Act of 1959, 138
Choctaws, 47, 48, 62, 63, 82, 134, 136–38, 210–11
Chrétien, Jean, 204
Christianity, and theory of just war, 4, 12
Christianity, message of peace and non-violence, 3
Church, Senator Frank, 94
Citizens' Advocate Center, 213
Citizenship and the Indian, 62–63, 139–40, 163–65
Civil War and the American Indian, 70, 135
Clark, Ramsey, 184
Clement VI, 10